Frank Walker has worked as a journalist for 32 years, most recently as chief reporter for the *Sun-Herald*, covering defence, security, military and terrorism. He has worked on the *Sydney Morning Herald*, for News Limited in New York, Deutsche Welle radio in Germany, the *National Times*, and he has been the New York correspondent for the *Sun-Herald* as well as chief of staff. He has reported from the war in Afghanistan, the disaster after the tsunami in Thailand, terrorist attacks in Indonesia and a military coup in Fiji. This is his first book.

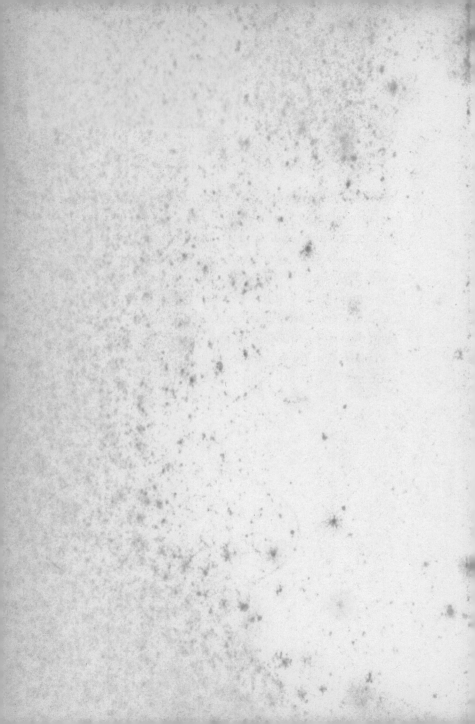

FRANK WALKER
THE TIGER MAN OF VIETNAM

First published in Australia and New Zealand in 2009
by Hachette Australia
(an imprint of Hachette Australia Pty Limited)
Level 17, 207 Kent Street, Sydney NSW 2000
www.hachette.com.au

This edition published in 2010

10 9 8 7 6 5 4 3 2

Copyright © Frank Walker 2009

This book is copyright. Apart from any fair dealing for the purposes of private study, research, criticism or review permitted under the *Copyright Act 1968*, no part may be stored or reproduced by any process without prior written permission. Enquiries should be made to the publisher.

National Library of Australia
Cataloguing-in-Publication data:

Walker, Frank.
The tiger man of Vietnam / Frank Walker.

978 0 7336 2655 5 (pbk.)

Petersen, Barry—Career in armed forces. Australia. Australian Army Training
Team, Vietnam—Officers—
Biography. Australia. Royal Australian Regiment. Battalion, 2nd. Company,
C—Officers—Biography.
Vietnam War, 1961–1975—Participation, Australian. Vietnam War,
1961–1975—Participation, Montagnard
(Vietnamese people).

959.70438

Cover and picture section design by Christabella Designs
Cover photograph of Barry Petersen courtesy of Barry Petersen
Cover photograph of helicopter courtesy of Corbis Australia Pty Limited
Picture section photographs courtesy Barry Petersen collection except as marked
Maps by Christabella Designs
Text designed by Bookhouse, Sydney
Typeset in 12/16 pt Simoncini Garamond by Bookhouse, Sydney
Printed and bound in Australia by Griffin Press, Adelaide, an Accredited ISO AS/NZS 14001:2004
Environmental Management System printer

The paper this book is printed on is certified against the Forest Stewardship Council® Standards. Griffin Press holds FSC chain of custody certification SGS-COC-005088. FSC promotes environmentally responsible, socially beneficial and economically viable management of the world's forests

CONTENTS

Map of Ban Me Thuot and Darlac Province	*vii*
Map of South Vietnam	*viii*
Preface	*ix*
1 Surprise Attack	1
2 Torture Training	14
3 Vietnam and the CIA	37
4 The CIA coup	62
5 Tiger Hunt	71
6 Montagnard Rebellion	101
7 The Johnnie Walker Miracle	140
8 Meeting Menzies	154
9 Fired	166
10 Farewell	193
11 A Pain in the Ass	218
12 Action in Exile	232
13 Return to Vietnam	242
14 Phoenix Rising	260
15 Stirred, Not Shaken	285
16 Betrayal	300
17 Back to Asia	306
18 Old Soldiers Never Die	312
Endnotes	*321*
A Timeline of Conflict	*326*
Bibliography	*337*
Acknowledgements	*341*
Index	*345*

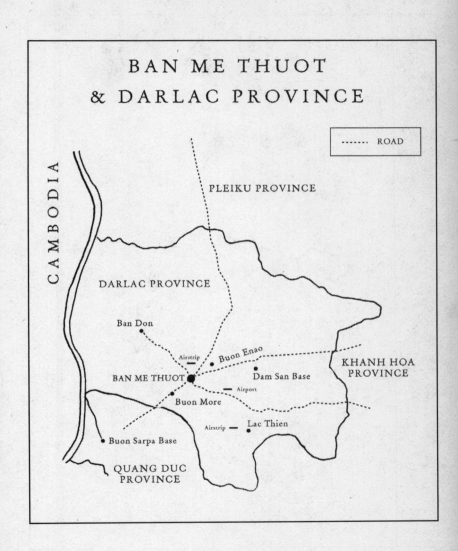

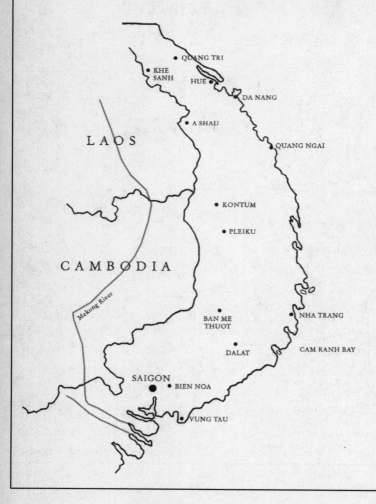

PREFACE

Stiff and with the tensed, squared shoulders of an old soldier, Barry Petersen stepped forward to lay his wreath at the War Memorial at Thailand's Hellfire Pass. His leg gave a twinge as he put his weight on it and bent down to lay the wreath, but he refused to let the pain of an old war injury show. The medals pinned to his chest jangled in the stillness as he straightened back up and dipped his head. He turned in perfect military step and resumed his place in the line of dignitaries.

An observer looking at the men proudly displaying their medals this Anzac Day might have noticed that Barry Petersen's row of 13 medals, stretching 20 centimetres across his chest, was the longest of them all. Those who know medals would acknowledge with respect the white and purple ribbon holding the Military Cross. This medal ranks two below the Victoria Cross, and it is only awarded for bravery in the face of the enemy. Further along the row of medals was a small brass oak leaf pinned to the Vietnam campaign ribbon. That one is for a Mention in Dispatches, given for courage in action against the enemy.

Few in Australia are aware of Petersen's place in our military history. His life could easily have been the inspiration for the controversial film *Apocalypse Now*. The parallels are there. Like Colonel Kurtz, played by Marlon Brando in the film, Petersen was eventually regarded by the CIA and senior American military men as having 'gone native'. Long before Australian combat troops set foot in Vietnam, the young Australian officer had been sent alone into the darkest, most remote part of the country to build a guerilla force of primitive local tribesmen to harass and attack the Viet Cong. It was an extraordinary secret mission, overseen by some of the most ruthless CIA agents who developed the Phoenix Program, which would later be linked to the worst atrocities in the Vietnam War.

Over two years in the Central Highlands of Vietnam, Petersen became so successful training and leading the indigenous Montagnard tribesmen against the Viet Cong that the communists put a price on his head: they wanted him dead or alive. It was true, the Montagnard were in awe of the young Australian, declaring him a demi-god, and in a remarkable traditional blood-spilling ceremony, anointed him a paramount chief. When news of this filtered back, the CIA began to fear the mountain tribes were more loyal to Petersen than to the US or the corrupt government in Saigon. To them, he was becoming a 'Lawrence of the Highlands'.

Petersen was neither a god nor native. He was an army man in a difficult position. He had learned some of the CIA's darkest secrets. He'd uncovered top-secret illegal US military operations and the training of special assassination squads and when he was asked to do the same he refused. His defiance was not expected and his CIA bosses were furious. They wanted him removed (like the Viet Cong – one way or another).

Barry Petersen's life is an astonishing tale of one man's courage to stand up against what he saw as wrong in a place where it was hard to tell who the real enemy was, where murder and torture were the order of the day. The fact that Petersen has lived to lay a wreath at Hellfire Pass in 2008 is testament to a little luck and to his courage, moral fibre and tenacity. This is his story.

1
SURPRISE ATTACK

February 27, 1965: The first rays of dawn slowly started to light up the Vietnamese village of Thang Thanh, tucked away in the valley below. Mist that had collected overnight in the clearings and fields began to lift. Mountain birds, silent during the long dark night, opened up with their morning chorus.

Lying in a patch of thick cover on top of a hill overlooking the village, Captain Barry Petersen brought his binoculars up to his eyes. The 29-year-old Australian Army officer looked down on the village as people dressed in their traditional Vietnamese black pyjama-style attire rose from their thatch huts to wash, greet neighbours and begin their daily business. In pairs and small groups, they started heading out to work in the fields before the day heated up.

Petersen watched closely, searching for villagers who might be making their way to guard posts on the perimeter, looking for anybody approaching hidden bunkers, any sign of weapons, any hint of where the leaders of this village of about 500 people might be. He'd been informed by South Vietnamese army intelligence that Thang Thanh was under the control of the Viet Cong – a small force, with no North Vietnamese regular troops. But that information wasn't always reliable, and Petersen was determined to be cautious. He and his men were a long way from any United States or South Vietnamese army support if anything went wrong. This was not the place to be caught in a trap.

The heat and humidity rose steadily. Sweat dripped from Petersen's brow and his camouflage shirt started to stick to his slim frame. Slightly resembling Aussie film idol Errol Flynn, he was the only Westerner around for more than 50 kilometres. Being white and taller than the Vietnamese was a curse in this war. He stood out clearly as a target. Any VC who saw him coming would take aim at him first, not just because he was a bigger target, but to kill a 'Yankee' was the ultimate prize. Few knew, or cared, that he was an Australian. To them, any gun-toting Westerner was considered an American. The Vietnamese communists were determined to defeat the Yanks just as they had beaten the French.

Lowering his binoculars, Petersen reached for his water bottle, took a sip of stale, warm water and looked around at his soldiers. He was in the same camouflage uniform as them, sharply striped like a tiger, clothing markedly different from Australian or American uniforms. There was no sign of rank or anything displayed to show he was an Australian Army officer. Petersen's troops were all Montagnard, fierce mountain tribesmen of Vietnam's Central Highlands. In just one year he had moulded a motley group of 100 volunteers into what amounted to a private army of 1200 guerillas, and with them he had taken the fight to the Viet Cong in the remote mountains 260 kilometres north-east of Saigon.

Back in Australia hardly anyone was aware Australian soldiers were engaged in fighting in Vietnam. It would be another two months before the Menzies government announced its intention to send combat troops there and another six months before the first Australian troops arrived. At the time Captain Barry Petersen was scoping out the village, the first United States combat troops were four weeks off arriving in the country.

Petersen's mission was highly classified. It's doubtful whether even the Australian Prime Minister Sir Robert Menzies knew an Australian soldier was fighting Viet Cong in the mountains of Vietnam. Had he known, it's likely Menzies would have been surprised who the Australian was taking orders from. Petersen was not operating under the command of the Australian Defence Force. In a top-secret move 18 months earlier, Petersen had been told by his Australian commanding officer in Vietnam that he was to work for, and take orders from, the United States Central Intelligence Agency (CIA).

The CIA had given Petersen an extraordinary mission – go into the mountains and build a private army of tribal warriors to take on the communists. The Montagnard people were a distinct ethnic group from the Vietnamese, they were herders and farmers who lived communally in long thatched houses. Their prime weapons were handmade crossbows and arrows and machetes. Petersen's mission was to train them to use modern carbines and machine guns to take on a battle-hardened enemy with decades of experience in guerilla warfare.

There was good reason for his task. The Central Highlands were strategically vital to the survival of the South Vietnamese government in Saigon. For years the North Vietnamese had been sending supplies south through the Highlands – a meandering string of paths through jungle and mountain passes that at times ran down the other side of the border inside Laos and Cambodia. These paths were later dubbed the Ho Chi Minh Trail.

The village below Petersen lay directly in the path of that trail. He had been told the Viet Cong were using it as a base to harass and ambush South Vietnamese forces trying to battle the infiltration. The village was officially called a 'Land Development Centre', part of the South Vietnamese government's plan to shift thousands of Vietnamese from the heavily populated coastal lowlands into new settlements in the sparsely settled Central Highlands. The Montagnard hated the Land Development Centres as they took over their land.

The settlement scheme was a disaster. The Vietnamese resented being forced to move to the Highlands and had difficulty farming in the mountain conditions. Many had relatives who had joined the Viet Cong and were living in the jungle. The VC relied on this resentment and the family ties within the villages for food, support and recruits.

Although a lowly captain, at this point Petersen had more troops serving under him then than any other Australian officer in Vietnam. The Australian military commander in Vietnam, Cold War warrior Colonel Ted Serong, had only 30 army trainers under him. Petersen was one of them, and he had unique talent and experience. It was Serong who had told him he was being seconded to the CIA, and to take orders from them. Petersen was on his own, far from any help, leading hundreds of rebellious armed tribesmen with a brimful of bloodlust. He was walking a deadly tightrope and he did not know how close it was to snapping.

Petersen looked at his watch. It would be another six hours before the villagers of Thang Thanh returned to their huts to settle down for their midday siesta – the perfect time to attack. Get them when they are sleeping, a tactic Petersen had learned from the Viet Cong. Petersen had also learned the best way to fight the small mobile units of Viet Cong was with his own small, mobile eight-man units. His force had used these tactics so successfully that the VC called them 'Tiger Men', referring to their striped, CIA-issued camouflage uniforms and perhaps also to the ferocity of their attacks. Petersen latched on to the name and gave his troops tiger beret badges made by a local metalworker. His men wore the badges with pride.

The Montagnard under his command were mainly from the Rhade tribe, just one of the dozens of tribes living in the highlands of Vietnam. The Vietnamese despised the Montagnard regardless of what tribe they were from. They called them *moi*, savages. The feeling was mutual. The Rhade still seethed with anger that lowland Vietnamese had been forcibly resettled in the Highlands, pushing their tribe out of the more fertile valleys. This village, Thang Thanh, had been resettled – even more reason for the Rhade to hate the villagers.

With the enmity going back hundreds of years, the Rhade were ready to kill the Vietnamese in the village, communists or not. Petersen knew from bitter experience that if he was not there to oversee the attack, his force would probably slaughter the entire village. A previous unsupervised assault on a village had resulted in more than 200 deaths. Not one prisoner was taken. His men told Petersen they all died in the fighting. He didn't believe it; he knew his men had slaughtered every villager they could lay their hands on. Even though he was operating outside the Australian rules of war, that wasn't the way Petersen chose to play the game.

For this attack Petersen had around 80 men with him hiding in the jungle overlooking the village. They were geared for travelling light: a few grenades, a World War Two vintage M1 carbine (more sophisticated guns came later), a dozen fresh magazines to reload, and a day pack with rice for one day, water bottle, matches, knife, pistol and medical pack. They travelled light for hit-and-run operations. Get in and out quickly. This attack was different, but Petersen was relying on surprise to help him and his force. He could not see any machine guns defending the village, but he knew they had AK-47s, grenades and mortars. He had ordered another 50 or so men to hide on the roads and paths leading out of the village on the flatlands. Those men were to stay put and catch or kill VC who tried to flee. Petersen's aim was to take as many VC prisoners as he could, and turn them over to the Vietnamese.

The Australian's main offsider, a battle-scarred veteran Rhade tribesman called Y-Liu, crawled his way up to him. Y-Liu had served with the French expeditionary force battling the Viet Minh. After the Vietnamese kicked the French out of Vietnam

Y-Liu joined the French Foreign Legion and fought in northern Africa. Fighting was in his blood, and he was happy to be killing Vietnamese again.

'The guards at the kilns have taken three prisoners, Aey,' Y-Liu said quietly, using the Montagnard expression for sir.

'Make sure they are held securely,' Petersen replied.

He had put guards on the charcoal kilns and paths heading up into the hills. Any villagers gathering firewood for the kilns or tending hunting traps would have to be detained to keep them quiet.

It had taken two days of trekking for Petersen and his force to reach the hill overlooking this remote village. His men knew the jungles of the Highlands well, and could move unseen through the thick forests without making a sound or leaving a trace. Petersen called in his key squad leaders and gave them last-minute instructions on how they were to approach the village. They returned to their eight-man units spread out to the left and right of him. The aim was to use whatever cover they could, such as ditches and corn and cassava fields, to get as close to the village as possible undetected.

Petersen's order not to open fire until fired upon was not some gentlemanly code: holding fire as long as possible enabled the troops to get as close as they could without being seen. It was simple. The closer you were to your target, the more likely you were to hit them.

The sun was now high in the sky and Petersen watched the villagers returning to their huts, finding shade to sleep off the midday heat. Having identified gaps in the makeshift fencing around the village, he'd pointed them out to his squad leaders. The village was supposed to have a defensive wall. Ironically, it was insisted on by the South Vietnamese authorities to keep out the Viet Cong. That had turned out to be a bad joke. The VC were now the ones inside the fence and the Aussie-led, CIA-financed mountain tribesmen were about to attack. Petersen looked at his watch: 1.30pm. The villagers were dozing. It was time to move out. Petersen signalled to the teams to the left and right of him. The long line of 80 men picked up their weapons and moved stealthily down the hill, taking care to stay under cover. At the base of the hill they fanned out in smaller groups of two and three so they could approach the village across a broad front. Petersen was in the commander's slot in the centre of the line, slightly behind the rest so he could see how they were advancing.

He had a radio operator with him to keep in touch with his squad leaders further out, as well as with the units in the jungle on the other side of the village waiting to trap fleeing VC. The men melded themselves into the gullies and vegetation cover as they moved in towards the village. Apart from the bleating of a goat, all was quiet. They'd got to within 10 metres of the first huts and the force still had not been seen. Petersen left cover, broke into a trot and reached the thatched huts on the edge of the village.

Suddenly the sharp rapid cracks of an AK-47 rang out about 200 metres to his right. He heard his own troops return fire with their M1s. All hell broke loose. Villagers ran from their huts in every direction, women and children screaming and heading for bunkers, the men heading for cover and defensive positions. With his gun poised to shoot, Petersen's eyes shifted left and right: anyone with a gun was now a target. He moved towards the rendezvous point, a VC-erected stage in the centre of the village where their leaders harangued the villagers with communist propaganda and signed up volunteers under threat of torture or execution. Petersen had a deep sympathy for the villagers' plight. He recognised they were damned either way. The communists burned their huts and killed those who would not join them. Now Petersen and his band were doing much the same.

He was moving around the outside of a hut when suddenly bullets whizzed towards him, ricocheting off the ground at his feet and hitting the hut behind him, splattering him with dirt and wooden splinters. He spun towards the direction of the shots and saw gunsmoke in a clump of banana trees just metres away. Instinctively he fired a burst from his semi-automatic. The banana clump trembled, then fell still. Banana trees are not great places to hide as they are too soft to give protection. No more shots came his way. Petersen moved forward and as he got closer he saw a badly wounded Vietnamese man crumpled on the ground. Blood was pouring from his chest. He was dying, his gun lying beside him. Petersen picked up the weapon and started to move on, when from behind him he heard a shot. He turned and saw that Y-Bu, a Montagnard and former VC, had finished off the wounded man. Y-Bu grinned at Petersen. 'You should have done the job properly,' he said and laughed.

Petersen said nothing. He had no particular aversion to finishing off the enemy: after years of guerilla war in Vietnam, and Malaya before that, Petersen had seen death and killed. But as he later reasoned, if he had executed the wounded VC the Montagnard would have had just a little bit less regard for him. In his eyes, and theirs, an Australian military commander was supposed to be above such things.

Petersen moved towards the sounds of fighting on the other side of the village and joined a group of his men clearing out an underground bunker. They were calling on the people to come out or else they would drop grenades down the trapdoor.

One by one the villagers came out. None of them had a gun, but when one woman carrying a baby saw Petersen she instantly started screaming, dropped the child and cowered on the ground.

A startled Petersen turned to his translator, Y-Jut.

'What is she screaming at me?' Petersen demanded.

Y-Jut shouted at the woman. 'What is the matter, why are you screaming?'

She jabbered at Y-Jut, hysterical with fear. Petersen knew she had more reason to be scared of the Montagnard than him. Petersen's presence was probably the only thing stopping a slaughter.

'She says Americans eat babies. She's terrified you will eat her baby,' said Y-Jut.

Petersen shook his head in disbelief. Communist propaganda constantly told stories of American atrocities, but eating babies was a new one.

'Tell her I am not an American, I am an Australian,' said Petersen. Someone picked up the crying baby and handed it to its terrified mother. She clung to it tightly and moved away, pressing against the wall of a hut, closing her eyes so she could not see Petersen.

The guns had fallen silent. Petersen's squad leaders reported that most of the fleeing villagers had been caught by the troops waiting to spring the trap and were being held at gunpoint in a field. Several villagers had been killed in the firefight – four would be the official tally. It might well have been more. Petersen did not think it wise to go around counting bodies – it was better not to know some of the things his men did. And besides, the number of enemy killed was not what made it a successful raid for him, having none of his men killed or wounded was what mattered more.

The Vietnamese provincial chief who had authorised the raid on the village had ordered that any hut containing communist propaganda be burned to the ground. All males of military age – which in Vietnam meant anyone between 15 and 50 – were to be rounded up and taken to the provincial military headquarters for questioning. Most of these men would not be coming back to their village. Those deemed to be Viet Cong faced a tough future in prison, or worse. Many found to be clear of communist contamination would be forced to serve in the South Vietnamese army.

Petersen's men searched the village and set fire to about a dozen huts where they found signs of VC propaganda – this could be anything from a pamphlet to a flag. Finding a weapon would have meant instant arrest. The men of the village were all rounded up and forced at gunpoint to squat in the dirt to wait for trucks to arrive which would take them far away to the regional capital Ban Me Thuot for questioning, not knowing if they would ever see their families again.

The aftermath of a firefight is an ugly time. For the victors there is the selfish elation of success and that they survived. But around them the wounded wailed in agony, women and children screamed and cried in shock. Smoke from burning huts choked the air. The bodies of those killed in the attack were left to lie in the fields and trenches where they fell. With merciless eyes the Montagnard troops kept their guns trained on the villagers – both men and women – in case of a sudden suicide attack with a grenade or a lunge with a hidden knife.

Amid the chaos in the village, Petersen saw an old Vietnamese couple crouching on the ground, shaking with fright. He walked over to them. In his mind, enough damage had been done for the day. Squatting down, he politely asked the old man if his wife could make them a pot of tea. The couple looked up at him, disbelieving. Petersen asked again with his few words of Vietnamese. He was polite and courteous. The old couple looked at each other and then the old man motioned to his wife to make the tea. She set about the task, hands trembling so much that she spilled the water as she filled the pot.

Through his puzzled translator, as the woman poured the tea, Petersen gently asked the man about his farming, his children, how long he had lived there and about village life. Gradually the couple calmed down. This was not the brutal interrogation they expected, but the passing of pleasantries in a bizarre moment of a crazy war. Petersen's Montagnard warriors watched on, scratching their heads. But there was method to the mad tea party. Petersen hoped that word of the courtesy and humane treatment from this white man in the feared Tiger camouflage uniform would spread around the villages. Perhaps they would learn that this particular Australian was not an ogre who ate babies, but a soldier doing his duty as best and as honourably as he could.

The Montagnard fighters would indeed spread the story among the Highland tribes of this extraordinary scene, but it was not with the message that Petersen intended. The story they told of the white warrior who led a successful surprise attack then sat down with his defeated enemy to discuss crops politely over a cup of tea was to give birth to a legend. It was a further step in the minds of the Montagnard to elevate this young Aussie captain to the honoured status of demi-god. The legend of the 'Tiger Man of Vietnam' had begun.

2
TORTURE TRAINING

From an early age Barry Petersen got on easily with people from different cultures. He was born in the tiny but pretty sugarcane town of Sarina in the hot tropics, 990 kilometres north of Brisbane. At the time of his birth in 1935, the sugarcane fields of northern Queensland were a multicultural place.

His father, Arthur, who preferred to be known as Fred, ran a radio repair business and when World War Two broke out he joined the army. Fred became a staff sergeant, keeping radios running in New Guinea and Borneo. When he returned to Australia after the war the family moved to the banana and sugarcane town of Innisfail, where Barry went to school with Italian, Greek, Chinese and Aboriginal kids. Here, he learned how to get along with them all and developed respect for their cultural taboos. His easygoing attitude was to stand him in good stead in later life as he mixed with indigenous peoples in Asia.

But as a youngster Barry Petersen's first interest was Africa.

He was fascinated by stories of British district officers serving in Africa, stories of African natives and lions and hippos and elephants. As a young teenager he even wrote to the Colonial Office in London asking if he could become a ranger and go to Africa. They wrote back a polite letter saying he should wait until he was 20 years old and recommended he do a degree in anthropology. At the time he didn't know what that was.

Barry finished his schooling in Brisbane at the Industrial High School and here he came into contact with students from Asia studying in Australia on the Colombo Plan (a Commonwealth bilateral aid scheme). It was then his interests switched from Africa to Asia.

Petersen always liked the outdoor life. During the years his father was away at the war Barry and his two younger sisters were raised by his mother and grandfather, Hans Christian Petersen, an Australian-born son of Danish migrants, who often took young Barry fishing in the waters off Sarina Beach. The old man was a hard taskmaster and instilled in young Barry the need for self-reliance. He forced him to take a stand against his fears, teaching him to catch fish by wading out from the beach with long drag nets with a pole at each end. Corks kept one edge up and weights were attached to the bottom end of the net so it dragged on the sand. Barry always had to take the deep water end of the net, forcing him out to where the water was up to his neck before looping around to catch the fish in the shallow water.

The trouble was these were shark-infested waters. Hammerhead, reef and grey nurse sharks could be seen cruising for their own fish in the crystal-clear water. Barry was terrified of them, but his Pop would say: 'They won't touch you while you drag the net.' Jumping at every shadow around him, Barry always came back onto the beach with huge relief. He was desperate for Pop's praise and approval, and proud when his courage was acknowledged. The young boy wanted to prove to him he was a man.

His grandfather's lessons did not go to waste. Barry joined the Boy Scouts, and threw himself into the outdoor activities, earning just about every outdoors badge he could for his uniform. His sense of adventure didn't wane as he got older and his first job after school was with a survey company. He liked that it kept him working outdoors.

In 1953, like all young Australian men, Petersen had to enlist in the army for a compulsory three-month stint of National Service. The Korean War was in full swing, and while National Servicemen were not sent to that war, it was constantly in the news and made a deep impression on young Barry.

He loved his time in the service and thrived during the military training, learning fighting skills, shooting rifles and the orderliness of army life. At the end of the three months, he volunteered to join the army and was sent to officer cadet school in Portsea, Victoria. In 1954 he graduated as second lieutenant and a trained signaller.

Petersen soon realised this deskbound job was not for him, so with the Korean War over, he transferred to the infantry and was assigned to training National Service troops. He fitted straight in and with a new batch of men arriving every three months, he learned quickly and could correct his mistakes with every new intake.

It was clear that Barry Petersen was well suited to army life and in 1957 he was transferred to 1st Battalion Royal Australian Regiment, based in Queensland. His first mission was to join Australia's support for the British in Malaya against Chinese communist jungle guerillas, who were fighting the old Imperial colonial power moving back in after World War Two. Britain was battling to re-establish ownership of the country's rubber and tin industries. Petersen learned Malay and trained in anti-guerilla jungle warfare. He was a natural. He picked up the language quickly and readily adapted to working with the Malays, training them to act as guides and jungle fighters.

In Malaya, plantation owners had insisted the conflict be called an 'emergency' as their insurers would not pay up if it were declared a war. It didn't matter what label was used, the situation had all the hallmarks of a war as the Malay government, the British and their Australian allies rounded up hundreds of thousands of ethnic Chinese Malays and put them into guarded camps surrounded by floodlights, police posts and barbed wire. The aim was to stop them joining the communist guerillas, a tactic the British first learned in the Boer War some 50 years earlier. The British camps for the Boers were the world's first concentration camps.

Once he arrived in the country, Petersen was made a platoon commander with the task of pursuing communist guerillas in the jungle. It was an arduous two-year tour that saw him going up and down the mountains carrying heavy equipment. He was working with indigenous tribal groups called the Orang Asli (Malay for 'original people'), who were looked down on as primitive savages by Malays and ethnic Chinese. Petersen did not look down on his men, for him they were superb in the jungle. They knew how to stalk silently, track human or animal, and could survive quite happily on what the jungle provided for food, shelter and water.

The communists had long acknowledged the strengths of the Asli people and had been living among them and getting their forces resupplied by them. The job of Petersen and his men was to win back the Asli, train them in modern warfare and arm them to fight the communists who were coming over the border from the jungles of southern Thailand.

Over the two years Petersen trained and patrolled with the Asli, he developed a deep and abiding respect for them. He applied the skills he learned as a schoolboy to observe and respect their customs, to avoid breaching the social taboos and behaviour that other cultures might see as bad form.

Petersen's commander in Malaya, Colonel John Milner, saw that Petersen had an easy affinity with the Asli and urged him to stick with this type of military work. This suggestion must have been noted officially as later Petersen was recommended for the Special Operations group when Australia was gearing up to send a training team to Vietnam.

Petersen was back in Australia as a captain when he received a letter asking if he would be willing to join four other officers and volunteer to go to South Vietnam as military advisers. This invitation came several months before the conservative Liberal government of Sir Robert Menzies publicly announced on 24 May 1962, that Australia would send a small army training team to Vietnam.

The timing of the letter to Petersen is particularly revealing, as the Australian government claimed at the time that the Australian advisers were only being sent at the invitation of the government of the Republic of Vietnam. Menzies said the Australian Army trainers were to help teach jungle warfare and village defence to Vietnamese forces in their struggle against communist armed insurgency.

This is not to suggest Menzies had great vision, anticipating the invitation by several months and starting the ball rolling by ordering the army to be prepared to send a skilled training team to Vietnam. The truth was that the invitation from the Vietnamese government was quickly cobbled together after Australia had already decided to send troops. For many years it was believed Australia only became involved in the Vietnam War because of political and diplomatic pressure from the United States. On the contrary, it was later revealed that the Menzies government had always been extremely keen to get the US more deeply involved in the Vietnam conflict, in the belief this would tie the US to the South East Asian region.

Senior Foreign Affairs official Gordon Jockel wrote in a note two years later: 'Although we have stressed the fact publicly that our assistance was given in response to an invitation from the Government of Vietnam, our offer was in fact made following a request from the United States government that Australia provide some military assistance to Vietnam in the form of a Services "presence".'[1]

Senior lawyer Michael Sexton, who later became solicitor general of NSW, put it bluntly in his 1981 book *War for the*

Asking – How Australia Invited Itself to Vietnam: 'The Vietnam War began with a betrayal of truth.'

Petersen knew nothing about Vietnam when he volunteered to go there. 'A lot of people at the time didn't even know where Vietnam was. I didn't know what the issues were – I thought it was something similar to Malaya and I knew I had experience in that sort of conflict. I was very keen to be part of the training team. When we assembled there were about 35 of us; they read out the names and I was certain I was going as I had been one of the original five approached to go. They called out the name Peterson, and I thought it was me but then they spelt it out with 's-o-n' and it was another bloke. I was stunned when I was not included in the first 30 names called out.'

But the army had other plans for the Petersen with an 'e'. He was invited to apply for Special Operations training, top-secret military operations that included cloak-and-dagger spying. Petersen jumped at the chance. He was ordered to tell no one, and to report to an address in Melbourne. It turned out to be a nameless, nondescript building buried among other dull office blocks.

Inside he registered at a rather bland reception desk and was shown to a room where he was given a thorough medical check. The medical officer offered no hint of what the health checks were for. Petersen had been in the military long enough, particularly in the secretive side of Special Operations, to know not to ask questions. Nobody volunteered any hints of whose office he was in. He was then shown into a room with a chair in the middle facing a panel of five nameless men. The men did not introduce themselves to Petersen, nor did they say what the interview was for.

Petersen sat down and the five men began questioning him. They asked, 'How would you feel if your sister married an Aboriginal?' Petersen replied that it would be entirely up to her. He thought the interview was just a formality because they had the records of what he had done in Malaya in front of them. They didn't ask what he thought of communism, or what he thought about the situation in Vietnam. At the end of the interview they asked if he had any questions. He said, 'Yes, when will I know if I have been selected?'

'Soon,' came the answer.

A few hours later he was called back to the building and told to wait in the same interview room. The lead man of the panel of five came in and gave him papers to sign. It was an official pledge to keep what he would subsequently learn secret. What Petersen was about to be told had the very top level of secrecy, classified 'Oyster'. Should he ever breach the agreement he could be jailed. The man then revealed to Petersen that he was a member of the Australian Secret Intelligence Service (ASIS) and that Petersen might be working for them in the near future. The signing of these papers marked the beginning of Barry Petersen's work in the murky shadows of covert services, which would continue for the rest of his life.

Formed in absolute secrecy in 1952 to undertake spying operations overseas, ASIS was so secret that few in the government even knew it existed for the next 20 years. In fact the organisation was so top secret that officially it did not actually exist. There were no records, it was not answerable to anyone. Its name was not to be spoken. The government denied its existence, and if anyone in the media learned of it they were threatened with jail to keep it out of the headlines. The identity of the person who headed it was classified top secret, and its members were legally protected from being named in public.

Petersen was told the building they were in had the classified codename MO9. In typical bland bureaucratic language it stood for Main Office 9. The man Petersen met in that interview room never gave his name. He told Petersen ASIS ran the secret training school that prepared agents and military men like him for clandestine overseas operations.

The man also informed Petersen that his name would be placed on a classified list of those who had been told the identity of the director-general of ASIS, Major-General Sir Walter Cawthorn. Hearing this name instilled confidence in Petersen as Cawthorn had a good reputation as an army officer.

The military have always had a close relationship with the world of spies. Many secret agents and their shadowy colleagues are former military men – even the fictional James Bond was a commander in the Royal Navy Reserve.

Australia's spy school was at Swan Island in Victoria – a small 1.4-square-kilometre island at the mouth of Port Phillip Bay, connected to the mainland only by a one-lane bridge. A fort was built on the island during the Crimean War in the 1870s in case of a Russian attack on Melbourne. It worked, as no Russians ever tried to invade the city.

Swan Island has a long history of training both the military and civilians for covert operations. The first trainees on the island were inducted during the Cold War. It is still used today to train secret agents and Special Forces in counter-terrorism operations.

Petersen's intensive course in spycraft covered operating codes – both sending and decoding, how to make message drops and collections, how to run a surveillance operation, how to check rooms for bugs, how to secretly tape-record meetings and conversations, how to follow someone unseen, how to spot someone following you. It was all new to him, and he loved it. The handful of men in the course were told they were getting the same training as that undertaken by the British MI6.

While at Swan Island Petersen was told he may be required to operate behind enemy lines and work with guerilla forces, but he was given no hint of where he would be sent or what he would be doing. He was enthralled.

But being a spy was not as easy as he thought. In his first practice field trip he and a few others had the task of gaining information in a small Victorian town without being detected. After checking in to a modest hotel Petersen and his colleagues went about their business. Thinking they had been very secret and clever, they returned to the hotel at the end of the day only to overhear locals talking about the secret agents sneaking around town.

Petersen soon learned the lesson that it's far easier to hide in a big city than in a small town. Locals in a small town notice strange faces and things out of the usual. In big cities spies can be much more anonymous.

Despite this initial failure he soon developed his own spying methods and sources. His mates' network came good after the course at Swan Island when he got a letter from fellow officer and friend Captain John Healy, who had gone to Vietnam some months earlier. Healy wrote that he had been working for the innocuously named Combined Studies Division, a cover for the

CIA's Covert Action Branch, and that Petersen would be his replacement when he came over to Vietnam. Thanks to his own spy network, Petersen now knew where he would be going, and that it was going to involve serious skulduggery. He realised he could get in some tough positions, and possibly captured. Knowing what could be at stake he volunteered to do one more course – this one run by the military. It had an innocent enough official name – the Code of Conduct Course. To the troops it had a more accurate moniker: Torture School.

The course was run on military land at the School of Military Intelligence at Middle Head in Sydney. The site has magnificent views up Sydney Harbour, but that is not why the military chose the old installation. Running through the land are tunnels and underground storage rooms dug for gun emplacements. Just like Swan Island in Victoria, Middle Head fort was built in the 1870s to stop the Russians invading Sydney during the Crimean War. Another fort, Fort Denison, was built on a tiny island called Pinchgut, which today stands just before the world-famous Sydney Opera House. Once again the ploy proved a brilliant military move. The Russians never came.

As the military geared up for the Vietnam War, the damp, dingy old tunnels were used for training Australian soldiers to withstand interrogation if they were captured by the enemy. The aim was not to train them to withstand physical torture. Nobody can do that. There were no needles under fingernails or electric shocks, but there were beatings, humiliation, days of pain and agony, sleep deprivation and psychological torture to break down confidence and resistance. Most of the techniques were based on what had happened to Allied soldiers taken prisoner in the Korean War. The military wanted their men to have some idea of what would happen to them if they were captured in Vietnam. It might not stop them from breaking down, but at least they would have the satisfaction of recognising the torture techniques and perhaps help them withstand the horrors a little better.

Petersen was one of 14 nervous young officers who entered the course in early 1963. When he arrived he was stunned by the spectacular views of Sydney Harbour, but the thought of what he was about to go through soon took away any enjoyment of the view.

He had been warned by others not to trust anyone in the course: not the friendly guards; not the good-cop/bad-cop interrogators; not even the other officers doing the course with him. They could just as easily be plants trying to get information from him. Trust no one, say nothing, he was told, just give name, rank and serial number. He was terrified that if he broke down or failed he would not be allowed to serve in the Special Forces in Vietnam so was determined to bite his tongue, stare straight ahead, cut off the world and get through it without disgracing himself.

On his first day the commander of the course addressed the small group gathered in the mess room, reminding them they were volunteers, that they could ask to leave the course at any time and would be released instantly 'without prejudice'. Petersen doubted what he heard. He was certain there would be a black mark against anyone who failed this course, and they could say goodbye to any Special Forces assignment. Surely it would be back to regular duties for any drop-out.

The commander looked around, nodded and left the room. Suddenly the doors burst open and a squad of mean-looking soldiers dressed only in khaki with red stars on their caps stormed in, shouting and ordering the volunteers to stand and line up against the wall. One by one the 14 men were seized, dragged out of the barracks and down into a maze of underground tunnels and cells. They were pushed and shoved towards the deepest, darkest and coldest part of the old fortifications. Once there, shouting guards ordered them to completely strip off their crisp military uniforms and pull on bedraggled prison garb, ill-fitting, torn and stained smelly pants and shirts. With no belts or elastic in their pants, the 'prisoners' had to clutch them to stop them falling down. This was the first step in the process of breaking down the prisoner – humiliation.

The men were thrown into separate cells, but these were not to be their own cells. Nothing could get to the stage where it was considered safe or familiar. The prisoner had to be kept on edge, anxious and apprehensive about what would come next.

Petersen got to know many cells and each one had its own particular offensive characteristic. One room he dubbed the Music Room as a loudspeaker up near the ceiling constantly blared communist anthems such as *The Internationale* and *The East is Red* interspersed with loud rants of communist propaganda. He called another room the Whistlestop as it had a loudspeaker that emitted a series of grating high shrieks, making it virtually impossible to sleep or think clearly. Harsh interrogations were conducted in the Conversation Suite. The Pit was a cellar room accessed only by a ladder. It had ankle-deep water and plunged the prisoner into total darkness and absolute silence, putting them in isolation to ponder the next step in their torture.

Over the first eight days Petersen was dragged in and out of these cells, he was kept moving to keep him disoriented. Each time he was removed from a cell, the guard placed a calico bag over his head then grabbed him, shoving him along the corridors, spinning him around, taking a different route each time, backtracking, standing for a minute, then moving on again. He was ordered to get on his hands and knees to crawl under something that wasn't there before. It was all part of the process of disorientation so he could not recognise the layout or work out the passage of time.

The treatment intensified as the days wore on. This was no play acting, it was ugly and sadistic. Petersen was bruised, cold, filthy, in pain and degraded. He had not been allowed to sleep for days. He had only cold, wet floors to lie on. His pitiful clothes were only just hanging on him. His jacket was far too small for him and his pants fell around his ankles, but he had used his ingenuity to work a piece of wire loose from a disused light fitting to act as a belt to hold them up. He did this despite knowing it was against the rules; a small undiscovered bit of rebellion that gave him a shred of dignity.

Time and days blurred and once more Petersen was dragged into the interrogation room. It was windowless, cold, dank and stank of stale rotten air. An incredibly bright light shone directly into his face. A broomstick lay on the floor and Petersen was forced to kneel with his whole weight on it just below the kneecaps. It was an extremely painful position, he later described as 'like a carnivore gnawing at your joints and thighs and threatening to devour your whole body'. Determined to tough it out, he knelt motionless, back upright. He was ordered to keep his arms held out straight in front of him until his shoulders screamed out in agony. It seemed only to increase the pressure on his knees. The pain was excruciating.

The chief interrogator barked out questions. 'Name? Rank? Number?' Petersen concentrated on giving only the regulation answer. 'Captain Arthur Barry Petersen, Australian Army number 13668.' He could sense, rather than see, the interrogator. He could tell there were others in the room, but the blinding light made them only shadows. They wielded batons and punched and prodded him as he knelt. God, they hurt.

The interrogator spoke in clipped tones, his voice void of any emotion. 'Today Petersen, you will tell us more.'

'The others have told us,' a second voice said.

'The others have told us,' the interrogator repeated.

Petersen stayed silent. He knew this was a trick. His knees were on fire and he felt as though bayonets were thrusting up through his knees into his thighs, but he kept his back straight and his arms thrust forward as ordered. He hadn't broken yet, and he was determined to tough it out.

'Petersen, Captain, number 13668,' he shouted back, retreating to the traditional formula of prisoners of war. One word more, even to ask a question, and his torturers would have opened a tiny crack. They would work it, work it, and the dam he had built in his mind would break open, and the words come tumbling out. He pursed his lips and repeated the formula again: 'Petersen, Captain, 13668.'

The interrogator told him with disgust that he stank. After eight days of no washing and lying in putrid human waste that was certainly true. 'Have you no pride, Petersen?' the interrogator shouted at him. 'Have you no sense of decency, you dirty, filthy man?'

This too will pass, thought Petersen. It must end sometime. There will be a hot shower at the end of this torment. This is only training. He knew he could end it all by saying he had had enough, that he wanted out. Instead, he said nothing. But the physical toll was showing. The arms he was ordered to hold out in front of him started to droop with the strain.

'Get them up!' screamed a guard, and a baton whacked him in the back above the kidneys. It was expertly placed, just above the spot where it would cause lasting damage, but hard enough to cause a painful jolt to course through Petersen's body. He jerked upright and his arms shot out in front of him. His trousers fell to his knees revealing the wire that had been holding them up.

The guards shouted: 'He's got wire, he's got wire. Grab him. Get it off him.'

Rough hands seized his arms and forced him to the ground. Another guard grabbed the wire and the pants. He was pulled back to his knees, his nakedness exposed to his abusers, adding to the degradation.

'Where did you get the wire?' the guard demanded, his face right in Petersen's ear.

Petersen said nothing.

'You have been vandalising this prison. You were going to use it to attack us. You broke the rules. Why did you do this?'

Petersen looked steadily ahead, saying nothing.

'You know this means more punishment,' the interrogator said more softly. 'Why do you do this to yourself, Petersen? The others are far more cooperative.'

That may be true, thought Petersen. He had heard at least one of them screaming at night from another cell. He seemed to be going out of his head. Or was it another trick?

Name, rank, serial number.

The guards dragged Petersen to the Pit for punishment. This was like a torture cell in a medieval castle. The only way in was through a trapdoor in the roof. Petersen was ordered to climb down the ladder to the floor then the guards pulled the ladder back up again and the trapdoor slammed shut. He was alone in the darkness. The water level in the bottom of the cell varied from ankle deep to above the shins. Water dripped constantly and ran down the slimy walls. It was bitterly cold. And there were rats. Petersen could hear them scurrying in the dark.

What was a rat doing in a place like this? he thought. What do they eat?

Maybe the guards dropped them in to add to the atmosphere, he thought. Petersen didn't like rats. When he was in the Malayan jungle rats had run over him as he'd slept. It added to the horror.

In the darkness he rummaged around and found a couple of loose bricks and planks of wood on the floor of the Pit. After rigging himself up a makeshift bed just above the waterline he settled to lie down on the wooden planks. Then he discovered the downside – his makeshift bed was also just above the waterline for the rats. Only exhaustion finally let Petersen fall into fitful sleep. At least the Pit was quiet. His nerves were raw from endless replays of recorded rants and the screams from neighbouring cells going through the night. Or he thought it was night. It was impossible to keep track of time in this place. Food came at no regular interval. Sometimes it seemed six or eight hours had passed. Other times it seemed the gap was only one or two hours. Again, it was all part of the effort to disorient the prisoner. The meals never came with a bowl or fork, Petersen had to hold out cupped hands and the guard would drop a dollop of gluggy rice into them. At first Petersen ate it all in one go, but after a while he learned to store some away by rolling it into a ball and hiding it in his jacket pocket for those times when the ration came late.

On one occasion he was blindfolded and taken into a room. They took off the blindfold. They sat him down and offered him some decent food. A smiling man sat at the table, telling him to go ahead and eat. He said all the other prisoners had eaten, that there was nothing to lose. But Petersen refused to eat or to talk. There was probably nothing to lose by eating the food. It didn't give any secrets away. But it would have opened a crack, it could have led to conversation he did not want.

The interrogators tried another tactic. Petersen was brought up from the Pit and told he was going to see the 'counsellor'. He was taken to a different office, a warm dry place and behind a desk sat an affable-looking man who smiled and motioned Petersen to a chair.

'Sit down please, Petersen. Would you like a cigarette?'

Petersen didn't smoke, but even if he did he wouldn't have taken it.

'No thank you.'

'Well, how about some coffee?'

Coffee! He would have given his eye-teeth for a cup of coffee.

'No thank you.'

'Water then?'

Petersen felt he couldn't be compromised by accepting a glass of water.

'Yes please.'

The kindly man smiled and said, 'Good.' He went to the door and told the guard outside to fetch a glass of water and came back to the desk.

'Now Arthur Barry Petersen. Captain. What do you prefer to be called, Arthur or Barry?'

Petersen had never liked the name Arthur. He was always Barry, and everybody in the army knew that. He recognised this as a question to get him talking. The wedge to open him up.

'Captain Petersen will do.'

'Oh, come now, there is no need to be so formal,' the man said pleasantly with a little laugh.

Petersen stared straight ahead, saying nothing.

'Well then, how are you feeling?'

'I am well thank you.'

'Not too cold, hungry?'

Petersen said nothing.

The friendly interrogator smiled and shrugged his shoulders. 'I only ask because I know how miserable this place can be. It's all right for us cold-blooded southerners, but no place for a Queenslander.'

Petersen stiffened. He said nothing, but inwardly he asked himself how this man could know he was from Queensland. Had he let something slip? The counsellor was watching Petersen closely.

'Oh come on, relax, I am not asking you for military information.'

Silence.

'I don't need you to tell me you're from Queensland. I have it right here.' He held up a piece of paper, but the blank side was towards Petersen. Petersen believed the counsellor was cheating. He'd been told the rules of the game were that the interrogators could only use information against them that the prisoners had given them. Had he said something other than name, rank and serial number the whole time he had been in there? Had he let something slip? He couldn't remember.

He stayed silent.

The counsellor smiled. 'You are aware that the Australian Army Staff Corps list is freely available and anyone can look it up?'

He stayed silent.

'You know that I can look up that list and find, as I've got here, your date of birth, your qualifications, when you were promoted, the units you served with. I have all that.'

The counsellor waved his piece of paper. Petersen knew he must be lying.

'Let's try this another way. Tell me about your parents. Are they still living in Queensland?'

Petersen was anxious now. How did he know his parents were in Queensland? That wasn't in any of his army records. Where had he slipped up? The counsellor must have recognised the concern in Petersen's expression. He leaned forward with a glint in his eye. He had opened a crack in Petersen's wall.

'Well?' he demanded.

Petersen pressed his sweating lips together. 'Petersen, Captain, 13668!' he almost shouted back. But both men knew Petersen was on the verge of panic. Had he slipped up and said something to himself in his cell? What about his wallet when he was 'captured' in the barracks. Was there something in there that shouldn't have been that gave away more information than name, rank and serial number? Petersen was sure he had removed everything with any personal details before he came to the Middle Head base. All he had was a few banknotes, a watch and a pen. He stayed silent. After a while the convivial interrogator ordered the guards to take him back to his cell.

This time it was the cell Petersen had dubbed the Whistlestop. It had incessant screaming from cells next door as though someone was being tortured. He sat on the bunk and waited to be called to the interrogation room, where he knew they would bore into him again and try to split open the crack that had appeared in his façade. But nobody came. They were making him sweat.

Crazy though it might be, Petersen wanted them to come. He wanted to face his cruel interrogators and their baton beating and vile broom handle. He was convinced he was winning. He had not broken. At least not so far. How many days had it been? How much longer could it go on? This was a test. He wasn't a real prisoner. It had to end at some point. Petersen silently made a pact with himself again. No matter how many times they mentioned Queensland, no matter what questions they asked, he would answer only name, rank and serial number. That recitation was his salvation, and he would hang onto it with all his strength. But how did they know about Queensland? It nagged at him.

Nobody came. He waited and waited. Nothing happened. The shrieking was turned off. There was silence. Then his whole body started shaking uncontrollably. He was drenched with sweat as though overtaken by a profound fever. When he was at his lowest, he suddenly saw the answer to how the counsellor had found out about Queensland.

Regimental number 13668. Captain Arthur Barry Petersen.

That was it! The number! It was prefaced by the number one. The one signified Queensland. The first numbers two, three, four, five and so on signified other Australian states, indicating the point of recruitment and therefore possibly the place of birth. A wave of relief swept over him. He had not slipped up. He had not fallen for their trick. He had not revealed a secret. The wall he had erected had not crumbled.

A short time later the guards came in, pulled a hood over Petersen's head and dragged him from his cell. He could hear other prisoners in the stone corridor being brought from the other cells. The guards shouted at them to move forward, and they shuffled like blind sheep up the hall. Petersen could feel they were emerging into the open air. He tried to take deep breaths of the fresh air through the rough calico hood. What now? An execution? The guards herded them into some sort of line and suddenly they ripped off their hoods announcing, 'It's all over, you're through.' The prisoners were lined up outside in an old gun emplacement.

In front of the prisoners was a table laden with food and drink. Petersen looked warily at his fellow prisoners who were just as dirty, drawn and dishevelled as he was. They looked just as warily at him. Was it another trick? An officer in Australian Army uniform walked up and assured them the training was indeed over. The group broke out in laughter and, half-crying with relief, clapped each other on the back. But they did not number 14 any more – a couple had not made it through the ordeal. Petersen thought one of them must have been the prisoner he heard screaming as he was taken past his cell door. Later they found out another one had broken down and the instructors had intervened to get him to hospital. The Torture School had lived up to its name.

But Barry had got through. Sticking to his mantra – name, rank, serial number – no matter what happened had given him the strength to survive everything the torture school had thrown at him. Sure, he'd known it was only an exercise, that they would not physically torture him or abuse him as they would a real prisoner. He knew he only had to hang on for the duration of the exercise rather than the endless incarceration of a prisoner of war facing the real possibility of execution. But he had learned the importance of keeping hope alive against all the odds, and some basic strategies to stay alive and keep sane. At this point he felt he was as ready as he could be for whatever Vietnam could throw at him.

Barry Petersen grew up in northern Queensland, starting a lifelong love of the tropics. The eldest of three children, here he is in 1938, aged three, with his sister Coralie.

During World War Two Barry was raised by his Danish-born grandfather while his father, Arthur, was in the army in New Guinea. This photo was taken in 1943 with his mother Ivy, sister Coralie (RIGHT) and youngest sister Carmel.

As a youngster Petersen loved the outdoors and relished the Boy Scouts (ABOVE). A proud Private Petersen (RIGHT). When called up for his three months' National Service in 1953 he decided to stay on in the army and volunteered for officer training. In 1954 he graduated as second lieutenant and was assigned to training new National Servicemen.

In 1959 Lieutenant Petersen was sent to Malaya in Australia's campaign with the British against communist insurgents, in what was known as the Malaya Emergency. He adapted quickly to working with Malayan tribespeople on long anti-guerilla jungle patrols, learning their language and bush survival skills. In this formal 1961 photo (ABOVE), Lt Petersen is seated in the bottom row, sixth from the left, between sergeants with his platoon in B Company, 1st Battalion, Royal Australian Regiment. Petersen's unit (BELOW) train for riot control with Malayan soldiers playing the part of protesters.

In 1963, while Captain Petersen was in Sydney undergoing training to survive torture if captured in South Vietnam, there were protests at President Ngo Dinh Diem's repression and corruption. Shortly after Petersen arrived in the country and was seconded to the CIA to set up a Montagnard guerilla force in the Central Highlands, Diem was overthrown and killed in a US-backed military coup.

An aerial shot of the Central Highlands town of Ban Me Thuot in 1963. The dirt airstrip at the bottom of the picture was used by Air America to fly in Petersen and CIA operatives. Everybody else had to use a public airport well out of town.

Petersen in the typical CIA garb – white shirt and thin black tie – with US Army Captain Bill Amies, an adviser to the local Vietnamese province chief.

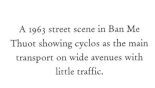

A 1963 street scene in Ban Me Thuot showing cyclos as the main transport on wide avenues with little traffic.

Guards stand at the front of the house Petersen turned into his headquarters in Ban Me Thuot.

Petersen's cook and housekeeper, sisters Ba Hai (LEFT) and Ba Nam.

The American military and intelligence headquarters in Ban Me Thuot known as the Bungalow. It covered an entire city block with its own shops, sports complex, cinema, canteen and secure concrete-hardened buildings for communications.

Courtesy Peter Jarratt

Petersen (RIGHT) at the handover to him of the 100 members of the armed propaganda and intelligence team previously run by the regional police. With him is his CIA handler Bryan Mills and provincial police chief Phan Tan Truoc (LEFT), who resented losing the team and the US dollars that came with it. Petersen believed Truoc twice tried to have him killed. In the background are their drivers.

Military training starts for the Montagnard force. At first they were called the Truong Son Force after the local mountain range. As their fighting reputation grew they became known as Tiger Men.

Montagnard village life had been unchanged for centuries before the war. They lived communally in thatched longhouses raised up from the ground. These pictures show the entrance to a Highlands village (ABOVE) and Petersen surrounded by villagers during a visit (BELOW) – note the precarious steps dug into the log.

3
VIETNAM AND THE CIA

While Captain Barry Petersen was undergoing the mock torture sessions in Sydney, far to the north in Saigon, a 76-year-old Buddhist monk was preparing himself for an horrific protest that would reverberate around the world.

Thich Quang Duc, a venerated senior abbot, made the drastic decision to do something spectacular to bring world attention to the repression of the Buddhists by the harsh and corrupt regime of President Ngo Dinh Diem. Diem was a fervent Catholic intent on forcing Catholic rule on South Vietnam even though the country was 90 per cent Buddhist. A month earlier government troops had opened fire on a crowd of Buddhists who were flying the Buddhist flag in defiance of a ban by Diem. Nine people were killed. When Diem tried to blame the Viet Cong for the deaths it was the final straw for the monks.

On 10 June 1963, Duc was driven by his monks to a small square in front of the Cambodian Embassy. He calmly walked to the footpath with two younger monks. One placed a cushion on the ground and Duc sat down on it, cross-legged in the lotus position. It was the traditional image of a man at peace. Those who had gathered to witness the protest, including American correspondents David Halberstam of the *New York Times* and Malcolm Browne of the Associated Press, had no idea what was about to happen. On the previous day, news reporters in Saigon had been sent a cryptic message notifying them that 'something important' would happen at the demonstration. Halberstam and Browne were the only ones who bothered to turn up. They saw another young monk walk forward carrying a five-gallon can of gasoline and watched in horror as he poured the contents over the sitting abbot. More than 300 monks and nuns surrounded Duc, blocking anybody from stopping what was about to happen and preventing anyone from getting too close. Halberstam and Browne looked on in shock as Duc recited a prayer while calmly rotating a string of beads, before reaching into his robes for a match. The abbot struck the match and dropped it in his lap. The flames instantly consumed him, burning his robes and his flesh, sending a plume of black oily smoke into the air. Duc did not flinch as the flesh burned off his skull. He stayed absolutely still until his flaming body slowly slumped to the ground, a charred black stump.

Browne's photo of the burning abbot went around the world and won him a Pulitzer Prize. The image had a resounding impact on world opinion and marked the beginning of the end for President Diem. In the White House, President John F Kennedy was increasingly concerned at how the war was going, and he was not sure he was getting accurate information from his military commanders in Vietnam. Kennedy was not questioning whether the US should be involved militarily in the country. He was an absolute believer in the Domino Theory, that unless the communists were stopped, they would spread out from China and South East Asian countries would fall one after another like dominoes. For him, it was not a question of whether the US should be in Vietnam, but whether the US was winning and whether Diem, not South Vietnam itself, was viable.[1]

Kennedy was right to be concerned; American military commanders were feeding overly optimistic accounts of the progress of the war against the Viet Cong back to Washington. In 1963 the US had a large contingent of 14 000 military 'advisers' in Vietnam. Their forces were training South Vietnamese troops and village militia and in the Highlands US Special Forces were training and fighting alongside Montagnard militia. But the US commanders in Saigon were ignoring reports from their mid-ranking officers in the field that the South Vietnamese army was simply not doing any fighting. The Vietnamese were wildly exaggerating post-action reports, falsifying the number of enemy killed or captured and villages made secure. South Vietnamese troops outraged villagers as they swept through, stealing chickens and livestock, ransacking their homes and bullying the inhabitants. These troops rarely caught Viet Cong as they only moved en masse, preceded by artillery shelling, giving the mobile Viet Cong plenty of time to disappear into the jungles or mingle with the populace. American officers in the field saw this clearly. They could also see that the Viet Cong controlled the vast bulk of the countryside. Areas marked on maps as peaceful were not controlled by the Saigon government at all, but by the Viet Cong. These areas were not safe.

The South Vietnamese commanders were under orders from Diem not to risk casualties, so they avoided combat wherever they could. So long as the US aid kept flowing, the Diem regime could live with the Viet Cong running around the rice paddies. American Saigon command did not want to hear any negative reports from its captains, majors and colonels in the field. Any field officer who tried to get the true situation across to the commanders was slammed as defeatist. The real burden of the war was being carried by local militia who encountered the VC in villages where both sides were struggling for control.

Like the American president, Petersen knew little of the true state of Vietnamese affairs as he prepared to go there. He read up on Vietnamese history and culture in the weeks before he left, but admits he could not understand the Buddhist monk's self-immolation. Several more monks followed Duc's lead and burned themselves to death. This level of sacrifice was totally alien to Australians and indeed most Westerners at the time, but it was to be seen again and again in Vietnam in both the cruelty of the terrorism and in the bravery of Vietnamese from both North and South charging into fatal situations with no hesitation. The sacrifice of Thich Quang Duc and other monks should have set alarms bells ringing among US and Australian leaders, as it showed the depth of determination and feeling they would be up against in Vietnam. No one realised the true power of fanaticism then.

In August 1963 Petersen travelled in civilian clothes to Saigon – first flying Qantas to Singapore, then Air France to Saigon. A year earlier the first contingent of 30 highly skilled and experienced men of the Australian Army Training Team Vietnam had quietly slipped out of Australia travelling in civilian clothes, but they had changed into jungle-green uniform shortly before they landed in Saigon. Petersen didn't bother changing. His mission was to go even deeper undercover, and he didn't want prying eyes to record the arrival of another Australian officer. He was hoping to fly below the radar. Briefed by ASIS, he knew he was destined to do something more clandestine than the previous contingent of officers. Officially he wasn't supposed to know, but again his mates' network had come to the fore and he had been told by his friend John Healy that he was going to be working with the CIA.

As he flew over South East Asia towards Vietnam, Petersen struggled to keep an aura of calm. Inwardly he was incredibly excited. Aged 28, highly trained, with experience in anti-communist guerilla warfare, he was about to embark on the biggest and most important mission of his life. He was a strong believer in the Cold War thinking of the time. Like President Kennedy and so many others, he was also a believer in the Domino Theory that depicted South East Asian countries falling one after the other to communism heading south from Mao's China. The accepted answer to this scenario was to prop up a wall of Western-friendly nations like South Vietnam, Malaya and Singapore, to stop the communist march. Like the Japanese in World War Two, the belief was the communists would head inexorably south towards Australia, as though pulled down by gravity.

The heat and humidity that struck Petersen as he stepped off the plane at Saigon did not surprise him. He was used to the tropics from his time in Malaya and he had grown up in the heat of Queensland. When John Healy met him at the airport and drove him into the city Petersen immediately fell in love with Old Saigon. Lush trees lined the streets and the mix of mango, poinciana, palm and rubber trees gave the boulevards shade and brushed the old colonial buildings, cooling them down and lending an atmosphere of stillness.

The smell of *nuoc mam* (fish sauce) used in streetside cooking pervaded the air. At first Petersen did not like the smell as it was stronger than the fish sauce used in Malaya and Thailand, but he soon got used to it.

Petersen knew how to handle himself in Asian cities and Saigon was no different. 'One of the things I have always done when I live in an Asian city is to find a good cyclo (bicycle-powered rickshaw) driver and ask them if they own or rent their cyclo. In Saigon I met this chap who was very helpful but he rented his cyclo. He said it would cost him $100 to buy his own. So I gave him $100. I had a friend for life, someone I could trust, someone who would not inform the authorities where I went and who I met. He would also tell me when authorities questioned him about where he had taken me. He would also ask me what I wanted him to tell them about where we went and who we met that day. It came in very useful.' Obviously some aspects of spymaking are instinctive and Petersen was showing innate skills in surviving in a conflict zone.

Saigon had yet to acquire the honky-tonk sleaze that was to come with the mass arrival of US troops in 1965. On the contrary, in 1963 Saigon was a rather puritanical town. Dancing in bars was banned and nightclubs were outlawed. Women were not allowed to wear clothing that bared shoulders, stomachs or legs and had to stick to the traditional but elegant *ao dai*, a long tunic worn over trousers. Adultery was punishable by jail, divorce was illegal, opium dens and brothels were closed and beauty pageants, boxing and animal fighting were banned. These were the edicts of Madame Nhu, wife of Ngo Dinh Nhu, brother of the President of Vietnam, Ngo Dinh Diem.

Diem was a bachelor, so his sister-in-law Madame Nhu was considered the First Lady of South Vietnam. She played the role to the hilt. A devout Catholic, she saw herself as the embodiment of Catholic Vietnam and the self-appointed 'angel' who would bring all of Vietnam to the Holy Roman Church. She was also cruel, manipulative, selfish and a complete hypocrite. While she dictated modest dress for Vietnamese women, she wore clothes that bared her shoulder, exposed décolletage, and was rumoured to have affairs. When the news broke of the self-immolation of Thich Quang Duc, she mocked it as a 'barbecuing'. In Marie-Antoinette-style, she declared: 'Let them burn and we shall clap our hands.' The people called her 'the Dragon Lady'. She had enormous power in the country and huge influence over her husband who ran the notorious secret police. Both President Diem and his brother Nhu were mystical Catholics, intent on making their ardent version of Christianity the dominant force over the Buddhists in their country. Their older brother, Ngo Dinh Thuc, Vietnam's Catholic Archbishop, was heavily involved in making investments in the country for the Church. Another brother, Ngo Dinh Can, ran central Vietnam like a feudal warlord.

President Diem promoted strong Catholics to key posts across the political, military and administrative hierarchy, while

Nhu ran a Gestapo-type secret police aimed at eliminating any opposition to the Diem regime. He used his secret police to suppress and persecute Buddhists and any other potential challengers to their dictatorial rule. The secret police was run by a strident Catholic, Dr Tran Kim Tuyen, who was known to have CIA advisers.[2]

According to historian Alfred McCoy, Nhu used the opium trade to finance his secret police. He placed Vietnamese intelligence agents in Laos to act as drug procurers, and flew the illegal drugs to Saigon in government planes of the First Transport Group run by Colonel Nguyen Cao Ky (later Air Marshal and Prime Minister). The First Transport Group also flew intelligence missions into Laos for the CIA.[3]

In the early 1950s while his countrymen were fighting to oust the French, Diem was overseas flitting from one monastery to another. In the US he made a valuable friend in Cardinal Francis Spellman of New York who introduced him to the influential Catholic politician Senator Mike Mansfield and a young Senator John F Kennedy.

The US government was firmly behind Diem and his corrupt ruling family, but only so long as Diem danced to the strings the US was pulling. The US would maintain their support if Diem and Nhu looked as though they were taking on the communists and the rising strength of the Viet Cong. The US had been pouring military advisers into South Vietnam since 1950 when they assisted the French against the Viet Minh national liberation movement. After the French were defeated and forced out in 1954, peace talks in Geneva ended with Vietnam divided into North and South on a demarcation line at the 17th Parallel, pending internationally supervised national elections in 1956. The US immediately backed South Vietnam and Prime Minister Diem with aid, military advisers and arms. CIA and Special Forces advisers arrived in their thousands to prop up the Vietnamese forces.

In August 1963 as Petersen was driving through Saigon for the first time, there were 16 000 US advisers in the country, most of them working with South Vietnamese troops. On top of that, the CIA had thousands of agents in the country carrying out clandestine actions against North Vietnam as well as trying to run the Diem government.

Twelve months earlier captains John Healy and Peter Young had been separated from the rest of the Australian Army Training Team Vietnam (AATTV) and told they would be attached to the CIA's Combined Studies Division (CSD) for very specific operations near Da Nang. The two officers were told to investigate how the Viet Cong operated, their hierarchy, how they supplied their units, their weapons, how they interacted with South Vietnamese villagers. Both men were given extraordinary freedom to travel around questioning US and Vietnamese army units. Healy later reflected that their biggest achievement was to gain the confidence of the suspicious operators of the CSD, secret service men who preferred to stay in the shadows. The CIA men did not trust their own soldiers, let alone foreigners. The commander of the AATTV Colonel Ted Serong regarded it as a major breakthrough that two Australian officers were able to work with the CSD and win their confidence. It was the first contact, and Serong was pleased it had opened the door for other Australian military men to work with the CIA.[4]

Once he'd arrived in Saigon, Healy took Petersen to meet Colonel Serong at his office inside the US command centre. Serong was a remarkable man, some say a brilliant military strategist. He was also an ideologue and fanatical anti-communist. Through his strong Roman Catholicism he had access and influence within the Diem government far beyond what his position would suggest. A serious 'player' in the freewheeling power politics of the US involvement in South Vietnam, he was a quiet man who kept a poker face, but he spoke with authority and people listened.

Serong seemed to relish the air of mystery and intrigue that surrounded him. He was supremely confident of his own ability, but did not display arrogance. He would keep silent while others discussed, gestured, ranted and raved, then chime in, speaking softly but forcefully, detailing everything right and wrong in the discussion, what should be done and how to do it.

The CIA respected Serong and valued his input. He had arrived in 1962, the first Australian military man in Vietnam. He'd come at the invitation of the CIA and impressed many of those he met with his capacity to sum up the situation. William Colby, CIA station chief in Saigon, said the Australian brought a unique and different ability to evaluate the problems facing them, in particular the importance of weighing Vietnamese political and social considerations as part of the military solution.[5]

Serong moved around the countryside extensively in 1962 and immediately recognised that the Viet Cong were winning the war. Northern Vietnamese troops and political cadres were moving south at will along the Ho Chi Minh Trail. The regular South Vietnamese army constantly avoided fighting and was poorly equipped and poorly led. Viet Cong controlled most of the rural areas; peasant villagers had little or no reason to fight them. Serong felt the US advisers, even US Special Forces training militia and the army, had little idea how to fight jungle warfare against guerillas. He had ideas that would make a difference.

The Saigon government was reluctant to arm local Montagnard militias in the strategically important Central Highlands, which the North Vietnamese used to infiltrate their forces into the South. Diem's Secretary of State, Nguyen Dinh Thuan, told Serong he had no intention of equipping the Montagnard adequately to take the fight to the Viet Cong. Serong later said: 'I suspect Thuan knows they will run out of ammunition and that he intends them to. He means to finish this war with no Montagnard problem.'[6]

Serong had met Petersen briefly after the captain had been selected for the AATTV, and knowing his capabilities had marked him early on for a very unique and special task.

Petersen was excited as he sat down before Serong.

'I have arranged for you to go to Ban Me Thuot – do you know where that is?' Serong asked.

'Yes sir,' replied Petersen. He'd studied maps of Vietnam for months, read every travel guide as well as all the military briefing notes he could find. Ban Me Thuot was 265 kilometres northeast of Saigon, a middle-sized town in the Central Highlands and capital of Darlac Province. Petersen was worried. It was a bit of a backwater, a long way from the demilitarised zone in the north and, to him, seemingly a long way from the action.

'You will be working with the Montagnard,' Serong went on.

Petersen's hopes rose. That would be interesting. The Montagnard were a primitive tribal people with a fearsome reputation. No ruler had managed to conquer them for long, and they had fought for independence for generations.

'I've managed to get the CIA to agree to let an Australian officer run his own field program. You're the first one. I want others to get the chance, so make a good job of it.'

Serong told Petersen he would be working for Combined Studies Division. He didn't spell out that this was just a front for the CIA, but both men knew.

'You will be working for the Americans and reporting directly to them. Your controller will be Bryan Mills, but you will give me a copy of everything that you report to them.

'I'll be up from time to time to see you, but you will be on your own. Good luck.'

It was the vaguest of briefings, and an absolutely extraordinary position for a junior officer to be put in. Many military officers are attached to foreign forces for training and cooperative military efforts, but not, as a rule, to foreign intelligence forces. Petersen was the first Australian to be given his own CIA field program in a relatively remote part of the country away from the watchful eyes of Australian and US senior military officers and civilian authorities. He did not know it at the time, but hardly anyone in the Australian government knew of his mission and even less that it was under CIA control.

Once his meeting with Serong was over, Healy took Petersen across town to report to his new CIA masters. The CSD headquarters were in a special concrete soundproofed, windowless box-like building at the rear of a nondescript villa not far from the centre of Saigon. The villa was also the home of the CIA Covert Action Branch chief in South Vietnam, Cliff Strathern, and his family. Healy knocked on a locked solid steel door which was opened only after someone had had a good long look at the two men through a spy hole. Once inside the bunker the atmosphere was buzzing. Maps covered the walls and were spread across the desks that filled the room along with piles of files. Large heavy-duty safes were up against the walls and used coffee cups littered tables and cabinet tops while a coffee percolator was operating on maximum power in the corner. The half-dozen American men in the room were clean-cut, mostly young, dressed either in dark suits with jackets discarded, or in khaki pants with crisp, white short-sleeved shirts worn loose over the pants to conceal the pistol and holster belted to their waists. This was the unofficial uniform of the South East Asian CIA secret agent.

Healy introduced Petersen to Strathern and Bryan Mills. The young Australian was immediately impressed with Mills and felt he was a person he could trust and work with. Energetic, friendly, educated and in his early 30s, Mills had spent 12 years in Thailand, Laos and Burma. He was unusually experienced in the region for an American intelligence agent. To Petersen, who was all fired up and enthusiastic about his new mission, Mills appeared quite reserved and cool. So was Strathern, who did not want to talk about anything beyond polite greetings. Finally Mills casually told Petersen they would fly up to Ban Me Thuot together in a week's time and he would brief him then. After handshakes and farewells, Petersen was out the door feeling somewhat deflated. It wasn't the momentous welcome he had expected.

Healy then took Petersen to Da Nang with him for a few days to fill in time and to see the large base near the coastal port used for training Vietnamese soldiers. There he met

Captain Peter Young and other Australians training Vietnamese troops. Young later became a key figure in military intelligence in Vietnam.

While in Da Nang Healy took Petersen to the CIA outfitters to be kitted out and given a handgun of his choice. He chose a 9mm Browning which he tucked into a holster under his loose shirt, just like the CIA agents he'd seen at CSD headquarters. The two men then joined a group of US Navy SEALS in a parachute jump to fill up the day. By the end of the week Petersen was back in Saigon to meet Bryan Mills at the Air America hangar for the flight up to Ban Me Thuot. He was ready for whatever came his way.

Air America was the CIA airline in South East Asia. Piloted by a rag-tag group of colourful characters from all over the world, it flew all sorts of planes on all sorts of missions, no questions asked, especially about passengers or cargo. For all concerned, it was best not to know.

The two-hour flight to Ban Me Thuot was a milk run for the small plane carrying only two passengers. Petersen watched as the landscape below changed from a patchwork of paddy fields, forests, dirt roads and villages to rugged, jungle-covered mountains. The Central Highlands were 1500 metres above sea level, and soon Petersen could see raging rivers and some isolated clearings with the thatched longhouses of the Montagnard.

Ban Me Thuot was a sprawling provincial capital of 45 000 people. The centre was well laid out with wide, tree-lined streets, large French colonial mansions and solid government buildings designed to represent imposing authority. From the elegant old town centre radiated ramshackle new homes built to house the thousands of Vietnamese forcibly relocated to the Highlands from the more densely settled coastal areas.

For hundreds of years the aristocracy of Vietnam had travelled to the Highlands to escape the heat of summer in the capital cities. They had left many crumbling, once grand palaces and hunting lodges in the town and on rundown estates scattered around the province. The French still had a little influence in this region. Several French families, who had settled here many generations before, had survived the Japanese occupation and the war against French colonialists and lived on large plantations in isolation from the Vietnamese government. They studiously ignored the increasing American presence and made little social contact. A French-run Catholic convent on the north-east edge of town housed closeted Benedictine nuns, including a great-grand-daughter of Emperor Franz Josef of Austria.

The Air America plane landed on a dirt airstrip, the smaller of the town's two airports. The major civilian airport was 14 kilometres east of town, but this dirt aerodrome was the quieter, more discreet way to slip into town. The CIA operative and Australian Army captain hired two cyclos to take them into town. Their destination was Madame Ly Tran Ly's Darlac Hotel, a modest, out-of-the-way, two-storey hotel where a new foreign arrival in town would not receive much obvious attention. The bar girls were young, demure country girls who lacked the hardness and sophistication of the soon-to-be infamous Saigon ladies keeping men company in bars, and providing other services on request. Petersen was given a simple room on the second floor, looking over an internal courtyard and garden and opening on to a veranda running around the hotel. This was to be his home until he settled in and set up his own house.

Bags dumped, Mills and Petersen sat down in the bar and over lunch Mills explained the situation in the province. The Viet Cong were bringing supplies and men down through the Highland jungles to supply operations in the Mekong Delta and Saigon. To combat them the CIA were supplying and funding two paramilitary operations through local Vietnamese authorities. Petersen's first task was to see if the forces the CIA were paying for actually existed, and to find out what they were up to.

Petersen listened intently as he was told the province chief was being paid US$2500 a month in salaries for 200 men who were supposedly in the Force Populaire, a local militia. The local police chief allegedly had a further 100 men in a so-called Armed Propaganda and Intelligence Team. Both were funded and supplied by the CIA. The key question was, did they exist?

Mills took Petersen to meet the Darlac province chief, an aloof army major called Hoang Thong, whose only foreign language was French. Petersen didn't understand the conversation but got the impression Thong was not pleased to have him around. Next stop was the local police headquarters, where Captain Pham Tuong came across as an intelligent, alert officer. Petersen liked him instantly. Tuong took the American and Australian to a nearby barracks to proudly display his 100-strong force. At least these troops existed, thought Petersen. He knew dealing with the province chief was not going to be so easy.

The next day over breakfast Mills reached for a bag and casually handed it to Petersen. He looked inside and was taken aback to see it was stuffed full of Vietnamese banknotes.

'Here, Barry, count this,' Mills said as he returned to his breakfast.

Inside was 35 000 piasters – worth about US$350 – a considerable amount in Vietnamese eyes. At that time a Vietnamese soldier was paid just US$13 a month.

'That's your operational fund,' Mills explained. 'You'll have a revolving fund. Just provide accounting with receipts every month and it will be topped up after whatever you spend.'

Petersen was surprised. As a mere captain he was not used to being given so much money to do with as he wished.

'I'll be back in a couple of weeks. I'll buzz the town in the plane to let you know when I am coming in.'

As Mills got up to leave, Petersen was nonplussed. 'But what am I to do here? What exactly are my instructions?' he asked.

Mills looked down at the young Aussie and smiled. The CIA worked differently to the military, and giving clearly defined, succinct orders was not the way of the secret agent.

'Oh, just get to know the locals,' Mills said nonchalantly. 'Find yourself a good interpreter and see if you can find a house to live in.

'But one bit of advice – there are about 80 Americans here based at the Bungalow. Try to stay away from them. You'll gain more credibility with the locals if they see you are not one of them.'

Petersen felt like a lost soul in a town where he knew nobody, didn't speak the language, and didn't have a clear set of orders. He realised that what he did, and how he did it, was going to be entirely up to him. He might be operating under CIA orders, but supervision was obviously to be very much at arm's length.

In those first days, Petersen was tempted to ignore Mills' advice and seek out some of the Americans based in Ban Me Thuot acting as advisers to the Vietnamese military. Their command HQ, the Bungalow, was a villa formerly used as a hunting lodge by Emperor Bao Dai with a set of ugly solid block buildings out the back surrounded by high walls and barbed wire. Inside the walls were accommodation, a communications centre with secure phone access to Saigon as well as radio and teleprinters, a map room, arms and a supply depot. More importantly, there was a social club where the Americans invited allied expats for parties and film nights.

For years the United States had used Ban Me Thuot as a place to experiment, to try out new methods of battling the Viet Cong and handling the South Vietnamese. In late 1961 the first Green Beret Special Forces arrived there to form hundreds of Rhade tribesmen in Darlac Province into a unit to prevent them from falling under Viet Cong control. By 1962 the US Army had 2000 Green Berets in the Highlands training Montagnard in militia units called the Civilian Irregular Defense Group.[7]

Barry Petersen had a lot to learn about those who had been there before him and how he was going to find his place in the existing order. There were about 200 000 Montagnards in the Highlands. Many were sympathetic to the Viet Cong after the South Vietnamese forced resettlements. Local police chiefs were so paranoid about the hostility of the Montagnard that they confiscated the tribesmen's spears and crossbows when they protested about being forced off their traditional lands.

Yet here were the Americans giving the Montagnard military training and providing them with modern weapons. By the time Petersen arrived more than 10 000 Montagnard had undergone training by the US advisers in camps springing up throughout the Highlands. South Vietnamese authorities watched this with some alarm, fearing the Montagnard could rise up and try to overthrow the Vietnamese in the Highlands. It was not an unfounded fear and the hatred between the two groups was palpable.

The American Special Forces troops lived a life divorced from those around them in the training camps. In a typical US training camp a dozen experienced US Green Berets acted as advisers and lived in a separate heavily defended area within the compound. They had mercenary bodyguards, mostly from the Nung tribe in the north, a fierce warrior people who were taller and stronger than most Asians and had a well-deserved fearsome reputation. Officially the camps were run by the South Vietnamese army – the Army of the Republic of Vietnam (ARVN). But everyone knew it was the Americans who were really in charge. Without them and their money the camps would not be there. The ARVN comprised about 200 soldiers and under them were around 200 Montagnard militia being trained by the Americans.

The ARVN sent the dregs of their army to these outposts, keeping their best soldiers for the defence of Saigon and President Diem. The ARVN troops hated being posted to the mountains far from their familiar rice paddies and lowland villages. Many deserted and some even slipped over to join the Viet Cong.

Meanwhile, the Americans had regular supplies of steaks, beer and music tapes flown in by helicopter. Their frustration with the pointlessness of their mission grew: they were making no inroads in patrolling the jungle outside the camp. It was so thick it could take eight hours to hack their way through a mile of it. They knew their shoddy bases running on low morale would be wiped out overnight in a determined attack by the Viet Cong, who ruled the jungle outside.

In Ban Me Thuot Petersen was starting to understand the reality of the situation in the Highlands. He felt the way the Americans were going about things was counterproductive, but since he needed them for technical help, he set out to acquaint himself with critical people such as the communications, intelligence and supply officers. The Americans had brought the comforts of home with them, and money appeared to be no object. They had a bar, post exchange, shops and tennis courts in their compound. If Petersen let things slide and just went with the flow, living could be easy in Ban Me Thuot. But then he met a couple of Americans who set up instant alarm bells. One was an American Special Forces officer who proudly told Petersen he was recruiting Montagnard deaf mutes.

'He told me his plan was to train these deaf mutes in unarmed combat, to kill with axes and knives,' Petersen later wrote in a confidential report to the Australian Army about his mission. He only wrote the report after his mission was completed and he'd left the Highlands as he did not want it to fall into the wrong hands.

'The idea was to strike terror into the hearts of the Viet Cong by killing them silently with knives and axes. The officer had designed badges depicting a hand and leaflets with a hand print. These would be left behind by the deaf mutes after they had slaughtered Viet Cong. They were to show stealth and power – the dreaded mark of "The Hand".

'I asked him how he trained his deaf mutes to identify Viet Cong. He replied that most of the Viet Cong were Vietnamese and racial identification was sufficient in Viet Cong controlled areas. I explained to him that the day would come when his deaf mutes would not differentiate between Vietnamese citizens and Viet Cong. What then? He replied that did not matter. He was very sympathetic to the Montagnard, as most American Special Forces tended to be.

'I told him he was creating a monster which he would leave behind when he returned to the United States after his six-month tour of duty. He merely laughed and ignored my advice. I therefore reported this program to Bryan Mills of Combined Studies Division in Saigon. I pointed out the resultant dangers of this program. Soon after this the SF officer was told by his headquarters to cancel his program . . .'[8]

After this encounter Petersen decided to keep as far away as he could from the Americans in Ban Me Thuot; he now understood Mills' advice to steer clear of the Bungalow – some of those inside were crazy. It was important to show the locals that he was an independent operator. He declined invitations to the American social club and stuck to his room at the Darlac Hotel.

The town appeared safe to Petersen so when he was out he left his Browning pistol behind in the hotel, locked in a drawer next to his bed. His few papers, including maps, cash and Australian Army orders were kept locked in a drawer at the bottom of his clothes cupboard. He naïvely thought the only enemy he had to worry about was the Viet Cong. He would learn quickly this was not the case.

Petersen's ability to operate independently was severely restricted by his inability to speak Vietnamese, let alone the language of the local Montagnard tribespeople, the Rhade. He had heard of a local American missionary, Reverend Rob Ziemer, who had been in the area for 16 years and who was preparing an English–Rhade dictionary. Petersen visited Ziemer and his wife, Marie, and found they were strict moralists. They disapproved of the Rhade traditional customs of sacrificing animals and drinking home-brewed alcohol, but they had translated the Gospels into Rhade and were working on the dictionary. Petersen was surprised to discover many Rhade words were similar to Malay, which he had learned while posted to Malaya. The Rhade must have similar ethnic origins. He found he could pick up a basic understanding of Rhade fairly quickly, but learning Vietnamese was to be more difficult.

Language wasn't the only stumbling block for Petersen – he ran into a brick wall when he started investigating the 200 paramilitary soldiers the local province chief was supposed to be organising for the CIA. Every time Petersen asked to see them he was given the run-around. He was told they were on manoeuvres, on leave, or given some other excuse. Vietnamese officials brushed him off, and became increasingly hostile when he pressed for an answer. Clearly the local province chief had a racket going and was pocketing the thousands of dollars of CIA money meant for a paramilitary force that simply did not exist. This was not news the province chief would want to get back to the CIA. Petersen knew officers had been killed for less, and it was soon clear how vulnerable he was stuck out on his own in Ban Me Thuot.

A week after Petersen arrived in the town a Vietnamese driver delivered an old battered army truck promised by Bryan Mills. Petersen was delighted and hoped that the affable driver, Bui Thi Vu, could serve as his interpreter. He found out Vu was related to the provincial chief, and almost certainly had been sent to act as an informant. Despite this Petersen decided to keep Vu, but he would make sure he didn't do or say anything in front of him that he would not want reported to the province chief.

Then things took a turn for the worse. Petersen had put to good use the tricks of the spy trade he had learned at Swan Island. Before he left his hotel room each day he arranged his papers in the locked drawer at the bottom of his wardrobe so that he could tell if they had been moved. He stacked papers so they left a certain word uncovered, arranged his pistol at a particular angle, left a human hair across the top of the drawer that would be dislodged when the drawer was opened – a secret service trick later shown in a James Bond film. After Petersen had been in the hotel for a week, he discovered the papers had been moved and the hair knocked away. He set the trap again. Again the evidence showed someone had been in his room and had looked in the drawer. He realised his room was being searched almost every time he left it to go into the town centre. No money was ever taken and his pistol was left untouched so he knew this was not the work of thieves. Petersen resolved to leave nothing in his room that could give the local Vietnamese reason to have him murdered. Better to play ignorant and naïve – and stay alive.

Then whoever was watching him stepped the game up another notch. Late one night, while lying in bed, he heard someone moving outside his door. He could see most of the room by the moonlight filtering through the curtainless windows facing onto the veranda. He watched as the door handle turned slowly, and quietly reached over to open the bedside drawer where he kept his gun. The drawer was locked. He looked aghast at the keys still hanging in the lock on the door. He could see somebody was trying to push the key out of the lock from the outside. It was an old-fashioned lock so that if they pushed the key out on his side they could put a key in on the other side and unlock the door. He would not have time to pull the key out of the door lock, run back to the bedside drawer and unlock it to get his gun out. So he grabbed the only weapon he could find – one of his heavy army boots. He stood, holding it up ready to defend himself.

Perhaps sensing movement, whoever was outside suddenly dropped any pretence at stealth. They kicked the door and hurled themselves at it, trying to crash their way through. But the door held. All went quiet. Petersen stood still, waiting. He watched, barely breathing as one shadow crossed the veranda window, then another. Two men stood there peering in. Petersen could see them clearly – stocky, tough-looking Vietnamese men staring at him with deadly cold eyes. Assassins. He knew they could see him as he stood in the middle of the room holding his army boot. Seconds ticked by as they stared at Petersen, and he stared back. No one said a thing. Then they left. Petersen rushed to the door, grabbed his keys and unlocked the drawer to pull out his pistol. He looked out to the veranda. Nothing. He unlocked the front door. There was no sign anybody had ever been there. It was clearly a warning: back off or else.

For the first time in Vietnam he felt fear. He realised he'd been too cavalier – never again did he allow that pistol to lie beyond his immediate reach. He also wanted to ensure he was legally covered should he have to shoot anyone who tried to break in. There was a difference between shooting somebody in combat and shooting somebody in the relative security of a town.

Barry Petersen reported the attempted break-in to Captain Pham Tuong, and asked if he should have his hand gun registered with the police. Tuong assured him it wasn't necessary. But Petersen had made his point. He'd made it known he would kill the next time someone tried to break in to his room. He was relying on the word filtering out to whomever was behind the attempt to intimidate him. It didn't happen again.

4
THE CIA COUP

Mills reappeared six weeks after he had dumped Petersen in Ban Me Thuot. An Air America Dornier swooped low over the town three times and by the second swoop Petersen was already on his way out to the airstrip in the truck driven by Vu. He watched as the little five-seater plane taxied to a halt and Mills got out. He was the only passenger on the plane. Petersen was relieved to see the American had a big bag of cash – he had chalked up quite a few debts around town, including his hotel bill, fuel for the truck and Vu's wages. The first thing on Bryan Mills' mind, however, was a good drink in a small, out-of-the-way bar for a discreet chat.

'Have you found those 200 troops we are paying for, Barry?' Mills asked.

'I don't think they exist, Bryan.'

'That figures. This sort of thing is happening all over the country.'

Mills confided that the CIA and the US government were fed up with the corruption in the ranks of their Vietnamese allies and had decided to stop giving financial aid to provincial governors and military commanders for what were called 'psychological' operations – propaganda actions designed to turn local people against the Viet Cong. Even more drastically, the US had closed off all funds for military units that were not actually involved in combat operations. This included the notorious Special Forces units that made up the presidential guard in Saigon – President Diem's personal bodyguard. Commanders and governors would be unhappy once the taps to the stream of US dollars were turned off.

It meant that the force in Ban Me Thuot that did exist – the 100 men in the police chief's propaganda and intelligence force – would not get paid.

'You've got enough money in that bag to pay for them for a few weeks. You'll just have to look after them,' said Mills with a wave of his hand, as though it didn't really matter to him.

The truth was Mills had bigger worries. The political situation in Saigon was rapidly deteriorating. More monks were burning themselves to death in the streets and demonstrations against the Diem regime were being put down brutally by Diem's thugs in the secret police. The US was losing patience with Diem, who seemed more obsessed with imposing Catholic domination over the Buddhists and extending his family's control than fighting the rising strength of the communists and the infiltration from North Vietnam.

'If anything does happen, Barry, you'll be OK up here in old Ban Me Thuot,' Mills said as he climbed into his plane to head back to Saigon. Once he took off, Petersen was again on his own.

A few days later a fit-looking young Rhade man approached Petersen as he left his hotel. This was to prove the turning point in his mission. 'I believe you are looking for an interpreter, Sir?' he said in perfect English.

The Rhade was 19-year-old Y-Tin Hwing, who had heard Petersen was asking around for someone who could speak English, Rhade and Vietnamese. Petersen hired the young lad on the spot. He was to be the first of half a dozen or so interpreters and fixers he used during his time in the Highlands.

The local Vietnamese police director, Captain Pham Tuong, was in a tough spot: without the CIA money he could not pay the 100 men in his Armed Propaganda and Intelligence Team. Having 100 armed men angry at not being paid was not a good position for a commander to be in, so he was relieved when Petersen offered to pay the men's wages until more money came from Saigon. Through this offer Petersen won himself an important friend.

However, storm clouds were gathering over Saigon that would have major consequences for Vietnam, and Petersen in Ban Me Thuot. On 31 October 1963, Colonel Ted Serong flew in to visit Petersen to get an update on what he was doing for the CIA. That afternoon they were talking in the hotel bar when they heard rumours that something big was happening in Saigon – possibly even a coup.

Serong was frustrated he was stuck in this provincial town while the action was breaking out in the capital. Fuming and pacing the room, he hit the phone desperately, trying to find out what was going on. He could not get through to anyone on the Vietnamese telephone system, so the two Australians went to the American Bungalow to get news.

The rumours proved true. Saigon was in turmoil; the airport was closed, Vietnamese soldiers were in the streets, but details of what it meant and where it was going were sketchy. Petersen and Serong returned to Petersen's hotel room and sat listening to Radio Saigon as Y-Tin translated what was being said. The big change in news came when the radio station was stormed by army rebels supporting the military coup, which was being led by the army's second-in-command, General Duong Van Minh. He was also known as Big Minh as he was unusually tall and hefty for a Vietnamese man. There were reports of fighting in the streets and the presidential palace under siege.

Serong wasn't shocked by the mutiny. He had got on well with Diem – both were strong Catholics and had mutual friends in high places, such as Melbourne Archbishop Daniel Mannix and fiercely anti-communist Australian Catholic political leader BA 'Bob' Santamaria. When Serong had first arrived in Vietnam, Diem pressed him to deploy his Australian Army Training Team in Quang Ngai in central Vietnam. Serong refused, wanting to spread his small training team around the country to have a more widespread impact. A broad deployment also gave Serong valuable eyes and ears in more parts of the country. He would later be stunned to discover the depth of Diem's deviousness; he had thought their mutual devotion to the Catholic cause and anti-communism made them close allies and personal friends. Just months before the revolt, Diem had asked Serong during one of their one-on-one meetings whether he knew why he had urged him to put all his trainers in Quang Ngai.

'I reasoned that if they were all killed your government would feel compelled to commit more troops to the defence of my country,' Diem told Serong.[1] Brutally, Diem and his brother would not have been above arranging a terrorist attack on the Australians using their hit squads dressed in black VC pyjamas to make them look like Viet Cong.

It was this sort of duplicity that turned the Americans against their erstwhile ally. Diem and his brother Nhu's ruthless crackdown on the Buddhists and photos of Buddhist monks burning themselves caused great unease in Washington. They felt they could no longer control the man. They were right.

The US Embassy was also increasingly alarmed at Nhu's growing influence and erratic behaviour. His secret police were arresting scores of dissidents every day, including children handing out anti-government pamphlets or scrawling slogans on walls.[2] Worse still, Nhu was becoming more and more nationalist, denouncing Americans in public and private almost every day. He accused American officials of 'destroying the psychology of our country' and 'initiating a process of disintegration'.

Nhu had even managed to plant listening devices inside the US Embassy, embarrassing US officials with remarkably accurate accounts of their confidential internal discussions in his English language newspaper the *Times of Vietnam*.

Nhu was playing a dangerous double game. His regime depended on US military and financial support to survive, but he was also dabbling with reaching an agreement with North Vietnam that would allow his family to stay in power. He made secret overtures to the North through French intermediaries in which he proposed backing off his persecution of communists if the North would stay out of the South. This signalled that despite his anti-communist rhetoric and arrests of communists, Nhu was ready to strike a peace deal with North Vietnam. The North had been pressing Nhu to recognise that the true enemy of both North and South Vietnam was the United States, that once the US military advisers were forced to leave, North and South could sit down and discuss a truce. The North was prepared to move to a gradual reunification and the establishment of a Western-style democracy in a neutral and independent Vietnam. Nhu was so keen on the deal he told the Northern agents he would be prepared to send his children to school in Hanoi as a gesture of trust. When the US got wind of this, Nhu claimed the US was forcing him towards the communists. Madame Nhu stoked the fires even further on a tour of the US where she denounced American liberals as worse than communists and dismissed Buddhist monks as 'hooligans in robes'.

For a short time an alarmed White House pondered whether Vietnam was really worth it. Robert Kennedy wondered if any Saigon regime could resist the communists, and whether 'now was not the time to get out of Vietnam entirely'.[3] The suggestion didn't go anywhere. To leave would be to admit defeat, and President John F Kennedy could not afford that humiliation as he looked forward to a second term in office; a peace deal between North and South could cost him re-election in 1964. He told a friend, Charles Bartlett, that he could not let South Vietnam go and then ask Americans to vote for him. 'Somehow we have got to hold that territory through the 1964 election,' he told his friend. Kennedy also told Bartlett he knew the US could not win a military war in Vietnam, and that eventually they would 'kick our asses out of there'.[4]

Petersen and Serong didn't know it, but the US decision to stop paying for militias under the command of regional governors and police chiefs was the secret signal for mutinous generals to go ahead with the overthrow of Diem. This was a US-backed coup, and the decision was made right at the very top by President John F Kennedy himself.

Kennedy approved the coup on the proviso that Americans were not directly involved in the plot. The frontman from the CIA and the US link to the coup generals was veteran CIA operative Lucien Conein, a colourful character and one of the CIA's top dirty-tricks performers. Conein had fought with the French resistance during World War Two. When the European war ended, he joined a company of French and Vietnamese commandos harassing Japanese posts in northern Vietnam. As Japan surrendered he entered Hanoi and had talks with Ho Chi Minh. Nine years later he covertly headed back into North Vietnam to sabotage the communist transport system. He had met many Vietnamese officers who later rose to become generals in key positions. Conein had been in Vietnam since 1962 as 'adviser' to the Saigon Ministry of the Interior.

Conein conveyed to the coup plotters that they had the green light from the US administration to depose Diem and Nhu. On 1 November the generals moved, isolating and killing key Diem loyalists and surrounding the presidential palace. Diem, hiding in the cellar of the palace, made a desperate phone call to US Ambassador Henry Cabot Lodge for help. Lodge feigned ignorance of what was going on, but offered safe conduct out of the country for Diem and his family if he resigned. Diem realised his time was up. He and his brother waited until dark, slipped out of the palace at around 8pm and drove to Cholon, the Chinese district of Saigon. They hid in the villa of a wealthy merchant who had backed them for years in return for lucrative deals. When the rebels stormed the palace at 9pm loyal palace guards fought back fiercely for hours. Many died on both sides not knowing Diem had already fled.

As dawn broke in Ban Me Thuot a desperate Serong was anxious to get back to Saigon to protect his family and oversee the position of the Australian military. The Ban Me Thuot army commander had stayed loyal to Diem until midnight, when he was forced at gunpoint by his deputy to surrender his division to the mutineers. The provincial chief held out longer, sending vans around the city until mid-morning with loudspeakers mounted on the roof broadcasting appeals to the people to stay loyal to President Diem. When the military switched sides, Serong was able to persuade a Vietnamese plane to fly him to Saigon. Petersen was left to his fate in the Highlands.

Diem had played his last card in Saigon by 6am. Desperate calls to generals he hoped had remained loyal were met with curses. Thinking he had secured safe passage out of the country, Diem told the coup leaders they could pick him up from St Francis Xavier Church in Cholon. There was just one big problem. The generals didn't have a plan to get Diem out of the country. They asked Conein for help, but he hadn't made plans for it either. The US would not grant Diem and Nhu asylum, and it would take days to find any other country that would.

The generals gave the job of picking up the deposed brothers to one of their most ruthless soldiers, former secret police thug General Mai Huu Xian. Xian took a couple of cold-blooded killers with him in two jeeps and an armoured personnel carrier. Diem and Nhu were suspicious of Xian and were upset they did not have a limousine befitting their dignity. Xian explained the APC was necessary as the streets were not safe. Diem and Nhu reluctantly got inside the armoured car. It was their death trap. At a relatively deserted point on the way back to Saigon the little convoy stopped. Two soldiers in the APC pulled out their automatic weapons and sprayed the brothers with bullets, then stabbed their bodies repeatedly. The hated Nhu came in for particularly grizzly treatment. The back of the APC was awash with blood and the bodies of Diem and Nhu were barely recognisable. The convoy then drove on to military headquarters.

General Minh told Conein the brothers had committed suicide, which Conein said was laughable as they were strict Catholics. 'There's a one in a million chance that people will believe your story. But if the truth gets out, I don't want to be blamed for leaking it,' Conein said.[5]

There were no tears for Diem and Nhu. People poured on to the streets cheering the coup leaders, and tore down Diem's portraits and slogans. Political prisoners scarred from torture were released from jail. Nightclubs opened up and in the countryside peasants demolished the fortified villages they had been forced to live in. Ambassador Lodge invited the coup leaders to his office to congratulate them.

Lodge sent a cable to President Kennedy: 'The prospects now are for a shorter war.'

Kennedy would not have long to savour the thought of victory. Three weeks later he was assassinated.

5
TIGER HUNT

The coup against Diem brought big changes to Ban Me Thuot and a marked improvement for Petersen. The regime change meant new cronies in key positions. The new Darlac province chief was an army officer, Colonel Le Van Thanh, a strong Catholic and seasoned soldier. Petersen felt he was a man he could deal with on a professional level. Thanh turned out to be a soldier Petersen would respect and consider a friend.

A new regional police chief also arrived, a tough, experienced professional called Ong Nguyen Binh who had served with internal security. Binh could not speak English, nor could his deputy and head of security, Phan Tan Truoc.

Petersen took an immediate dislike to Truoc, viewing him as a cunning schemer who was not to be trusted. Truoc was suspicious of Petersen and what he was up to. Petersen noticed Truoc resented his easy access to US-supplied cash and that he had been paying the 100 men of the police chief's Armed Propaganda and Intelligence Team since the money stopped coming from the US.

But Truoc had one big weakness – whisky – and Petersen knew how to exploit that weakness. Over the next few months he made sure his regular CIA shipments of supplies included crates of whisky to dish out to Truoc. Petersen also gave whisky and gifts to other officials in strategic positions. If they then passed these 'gifts' on to Truoc they won themselves favours, and Petersen had another grateful friend in the Vietnamese hierarchy.

Petersen then discovered the new police chief's passion was hunting. After they had been on a couple of hunting trips he arranged to get hold of some prized hunting guns from the CIA and presented them to Binh. He was fast learning the delicate art of diplomacy and bribery.

Petersen needed to get the 100 men away from Ban Me Thuot. They were doing very little, and certainly not patrolling the province, handing out propaganda and collecting intelligence as they were supposed to do. He was also concerned that Truoc had designs on turning the militia into his private bodyguard. Petersen went to Binh and convinced him the Montagnard members of the team should be housed in a village outside Ban Me Thuot where he could train them properly in jungle warfare.

The place he selected was Buon Enao, a half-empty Montagnard village a few kilometres east of Ban Me Thuot. It had previously been used by the CIA-sponsored US Special Forces as a training base.

But Truoc wasn't going to give up that easily, insisting on being present whenever the Australian visited the militia unit. When Petersen asked Bryan Mills for advice on how he could shake off Truoc, the unflappable CIA operator told him to tell the police chief he had received authority from Saigon to take over the team. The experienced Mills knew a trick or two. He produced a letter on US embassy letterhead signed by a senior US official thanking the police chief for his cooperation and praising him for his vision in the way he was running the province.

When the news was delivered, police chief Binh was puzzled, as he had received no instructions from Saigon personally. Mills said it must be a bureaucratic mix-up in either Saigon or Ban Me Thuot. Since he wasn't paying for the militia, Binh felt he didn't have much choice. Over the protests of his deputy Truoc, the police chief handed over the 100 men to Petersen at a formal ceremony in Buon Enao. The militia was given a new name to designate its new operation: the Truong Son Force, after the mountain range running along the ridge of the Highlands.

Petersen was surprised at how easy it had been. When he asked Mills about it, the American gave him a knowing smile and said it was best not to ask too many questions. As a result of Mills' trick Petersen now had total control of 100 men in the Central Highlands of South Vietnam.

With this force Petersen's mission gathered pace. He hired a second Vietnamese translator and fixer called Y-Jut Buon To, who found him a large rambling house to rent in one of the leafy tree-lined streets. With five large rooms in the main building and a rudimentary kitchen, laundry and servants' quarters out the back leading into a substantial walled garden, it was big enough for Petersen to use as both a headquarters and a home. Conditions were fairly primitive – a standard Vietnamese squat toilet, water had to be brought from a nearby well in a cyclo and the layout of the doors in the house meant you had to go outside and around the building to get into the neighbouring room.

Mills told Petersen to use his CIA operational funds to make the place liveable. Within a few weeks Petersen had running tap water, a pedestal installed in one of the toilets, and holes bashed in walls for doors to go directly from room to room. In the months ahead he converted these rooms into a living room, a classroom, an armoury, a radio room, a bedroom for himself and another for guests and bunk bed rooms for his security staff. Household staff were easily found, and two sisters, Nam and Hai, became cook and housekeeper. Petersen preferred to eat Vietnamese food and left them to run the laundry and kitchen in their own way. He hired several trusted Montagnard men from Truong Son Force as security to stand at the front gate and patrol the grounds. More importantly, he hired H'Chioh Nie, the wife of the local doctor, to act as his secretary and bookkeeper. She turned out to be invaluable to Petersen's operation.

H'Chioh spoke English, Vietnamese, French and several Montagnard dialects. She played a crucial role assisting Petersen typing up his reports, keeping accounts, interviewing potential interpreters and sometimes acted as an alternative interrogator of captured Viet Cong. Her gender and gentle nature made the prisoners feel they could trust her, so she regularly obtained more information from prisoners than the most severe interrogation.

The household steadily grew and became home to a small menagerie of animals. The police director deposed after Diem's fall had asked Petersen to take his peacocks and pet monkey and as Petersen toured the Montagnard villages further and further out from Ban Me Thuot he was presented with gifts of a deer, a gibbon ape, a young sun bear and even a tiger cub, which he called 'Tiger'. As Tiger grew, her roars became as effective against intruders as all the security guards put together.

The tiger cub was given to Petersen by a Chinese–Vietnamese merchant who provided the supplies for the men at Buon Enao – they always bought their own rice and food rather than expect it from the nearby villagers. It was an easy way to keep animosity to a minimum.

The tiger had been kept in a cage, and hadn't been played with enough by humans when she was a baby. Over time she slowly got used to her new home, but she was never a cuddly house pet – a broomstick was required to keep her off whenever anyone went near her. Her roars became legend around Ban Me Thuot.

Petersen was also given a female leopard cub by Montagnard tribesmen who had killed its mother in a trap. She was tiny and cried all the time. Petersen called her Fatima and slept with her next to him in his bed. She snuggled up to him for warmth and company.

The combination of young bear, roaring tiger and playful leopard created havoc in the military man's household. Fatima insisted on exploring every part of the house and garden and climbing all over Petersen and his guests. The bear and tiger lived outside and had cages to sleep in, but they all seemed to get on well together.

The leopard often crawled along the top of the garden wall and jumped into a neighbouring tree to descend on Vietnamese working in houses along the street. Every so often there would be screams and people running helter-skelter from houses and shops until one of Petersen's staff recovered the inquisitive animal. After a while they got to know Fatima and realised she was harmless and only looking for a cuddle.

The tiger, leopard and bear started to earn Petersen a reputation as a wild man of the mountain. Word spread of this strange Australian who had a leopard sleeping in his bed and a tiger and a bear living in his garden. It was not what the villagers expected and showed them that Barry Petersen was a special man.

Petersen knew not to take his safety for granted. From the beginning he gave strict instructions to his kitchen staff to buy only live chickens and pigs to slaughter themselves. This was not a problem for Vietnamese women, who usually slaughtered their own chickens kept in backyards. Petersen knew dressed meat could be easily poisoned, a favoured Asian method of getting rid of foreigners and high authority figures without having to storm the barricades and risk lives. If the Viet Cong wanted to kill Petersen it would be very easy to sell his staff poisoned chicken or pork.

One day Nam was walking to the market when she was approached by a merchant in the street who offered her a good deal on chicken meat. She thought it would be fine for the pets, so she bought some. When she got home she fed it to the leopard. Fatima fell sick and died very quickly.

Petersen took the leopard's death hard. At first he thought it was the communists trying to kill him, but then he realised it was more likely to be deputy police chief Truoc, who had men watching the Australian. He was still angry that Petersen had taken the 100 men of the propaganda team.

Truoc wasn't the only enemy Petersen was to earn among his supposed allies. But that he was to find out much later.

In the meantime he threw himself into training and equipping his Montagnard troops in the Truong Son Force. He was loaded up by the CIA with propaganda material – film projectors and propaganda films that mesmerised the tribesmen, a small printing press for printing up leaflets, as well as gifts such as children's toys, shirts, rice bowls and chopsticks, sewing kits, fishing rods – all marked as gifts from the government of South Vietnam. Petersen thought they were pretty useless in winning over the Montagnard, who he found were not as primitive and naïve as the Americans and Vietnamese believed.

Most of those in his Truong Son Force came from the local tribe, the Rhade, a tough, gritty people of Malay–Polynesian descent who were ethnically and culturally quite different from the Vietnamese. They had a reputation as fierce and ruthless warriors, and Petersen was keen to see what they would do with 20th-century weapons.

The term Montagnard was used by the early French missionaries to describe the hill tribes living in the mountain range stretching from the Yunnan plateau in China right down through South East Asia. The hill tribes and their rugged jungle tribal lands existed long before arbitrary border lines on maps were drawn through the Highlands. To the hill tribes, borders meant very little. The Rhade considered their tribal lands stretched from Vietnam right over the border into Cambodia, and they frequently wandered back and forth using jungle paths across the border without a second's thought.

In the 1960s the Montagnard were a major part of the population in many South East Asian countries and their traditional lands accounted for a large slab of the nations. In Laos they were half the population and occupied 80 per cent of the land area. In Burma the hill tribes were 20 per cent of the population and held more than half the land.

In South Vietnam around 30 Montagnard tribes made up 15 per cent of the country's population, but they occupied more than two-thirds of the land. That was before the Diem regime decided on a policy of forcibly resettling Vietnamese from the crowded coastal areas. Vietnamese authorities treated the Montagnard with disdain, riding roughshod over their land claims and treating them generally like dirt. The Vietnamese settlers hated being in the highlands as they found the environment hostile with its jungle animals and inferior farming land. They also looked down on the local hillpeople, calling them *moi* – savages.

But the Montagnard were the key to the survival of the US-backed South Vietnamese government. They lived on lands that sat astride the Ho Chi Minh Trail, the winding supply lines through the jungle for the North Vietnamese to get men and equipment down to the south. They knew the mountains and jungles like the backs of their hands and nothing moved in their area without them knowing about it. The South was not doing a good job in winning over the Montagnard; the North was promising autonomy and self-government if they won the war. Many Montagnard people had already defected to the North or cooperated with the local Viet Cong because of their poor treatment at the hands of the South Vietnamese.

Americans recognised the military importance of the Montagnard, and in particular the Rhade, whose traditional lands in Darlac Province were the gate from North to South leading down to Saigon. The CIA had been setting up Montagnard militia groups to take on the communists in the mountains of Laos, Cambodia and Vietnam ever since the French were defeated in 1954.

From the very start Petersen had a soft spot for the Montagnard. He spoke Malay and also knew some of the indigenous languages. So when he first heard Rhade spoken he was surprised he could understand many of the words. The dialect was different, but he could hold an elementary conversation with the Rhade people, most of whom spoke no language other than their own. This gave him an enormous advantage as he went out to make contact with the villagers to try to persuade them to supply troops for his force and intelligence on the movement of communist forces through their area.

He had learned about Rhade customs, that it was a matriarchal society in that the senior women held the land and property and therefore the real power, and that the men always consulted the women in community decision-making. The women mostly deferred to the men in public ceremonial duties and men led daily activities including farming decisions and, importantly for Petersen, whether to send young men to join a militia. He'd read up as much as he could on the formalities of Rhade ceremony and been briefed thoroughly by his translator. Having observed how Americans would usually drive right into the village in their jeeps, splashing mud and tearing up the streets as though they owned the place, Petersen was determined to show respect and win friends.

All this was tucked away in his mind as the earnest army captain from Queensland dressed in jungle greens tried to make a good first impression: he left his vehicle at the village gate and walked into the village with his translator. Chickens and small pigs scurried out of his way as he walked up the dirt lane that looked like the main road of the village. Rhade children stopped their playing and stared at him, fascinated at the good-looking young white man who walked without bodyguards and did not display guns. The Rhade live in longhouses, the extended family all having their own allocated space in the thatched building constructed on piles above the ground.

Petersen recalls that the Rhade did not need much of an excuse to open a jar or two of fermented rice wine, usually accompanied by the ritual sacrifice of at least one chicken or a pig, depending on the importance of the visitor. For very important occasions they slaughtered a buffalo. He tried to dissuade them from sacrificing their much-needed livestock, but to protest too much risked offending them.

The sacrifice involved waving a chicken over the visitor's head, then killing it and letting the blood drip on their bare foot, which rests on an axe head, while a shaman chants. Villagers come up and put a brass bracelet on the guest's wrist signifying friendship.

To refuse to drink their rice wine would be a major offence. In some tribal cultures refusing a drink would bring down bad fortune, curses from evil spirits, even death, on the headman. The Rhade drinking ceremony puts an Aussie skolling contest to shame.

The wine concoction is made by crushing rice, wild ginger root and bark into a paste which is rolled into small balls and left to dry. Then they are mixed with boiled rice and placed over a layer of bran and rice husks inside a jar that is sealed with banana leaves and left to ferment for weeks, or even months. To drink it the seal is removed, fresh green leaves are stuffed into it, water is poured into the jar, filling it to the brim. The host inserts a long bamboo drinking tube deep into the jar.

The first person offered a taste is the senior lady in the household. She takes a sip, then hands the straw to the honoured guest. Petersen found it pretty rough stuff. Sometimes it tasted like cider, sometimes sour, sometimes sweet, depending on the extra ingredients.

It was not a pleasant drinking experience. Sometimes grit and even wriggly weevils came up through the straw. It was a real test to keep smiling and get it down. The first time he was honoured with the ceremony Petersen could see the Rhade watching, examining how he took it as though it was a measure of his worth. He made sure a smile never left his face.

At Petersen's first village the headman announced the Australian would have to consume seven or eight glasses of rice wine before he could hand his jar on to someone else. Anxious to make a good impression, Petersen dutifully downed six or seven glasses before pleading that he was full, and passed the straw on. When the headman laughed and smiled he thought he had got out of it. Then they opened several other jars and the tribe was becoming very cheery.

With a bloated and rumbling stomach he retreated to the wall thinking he could sit and recover for a while, but to his horror they began to send him glasses from their own jars. Then he was handed a bowl of rice with some sort of meat and raw offal with fresh blood dripped over it like sauce.

His stomach did a double flip, but with the greater purpose in mind, and telling himself that if he survived the torture school in Sydney he could get through this, he ate some of the food and drank a little more of the rice wine. But just then one of the tribe laughed and showed how he was about to open another jar. On the verge of throwing up, Petersen got up and staggered to the rear entrance of the longhouse.

The only way up and down from the raised floor of the longhouse was via a log with steps cut into it. He knew he couldn't get down it in the dark, and his churning stomach had no time to lose, so he launched himself into space hoping he would land on something soft.

Petersen hit the ground just as his stomach lost its fight with its contents and lay there heaving. He was a complete mess and felt miserable.

Y-Jut descended the ladder nimbly and asked his commanding officer if he was all right.

'No' came the pitiful reply.

Y-Jut took Petersen down to the nearby creek to help him wash off the vomit. After a few long drinks of water the damp but gallant Aussie captain returned to the fray. The tribe greeted him with smiles and nods of approval and Petersen groaned as they held out several cups full of rice wine for him to replenish what he had just lost. He held out his hand and accepted a cup of the dreaded liquid, winning laughs and backslaps from the locals. He had won new friends.

It was a test of endurance, a matter of honour. Petersen felt this was a strange way to fight a war, but he upheld Australia's reputation in the drinking stakes.

He had to go through this ceremony every time he visited a Rhade village, but soon realised it was perfectly acceptable in local etiquette after a few drinks to get up from the circle and walk out of the longhouse to throw up in nearby bushes – so long as you returned for more. He also learned a few tricks to keep his intake as little as possible.

With his fascination for Africa, the young Barry Petersen fancied he'd grow up to be a famous game warden on an African wildife reserve protecting people from fierce lions, rhinos and leopards. So when he visited a remote Montagnard village and the chief asked him to hunt down a tiger which was stalking the nearby jungle taking their livestock he couldn't believe his ears.

With just spears and arrows as weapons, the villagers were afraid the tiger was going to take one of their children playing in the jungle, or even come into the village in search of easy prey. Petersen was going about his work spreading word of his mission and seeking intelligence on the Viet Cong so certainly didn't expect to be asked to protect anyone from a tiger. But he wasn't going to let this chance go by.

They took him to a bamboo grove in the jungle where this tiger had been seen. He could smell it. Tigers mark their territory and it had the powerful stink of stale urine; judging by this one it must have been a big male. Petersen had come across tigers in Malaya. While patrolling along a stream, he suddenly smelled the urine then heard a growl from the undergrowth. Backing off, he diverted the platoon in a big circle and they rejoined the stream further on.

Petersen remembered from adventure books he'd read as a kid that the best way to get a tiger was to find a clearing, stake out a goat or sheep as bait then let the tiger take one or two goats to let him think the clearing was safe. You'd build a hide up in a tall tree and shoot the tiger when it came in to take the next bait.

He recalls how he went out like a great white hunter and found the right sort of clearing with a big tree. 'We started building a platform up in the tree and covered it with branches. I remembered it was important to wait until it was raining to tether the goat so that it washed away the smell of humans. Luckily it rained that very night so after tethering a goat in the clearing we left it. When we came back in the morning the goat was gone. The tiger had taken the bait. We did it again a few nights later just before rain. Again the tiger took the goat.

'It was becoming one very well fed tiger so we waited a couple more nights before setting the trap. At dusk it was raining lightly, it was almost misty, and I climbed up to the tree platform with Y-Tin. We were both armed with Springfield .30-06 calibre sniper rifles – more then enough to kill a tiger at close range.

'The villagers tethered the third sacrificial goat in the clearing and we settled down to wait. The poor thing was bleating plaintively, but this was good as the tiger would hear it and be summoned for the kill.

'I remember the insects were bloody awful that night. The air was thick with termites, which had taken to the air. They swarmed on our sweaty skin and tried to crawl into my mouth and eyes. I hoped they wouldn't block my view when the tiger came.'

Time seemed to stretch forever that night as Petersen strained his ears to make sense of every faint rustle from the thick jungle. He dared not take his eyes off the goat in the centre of the clearing as he knew the tiger would move very fast, no matter how confident it felt. Then Petersen thought he saw something move in the bushes at the border of the clearing closest to the goat.

'I wasn't sure if it was the tiger or some other animal. I had to wait until it came out. If I missed with the first shot the tiger would get away and he wouldn't fall for the trap a second time. I waited, waited, staring at the spot where I thought the tiger would make its lunge for the poor goat.'

Suddenly the tense silence was interrupted by the sound of suppressed voices jabbering at the base of the tree. Petersen looked down and saw villagers beckoning to him to come down.

'I waved at them to go away, but they kept beckoning to me. I told Y-Tin to go down and tell them to go away, the tiger is near. Y-Tin shinned down the ladder and I saw him in a heated, hushed discussion as both sides waved their arms. I was furious as the tiger would have to be stone-deaf or drunk on rice wine not to hear the commotion.'

Y-Tin hissed up to Petersen, 'Sir!'

'Quiet,' Petersen hissed back.

'Sir,' Y-Tin said in a more anxious tone. 'VC coming.'

Petersen quickly assessed his situation. Here he was, stuck up a tree with a sniper rifle, villagers below him, a tiger in the bushes, and the Viet Cong coming for him. He was a sitting duck. He decided it was best to make a strategic withdrawal.

'I got down that tree faster than Tarzan of the Apes, and we scarpered out of there as fast as we could.

'Back at the village I learned that the Viet Cong had heard about my plan to kill the tiger days ago. They had prepared their own trap to snare the prize kill of an Australian officer. The great white hunter had become the great white hunted. I never found out if it really was the tiger in the bushes, but I never returned for a second go. The tiger lived to fight another day. I suppose I did too.'

Word spread about Barry Petersen's visits and the village headmen were usually pleased to see him. They offered him their young men as recruits, wanting protection for their village against the Viet Cong, who were also visiting the villagers and forcing them to hand over supplies and send young men to join their forces living in the jungles.

Across the country, particularly in the north, the VC often used terror and murder to force villagers into supporting them. They were particularly keen on killing Americans and went to great lengths to target white men they saw with groups of Vietnamese and Montagnard soldiers.

At first the Vietnamese and Montagnard saw Petersen as American. Every European-looking person was American in their eyes. Most of them did not know anything about Australia and even after they got to know him and that he was Australian, it still didn't mean anything to them.

When visiting villages looking for recruits Petersen was always trying to gather intelligence about movements of VC in their area, what they were up to and so on. Sometimes the visit was just to let the villagers get to know him so that next time he visited they might have intelligence to give him about what was going on around their village.

He usually travelled with one of his translators and a guard. They mostly stayed overnight as the drinking sessions would go late into the night, but he made a point never to stay two nights in the same village as word could get around to the VC he was there. Still, the VC had ears everywhere and could move fast. On several occasions Petersen was sleeping in a village after a big night on rice wine when he was hurriedly awakened to be told the VC were coming. He'd have to grab his boots and scarper. He never thought to stay and fight as he didn't want to put his hosts in danger.

Petersen could never really tell if the villagers were on his side. These people were caught in the middle of the conflict and having lived under the same primitive tribal lore they had used for thousands of years, neither communist nor democratic principles meant much to them. Their lives were governed by seasons and the demands of slash and burn farming and their beliefs centred on satisfying often competing demands of mythical jungle spirits and tribal legends. They did not support the government of South Vietnam, hated Vietnamese whether they be from North or South, and just wanted to be left alone. But that was not to be.

'We knew that VC would most likely come in straight after us the next night to spread their own propaganda and recruit fighters, and those VC would most likely be Montagnard themselves,' Petersen recalls. 'Many Montagnard went from one side to the other without feeling any guilt about it as they were not committed to the political causes behind either side.

The one big thing Montagnard on either side had in common was that they both hated the Vietnamese.'

Colonel Serong visited every few months to see how the Aussie captain was going. His region was not as violent as those further to the north, which were coming under increasing attacks from Viet Cong, sometimes bolstered by forces from North Vietnam.

After a short time in the Highlands Petersen strongly believed that the area held the key to the war against the communists and constantly tried to impress upon Serong that the Highlands were vital to the defence of Vietnam. Serong argued that a strong army in the north of the country was vital to stop the communists. Petersen noted that many years later Serong claimed in his biography that he realised all the time that the Highlands had been the key, but that was after the North broke through in Ban Me Thuot.

According to Petersen, the communists did not want confrontation in the Highlands. They wanted a clear run there so they could bring their forces and supplies down the Ho Chi Minh Trail to the coastal areas and Saigon. In the first few months Petersen was there he noticed the supply lines were constantly increasing. And it wasn't just fighting men in the forces heading down the trail, there were doctors, political officers, specialists in propaganda and communications and men trained in laying mines and booby traps. Petersen gained this information through defectors, from interrogations of prisoners and the local tribespeople who were talking to Montagnard working among the North Vietnamese forces.

Petersen's rigorous training of his 100 men in the Truong Son Force had gone well. He now had a disciplined unit, still untested in battle but well used to patrolling in eight-man teams in the jungles around Buon Enao and nearby Montagnard villages.

He asked Serong for an experienced warrant officer to help train the Montagnard troops. Serong sent him Danny Neville, whom Petersen knew from training in Australia, and he proved to be an excellent man for the job. WO Neville worked in Buon Enao for three weeks drilling the 100 men in weapons, jungle patrolling, combat training and camp discipline.

The men were mostly armed with the World War Two vintage M1 carbines, which in Petersen's view were not much better than slingshots. It is a close-quarter weapon, but they did have plenty of ammunition for it. Some of the men had also captured AK-47s from the enemy which were a much better weapon. The VC had a lot of captured weapons besides the AK-47, but had trouble finding enough ammunition, making them poor shots as they could not get enough practice.

Petersen was also issued grenades which they threw into trenches where the VC had dug in. When they were in action the aim was to continue the advance swiftly: once the firing started move swiftly to reach the target.

Petersen insisted his Montagnard force operate under the same military code of conduct instilled in him as an Australian Army officer. He would not allow his men to throw grenades into a hut before checking it to make sure no innocents, especially children, were inside. He could not be sure his force always followed his order, but he tried to impress on them the way to win over people was to fight with honour and to target only the enemy.

The VC often hid in tunnels and bunkers, and he instructed his men to call on them to come out before dropping in grenades. If they didn't come out, well, that was war. Petersen strongly believed his men were better trained than those Montagnard attached to American Special Forces.

His were trained to work in eight-man teams, while the US forces trained them to operate in 30-man platoons and companies of 100. The Americans called their units a strike force, as the aim was to strike targets in an overwhelming force. Petersen aimed to hit and run. Very rarely would the Americans try to ambush – they did not have regular patrols going out around their base to keep the area clear. Often the VC would stage an attack on a village and then lie low and wait for US-backed forces to arrive. Then they would spring out from the jungle and ambush them on the roads. They hit and ran, hit and ran, and the Americans rarely even saw them.

The Americans got to the stage where they would not leave their base to counterattack without air cover. The planes would scream in and napalm, strafe or bomb the area before the US and Vietnamese troops moved in. The trouble was they generally got there only after it was all over. The VC left as soon as they heard the planes coming. The village was destroyed, villagers were killed and a whole lot of possibly innocent people were left hating the US. Petersen, on the other hand, operated just like the enemy: his forces moved in small groups and engaged in hit-and-run tactics. He learned that from his training in Australia, from his time in Malaya, and from studying guerilla warfare like that of the Chindits, the guerilla force operating behind Japanese lines in Burma during World War Two. He knew how to fight a guerilla war, so all he needed was arms and supplies, and the CIA gave him those in abundance.

Colonel Serong was fully aware of the shortcomings of the way the US was running the war. Frustrated that his message was not getting through to those in power in Australia, he would take a carefully chosen reporter with him on a tour of northern US bases where members of the Australian Army Training Team were ensconced, training Montagnard.

One was Peter Smark writing for Rupert Murdoch's national newspaper *The Australian*, a new paper, and one of the few newspapers at the time questioning what was going on in Vietnam. It eventually became the first newspaper to speak out against the war. Australian military involvement was still kept under wraps as far as the public was concerned. In August 1964 *The Australian* published Smark's report of a tour he had made several months earlier.[1]

Smark did not report that he travelled with Serong. One of the men Smark spoke to at a base just 8 kilometres from the Laotian border was Warrant Officer Bevan Stokes, who was later to serve with Petersen. Stokes remembers Serong turning up at his northern base with a journalist and photographer. The base was A Shau, a heavily fortified former French fort with an airstrip, a dozen US Special Forces troops, their tough Montagnard bodyguards from the warlike Nung tribe, 20 or so Vietnamese Special Forces and around 200 Vietnamese militia.

'The militia was made up of total misfits,' Stokes remembered in 2008 as he sat in his semi-rural home on the outskirts of Sydney.

'The militia were the worst of the worst – Vietnamese deserters, killers, cowboys, thieves and cowards. If they had stuffed up somewhere, the Vietnamese sent them up to A Shau. There was no way out for them up there: the only way in and out was by air. The Americans had no faith in the militia. They relied on the Nungs to do the dirty work and protect them, not only from the communists but also from the cutthroats in the militia. The Nungs were big, fierce fighters, six feet tall, very tough fighters, absolutely ruthless. There were about ten of them and they stuck very close to the Americans, guarding the American section of the camp. They were a separate tribe from the local Montagnard, possibly from southern China. The Americans paid them twice what the Vietnamese got. The Vietnamese – both the Special Forces troops and the militia – were scared of them and kept out of their way.'

Smark got a sense of this when he visited A Shau and several other camps with Serong. He wrote one of the few articles about the Australian Army Training Team activities that appeared a good 12 months before the Australian government sent combat troops to the Vietnam War. He reported that the Australian military advisers were playing an important role breaching the gaps opening up in the war effort as the CIA argued with other US departments and army Special Forces. He told his readers men like Bevan Stokes were winning the admiration of the Americans and the affection of mountain tribesmen as they trained their men in effective guerilla fighting to block the encroachment of North Vietnamese down through the Central Highlands.

Serong must have been extremely happy with those comments, but he still wanted to get across a message that was more than a pat on the back for the Training Team. Smark went on to say the task the Australians had been set was 'almost impossible', that a big mistake had been made in October 1962 when the effort to dam the trickle of arms and supplies coming down from North Vietnam through Laos into South Vietnam was 'almost totally destroyed by squabbling in the US ranks'.

Smark told his readers earlier CIA secret operations to train thousands of mountain tribesmen in Laos and Vietnam had been extremely successful in taking the fight to the Viet Cong and that the CIA had built up a vast network of skilled indigenous scouts and armed guerilla units who were loyal to the Americans.

In October 1962 the US government decided to hand over the successful CIA mountain tribesmen program to the US Special Forces. Smark said these forces were highly capable and well trained, and the transfer of the program should not, on the face of it, have caused a problem. Under the protocol with the South Vietnamese government, as soon as control of the program ceased to be a secret CIA operation and became an official US military operation, US forces could only operate as military advisers to the South Vietnamese defence force, the ARVN. As a consequence, ARVN officers and their forces were officially in command of the operation. As the ARVN was almost entirely delta Vietnamese, old hatred and resentments flared again and the Montagnard fighters drifted away. They either went over the border to Laos to join other CIA-run militia units, or simply went back to their farms.

'Today's operation in which the Australians are playing a crucial part is more limited, much less successful and for the men who take part, much more dangerous,' Smark wrote.

Petersen was surprised when he was shown the Smark article in 2008. 'Obviously Serong wanted that message to get out. But the reporter did not know the CIA still had secret covert operations going on outside the US Special Forces. He didn't know Serong had placed one of his men to head up one of those top-secret operations. I don't know what the reaction would have been if the Australian public knew one of their officers was secretly in charge of a CIA-funded and supervised operation in Ban Me Thuot. No reporter knew what I was doing until the very end.'

Smark didn't quote Serong in his article, but he made sure Serong got the payoff he deserved for helping with the story. Smark concluded his report praising Serong as, 'one of the best informed, most influential and most respected military men in the country.'

Petersen was impressed: 'Serong couldn't have hoped for better if he had written it himself!'

Former Warrant Officer Bevan Stokes was also not aware of the article until he was shown it in 2008. He was surprised at the way he had been used by Serong to get his message out that there were serious problems with the way the Americans were running the war.

'I couldn't agree more with him,' Stokes said. 'I was scared at A Shau because of the way the US Special Forces were running things. The Americans did not want to patrol in small groups. They were Special Forces and very well trained in technical things like weaponry; their medics were first class; they were all very well trained in their specific field. But they had no idea of patrolling.

'We suggested making a snap-shooting course to train some of the militia and improvised a snap-shooting gallery in the jungle beside the airstrip. We rigged up metal plates that would jump out from behind a tree or bush at the pull of a cable and send the trainees down the jungle path shooting at the targets as they popped up. We trained them to point their rifle exactly where they were looking. We'd go along the path and pull on the cable as they approached a target and out it would pop and they'd have to fire and hit it. The Americans were amazed at this. They had never seen anything like it. This was normal for us. We had this in all our training bases in Australia. They'd do it and after a while got very good at it. You could tell if it hit by the ding; if they hadn't shot it within two seconds we counted them as dead.

'The Americans were just not trained to fight a guerilla war. We'd try to tell them to patrol in small groups: easier to move and harder to spot. They wouldn't be in it. They'd take out 30 to 40 people all armed to the teeth. You couldn't patrol that way in a jungle, especially in mountains. The enemy would hear them coming from miles away. They would go out on one of these big patrols and not see anything. But shortly after I left that base they were overrun with VC and I think only one or two Americans survived. The VC were bloody good jungle fighters – they'd be invisible, hidden in tunnels or covered in leaves. You could go right past them and not see them.'

Stokes said the American tactics cost many lives, including Australian.

'Three of us in the Training Team went to the bases in the mountains near the northern border. I survived, but the other two were killed.'

The first Australian soldier to be killed in Vietnam was Sergeant Bill Hacking, aged 29. He died in suspicious circumstances. On 1 June 1963, he was dropped into the highland jungle northwest of the central Vietnamese town of Hue with Captain Bob Hagerty to assist a Vietnamese search and destroy mission. The column was on a ridge deep in the jungle when they stopped for a break. Dropping their packs, Hagerty walked further on up the line of men while Hacking stayed back talking with a Vietnamese regimental sergeant major. Suddenly a shot rang out. Hagerty raced back to find Hacking dead with a bullet right through his forehead.

'Bill was killed when his own weapon discharged accidentally,' Hagerty told Bruce Davies and Gary McKay for their 2004 book on the Training Team, *The Men Who Persevered*. 'This was a tragic and inexplicable happening which defied any rational explanation,' Hagerty said. The authors slammed the investigation into the death as 'insufficient'. A court of inquiry was not held until six months after Hacking's death, and there were gaps in the forensic examination. The court found Hacking died by an accidental discharge of his weapon, but the authors said the angle of the bullet and powder burns on Hacking's forehead, in addition to despairing letters he had written to his fiancée describing his mission as a nightmare, suggest he took his own life.[2]

Stokes was furious when he read that. 'I knew Bill Hacking very well,' he said in 2008. 'We'd been in the army together for years. There is no way in the world he would commit suicide. He was a weapons expert, so snagging his gun on something was out of the question. Even if he was in despair about the war, he was anxious to get back alive to marry his girlfriend. That was all he ever talked about. He wrote to her just about every day.

'I believe Bill Hacking was killed by the Vietnamese soldiers he was with. They hated being taken out into the jungle to fight, and they resented foreigners like us taking them where they didn't want to go. The Vietnamese soldiers were a bunch of cutthroats, and many VC had infiltrated their ranks. I have no doubt Bill was murdered by the Vietnamese he was sent to train to defend their country.'

Bill Hacking had shared Bevan Stokes' poor opinion of the US army officers training the Vietnamese. Hacking wrote to his fiancée, quoted in Paul Ham's 2007 book *Vietnam – The Australian War*: 'Those stupid bastards from the land of the dollar are driving me around the twist. They are the real enemy up here, their complacency and super-man complex has got the Vietnamese hating their guts and we (at least I) are not far behind . . .'[3]

As Petersen said, the Vietnamese and Montagnard regarded all Western military advisers as American whether they were from Australia, New Zealand or any other allied force. Bill Hacking was probably a victim of fragging, an American army term that became common over the course of the Vietnam War for soldiers who murdered senior officers who were unpopular or resented for pushing them into action. The term came from the fragmentation grenades lobbed into tents while the officer or sergeant slept to make it look like it was a VC attack. Texas A&M University history Professor Terry Anderson, a Vietnam veteran, puts the fragging count by war's end as high as 600.

Stokes also blames the death of Warrant Officer Kevin Conway on the manner in which the Americans ran their camps. Conway was the only Australian in the Nam Dong Special Forces Camp in an isolated valley 50 kilometres northwest of Da Nang in July 1964 when it came under full-scale attack by North Vietnamese troops and VC. The base had much the same force as Stokes' base A Shau: 12 US Special Forces soldiers, 1 Australian, 16 Vietnamese Special Forces, 40 Nungs and 372 militia, or Civilian Irregular Defense Group, as well as an American 'anthropologist' studying the local Katu Montagnard. In the early hours of 6 July the camp came under heavy mortar and machine gun fire. Stokes was 60 kilometres away in A Shau listening in to the desperate pleas for help over the radio.

'We received their call for help at three or four in the morning. Nam Dong was similar to A Shau, but not as well fortified. The Americans would not go out and patrol in small groups and I knew that allowed the enemy to disperse around them as they stuck to travelling through the jungle. The Americans wouldn't keep patrols out for long, so they never got to know their piece of jungle to spot signs of change indicating the enemy was present.

'In Malaya we would be out for a week at a time. We knew when our area was clear of enemy and when it wasn't. The Americans didn't know much of what was going on in the jungle at all. Over the radio we heard them call for the US Air Force to bomb their attackers but the planes couldn't get through the thick cloud. The VC had picked their time well. The camp was overrun and poor Kevin Conway was killed along with the Americans and Vietnamese.'

The communists had launched an intense mortar attack which took out several key defensive positions, then charged and managed to get inside the perimeter wire. There was fierce hand-to-hand fighting throughout the night. The defenders held out until the cloud lifted, and the US Air Force arrived to bomb the North Vietnamese troops back to the jungle. Conway was believed to have been killed in the first minutes of the attack as he ran with his rifle to a defensive trench. WO Kevin Conway, aged 35, was Australia's first combat fatality in the Vietnam War.

'I was glad to get out of there,' said Stokes, shaking his head. 'Any fool could see the VC were everywhere in the jungles. General Westmoreland, the US general in charge of American forces in Vietnam, flew in to visit our base one day and you would think the Americans would have made sure the airstrip was secure. I got a picture of the general shaking my hand. I had got my camera and was watching as his Caribou was taking off when three or four VC suddenly stepped out of the jungle on the other side of the airstrip and started shooting at the plane. It took off and the Yanks went tearing into the jungle to try to catch them. But the truth was the Yanks had no idea how to fight against guerillas and no idea how to fight a jungle war. They didn't learn from the French, who lost because they stuck to static positions and tried to outgun the enemy, but you can't do that if the enemy just disappears into the jungle. Their soldiers were only posted to Vietnam for six months and had little chance to learn how to fight, let alone get to know the men they were supposed to be training.

'When Serong told me I was going to join Barry Petersen in the Highlands I was thrilled as I'd worked with him in Australia when I was a corporal. I would wake him early in the morning and we would go for a dawn jog together. I knew he was a fine officer and it would be really interesting work.'

Stokes left A Shau with huge admiration for the Montagnard soldiers, in particular the Nung.

'I owe one of them my life. We were on patrol crossing a creek bed when all of a sudden bullets came flying at us from everywhere. The jungle just erupted. We were crouching down and this big Nung who was shadowing me pushed me forward to the ground, at the same time firing into the bush killing the VC there.

'If he hadn't pushed me, the bullet would have gone right through my head. I saw the blast from the VC gun just a few feet away. Because the Nung fired over the top of me I couldn't hear anything for days. I don't remember his name, but I got a picture taken when we got back to camp and I still have it. Whenever I went out on patrol after that I got him to come with me. He was a bloody good soldier and a terrific fighter.'

A Shau was overrun by North Vietnamese forces in March 1966 after a fierce two-day battle.

6
MONTAGNARD REBELLION

Back at Buon Enao the 100-strong Truong Son Force was now a tight unit that Petersen felt he could deploy effectively in small patrols in the area around Ban Me Thuot. By now he had defined his mission in the province more clearly. He judged the best use for Truong Son was to continue with its mission of disseminating anti-communist propaganda and collecting intelligence, but also expand into disrupting Viet Cong activities with ambushes, small-scale raids and capturing Viet Cong agents. Petersen was confident his unit was capable of hunting down VC and killing them.

He believed the most effective way to run the Truong Son Force was by promoting its own Montagnard officers from the ranks. He knew this would cause concern among Vietnamese officials. They were wary of the Montagnard, especially of armed and trained Montagnard running their own independent military unit; now they would be trained as military leaders. There was a growing danger that local army or police commanders, in particular the suspicious police deputy Truoc, could try to wrench the Truong Son Force away from him. The Force was a valuable asset – 100 well-armed, well-paid, well-equipped and well-trained Montagnard with only one Australian officer in charge. Petersen realised he was sticking his head up well above the trenches, and men like Truoc had good reason to shoot the tempting target.

Knowing the attention his actions would bring, Petersen indulged in a bit of smart diplomacy. He approached the province chief and asked him to be commander-in-chief of the Truong Son Force. Petersen would be the deputy commander, running day-to-day training and operations.

'As province chief he was already nominally in charge of all militia in his region, but I knew he'd like the title commander-in-chief. I made sure he got a special badge and honorary salute from the men at a special military ceremony. From then on I had control of the unit without the fear of harassment from other Vietnamese officials.'

Bryan Mills was pleased with the arrangement. For him it was a matter of whatever worked.

'Go recruit another 250,' Mills told Petersen. 'The money will be on its way. It's going well, just keep building up the unit.'

With the force increasing to 350, Bevan Stokes arrived at just the right time. Petersen had plans to expand the force into other parts of the province and knew Stokes had the skills and ability to work on his own and get the job done. Three-quarters of the team were from the Rhade tribe, whose villages were scattered around Ban Me Thuot and in the highlands to the north and west of the city. But a quarter of the unit were from the M'Nong tribe who lived mainly to the southwest in the more isolated Lac Thien district. Petersen thought Stokes could set up a second unit made up primarily of the M'Nong.

He knew Stokes would have to deal with the M'Nong chiefs on his own and so would have to cope with the notorious rice wine drinking ceremony. He decided to 'blood' Stokes on a visit to Buon Enao where he would meet the M'Nong chief as well as the Rhade chieftains. He briefed Stokes on the drinking etiquette, but that did not prepare him for the reality. Petersen's heart sank when he saw the villagers had no less than 12 large rice jars lined up for them in the longhouse.

'Now we'll see what you're made of,' Petersen told Stokes. They sat cross-legged before the first big jar. The headman proudly thrust his hand into the depths of the vessel and pulled out a handful of the gluggy mush. It was heaving with maggots, writhing and twisting in his hand, but that wasn't going to prevent a hardy Montagnard from giving up his alcohol fix. The headman deemed it worthy of consumption.

Stokes was mortified.

'I can't drink that, Sir,' he whispered to Petersen. 'It's bloody alive.'

Petersen told Stokes the holes at the bottom of the bamboo drinking straws were small enough to stop maggots and grit getting through. 'Just strain it through your teeth as you drink. You'll be right,' he told him.

But Stokes had drawn his line in the sand. He would do a lot for Australia, but he wouldn't drink maggot-infested rice wine. Luckily there were some bottles of beer from Ban Me Thuot in their truck, so Stokes and the M'Nong chief started toasting each other with the local brew, Biere La Rue. Petersen persevered with the ritual of the rice wine jars, a bit disappointed in Stokes.

'I was upset with him and wondered how he would get on by himself if he couldn't handle the local customs. A few hours later I found him at the other end of the longhouse, arm in arm with the M'Nong chief, laughing and singing some silly song. They had knocked off all the beer and Stokes had lost his inhibitions about maggots and they were getting stuck into a jar. I knew then he was going to be OK.'

Stokes wasn't so sure. 'If you have ever used a drop toilet, well this looked just the same. The maggots were as big as your finger. The villagers didn't seem to care. They just pulled out the rotten leaves and twigs at the top, put in fresh leaves and filled it with water to the top and poked the reed right through.

'There was no way I was going to drink that. Barry was used to it, and was digging it. The M'Nong chief was an old toothless, betel-chewing old fella. So after a few beers I said, "OK I'll try it."

'I took a sip and it was strong, sweet and sickly. Boy it was strong. If it was a few months old it would have been 20 per cent proof. Every so often something solid and wriggly would slip through, and I just swallowed it. I was getting on really well with the chief. We didn't speak a word of each other's language, but you know how drunks can communicate all over the world no matter what the language, well, that was us.'

Petersen was pleased Stokes had passed the test and sent him down to Lac Thien with some M'Nong tribesmen to build a new base far from the Vietnamese stronghold of Ban Me Thuot. To win Vietnamese approval for the new base, Petersen asked the province chief for permission to name it after him. Flattery got him everywhere.

Though it was a mission filled with danger Stokes grabbed the chance. 'I was attracted to the tribespeople straight away I reckon, especially the young men, who reminded me of the Gurkhas I had met in Malaya serving with the British. The Montagnard were a tough, fearless, independent people who had been pushed around for hundreds of years, but they were still standing. I was looking forward to going out on patrol with them. They were keen, intelligent, eager to learn, and they learned quickly. I developed a great deal of respect for them. People said they were primitive, but not in my mind. They were forced to live in poverty like they did, and they wanted to stick to their traditional way of life. Loyal and disciplined, they did what they were told, they would not desert, and they would keep on going even if wounded. I trusted them.'

The new base at Lac Thien was off the main path of the Ho Chi Minh Trail, but the Viet Cong operating near there had recently overrun a Vietnamese army outpost, killing all those inside. The VC had a lot of Montagnard on their side, with many of them from the M'Nong tribe. The village people were caught in the middle. The VC would come in and tell the village chief he had to supply men for their unit. If he didn't, or if they ran off, the VC would come back and kill the village chief and his family.

'Barry told me we were not arming them for their own autonomy or their fight against the Vietnamese. But I must admit I sort of indirectly hinted to them that they would get their autonomy or some independence if they fought with us. I hoped it would bring them more on side with us. The VC were promising them all sorts of things, so I thought we had to offer them something too. Barry didn't do that. He was much more correct and played it straight down the line. But I know they thought they could get more say in their own future if they joined our force and fought against the communists.

'I am sure they thought the US would give them autonomy once the war was over if they fought for us. We gave them nice uniforms, good weapons and trained them. What's more we treated them with respect, which is something they never got from the Vietnamese.'

Stokes went out of his way to make sure the locals of Lac Thien knew he was Australian, not American.

'Australian soldiers have a knack of getting on with other peoples wherever they go, right from the diggers of World War One through World War Two and now with Timor, Iraq and Afghanistan. The Americans treat local populations like garbage. They take America with them wherever they go with their base shops, food, music, dollars and attitudes. In the case of Vietnam they appeared to make no attempt to understand the point of view of the locals. Australians on the other hand tend to live with the locals, eat their food, use their currency, get to know them and respect their customs.

'I was all on my own down there. The only link I had to Barry was through a two-way radio. It was an incredible position for a 25-year-old warrant officer to be in. I was going to make the most of it while it lasted.'

Stokes got stuck into building his fort in the jungle, surrounding it with trenches and barbed wire, positioning machine gun posts on the corners and sending constant patrols into the jungle to have ears and eyes well out from the camp. He had no heavy equipment like bulldozers to build an airstrip, so he contracted local men with elephants to clear the brush and press the dirt down flat.

'The independence I had at Lac Thien was wonderful. I could organise my own ambushes, decide on patrols and make decisions on the men. I ate the M'Nong food – I paid a wife of one of the soldiers to cook for me sometimes. Otherwise I ate camp food. Your stomach toughens up, but I was crook a lot of the time.

'I shared my hut with a couple of soldiers I trusted. You had to be ready for attack at any moment. I always had 526 bullets with me – a fully laden carbine with folding stock, two 28 magazines taped back to back – 56 bullets for the carbine. The safety catch was always off and I had a bullet up the spout. All I had to do was touch the trigger and I could fire 20 bullets in 2 seconds. I had four 28 clips in each pouch. In both of the other pouches I had two 12-round clips. In my pack I had a couple of rolls of bullets. I had that with me everywhere I went.'

Just about every night Stokes heard gunshots coming from the jungle. The VC were everywhere, but they were not keen on an open confrontation with the well-armed and well-trained M'Nong force. Nothing more than a small group could move in the area without Stokes' men knowing about it. There had to be constant vigilance, even when asleep.

'Going to bed at night I kept my boots on, my emergency belt and my little pack on. I held my gun and lay on my back keeping the muzzle just above my head, my finger along the trigger guard. I got used to sleeping like that. If you wake up and someone is coming to cut your throat you don't have time to even think. There is no second chance. It has to be instantaneous. You might not hit him, but you would scare him for a fraction of a second, giving you a chance to escape. All the time you just keep moving and firing.'

Stokes was determined to get the VC unit that had taken out the Vietnamese army post some months before. 'I felt we couldn't claim the area as our own until we hit back. Within a short time we had intelligence from the locals about where they were based and we tracked them down. We went out in a raiding party and got their commander.'

The Viet Cong posted a reward of 50 000 piasters – about US$600 – on the head of Bevan Stokes after his successful raid on the local VC commander. The pamphlets were put up at night on trees all around Lac Thien and Ban Me Thuot with a crude drawing of Stokes, his prominent nose making him look a bit like Pinocchio.

It was a huge amount of money for the locals, more than three years' salary for a soldier. It is a sign of the high regard in which the Montagnard held the young Australian that not one of his men turned traitor on him, or took the opportunity to shoot him in the back on patrol. As Stokes knew from his mate Bill Hacking, it did happen.

While Stokes was making enemies at Lac Thien, Petersen was also making his mark against the Viet Cong, leading his growing force on a number of raids and patrols. Soon the VC distributed 'wanted dead or alive' posters for both Stokes and Petersen.

One of the Viet Cong posters referred to Petersen's Montagnard force as 'Tiger Men'. It was only meant to identify them by their CIA-issued camouflage striped uniform, but Petersen seized on it as a badge of honour.

'On my next trip to Saigon I got a metalworker to make up a thousand shiny tiger head badges. At a formal parade ceremony attended by the province chief, their commander-in-chief, I told the men the enemy feared them and now called them Tiger Men and showed them their new emblem, a tiger's head.

'I handed out the badges to put on their berets, and you could see them swell with pride. They stood a little taller, marched a little snappier, thinking of themselves as a special elite unit. It was a good move.'

Petersen insists the name had nothing to do with the tiger cub he kept in his backyard. 'I don't know if the VC even knew about that. The poster had been handed in to US intelligence in Ban Me Thuot and they passed it on to me. Bryan Mills thought it would be a good idea to do something to make the unit feel it had its own identity, so the men would feel loyalty to their own unit and make them stand apart from other Montagnard forces in the Highlands run by the US Special Forces with Vietnamese officers.'

It was to be a smarter move than Mills or Petersen could have realised at the time. Behind the scenes trouble was brewing: Stokes and Petersen were about to have far more to contend with than the unseen communist enemy in the jungle. There were spies everywhere from all sides. Political movements were constantly building and erupting as agents of the CIA, North Vietnamese communist spies, Montagnard independence rebels and French agents with their own agenda were all busy trying to manipulate events to their advantage.

The first eruption came on 29 January 1964, just three months after the military coup that killed President Diem. The French-trained General Nguyen Khanh, aged just 37, head of the Vietnamese 2nd Army Corps in the north of the country, overthrew the military junta headed by 'Big' Minh – General Duong Van Minh.

Khanh was a cocky young officer who strutted and preened his goatee. An ambitious opportunist with designs on himself, after the war he ended up running a shabby Asian restaurant next to a petrol station in West Palm Beach, Florida.[1] Khanh proclaimed he was keen on taking the war into North Vietnam, telling the US Embassy Minh was an appeaser, as well as corrupt. Khanh allowed Minh to stay on as head of state, but he took over running the military junta, which had the real power. The Vietnamese met the coup with a shrug of their shoulders and went on with their lives. One general was much like another in 1964 South Vietnam.

Khanh had told CIA agent Lou Conein what he intended to do and kept the US Embassy informed on every move. The US had no objections as they believed they could control Khanh even more than Minh and US Ambassador Henry Cabot Lodge saw Khanh as less likely to seek a peace deal with North Vietnam. Stanley Karnow, author of the history of the war, *Vietnam*, commented: 'As regimes rose and fell in Saigon, nothing alarmed American strategists more than the prospect of a change that would bring to power South Vietnamese leaders prepared to reach an accommodation with the Communists.'[2]

In other words, the outbreak of peace was the worst possible result as far as the United States was concerned.

The first thing Khanh did after seizing power was to execute Major Nguyen Van Nhung, the officer who had murdered President Diem and his brother three months earlier. Khanh's killer took Nhung into his garden, had him kneel, and put a bullet through the back of his head. With a straight face, Khanh claimed Nhung must have been filled with remorse for killing Diem and committed suicide. The message to his rivals was clear.

Lodge sent a cable to Washington declaring the US needed a 'tough and ruthless commander. Perhaps Khanh is it'.[3] The US was happy to back murderous thugs, so long as they did what they were told.

One of Khanh's first political efforts to try to make himself popular was to order the release of most of the political prisoners imprisoned during the Diem regime. One of them was a respected Rhade leader called Y-Bham Enuol, a strong advocate of Montagnard rights. Diem had thrown Y-Bham into jail five years earlier after he'd led a Montagnard group demanding a level of autonomy – at least the same level of autonomy they had enjoyed under French colonial rule. The Darlac province chief Colonel Thanh convinced Khanh that, once freed, Y-Bham should be given an official position and unite the Montagnard behind the new government. Thousands of Montagnard people in traditional costumes turned up at Ban Me Thuot's sports ground to welcome Y-Bham home. Khanh arrived and with great fanfare returned Y-Bham to his people.

A few weeks later Y-Jut introduced Petersen to Y-Bham. The two hit it off and became firm friends. Much of this was cemented during a mammoth drinking session held at Y-Bham's home village, Buon Ea Bong, about 3 kilometres northwest of Ban Me Thuot. Y-Bham held a very large sacrifice of five water buffalo to celebrate his freedom and Petersen was the only non-Montagnard invited. Mindful of spies in the crowd, Petersen was careful not to sympathise publicly with Y-Bham's aspirations of Montagnard independence. The night got very boozy and Y-Bham and Petersen downed a great deal of beer, rice wine and CIA-supplied whisky. In the early hours when both were extremely drunk, Y-Bham revealed his aims were first to fight against the Viet Cong, then to work slowly and carefully towards self-government for the Montagnard. As the drinking dragged towards dawn Y-Bham proudly presented Petersen to his young daughter (actually his niece, as Petersen learned later). The young woman had to sit beside Petersen and share his straw stuck into the jar of rice wine. By 4am Y-Bham was affectionately calling Petersen his 'grandfather' and then later 'brother' before collapsing.[4]

Slowly but steadily, the Australian army captain was being sucked into Vietnam's domestic politics. He might not have seen any other outsiders at the ceremony, but the Vietnamese, the CIA and the communists would have had their spies there who took special note of the lone white man present.

The French were particularly interested in the release of Y-Bham Enuol. There were still French plantation owners in the Highlands and agents of the French government were quietly at work trying to manipulate events so that French authorities could sneak back into their former colony. In their day, the French had given the Montagnard a limited autonomy in the Highlands; now they saw opportunities to regain a toehold through the Montagnard.

Soon after he arrived in Buon Me Thuot, Petersen suspected the French were playing their own dirty games. While he steered clear of American advisers at the Bungalow, he did socialise with Bill Bouchart, a French–Canadian who lived in his street. Bouchart lived alone in an apartment on the first floor above a little shop. Ostensibly, he was working for a geographic study group, however, he admitted to Petersen this was a cover for his real role as the regional agent for the US Defense Intelligence Agency. Since Petersen was working for the CIA, they were natural allies.

'Bouchart's role was to infiltrate the French community in the region as we knew the French were secretly supporting the communists. He could speak and act like a Frenchman and he was a rather dashing fellow so had been accepted into the French social circle. It had taken him a long time to crack that circle. For years they would not let him stay overnight at their plantations after dinner. He had to drive back to town through the night, risking ambush from either the Viet Cong or bandits. But Bill stuck at it and diligently went out to the plantations for tennis matches and social events, something I was never invited to. I don't think they ever really trusted him, though.'

The French refused to have anything to do with the Americans or the military. Late one night after a few drinks in Petersen's house, Bouchart revealed his fears. 'They are trying to get me, Barry,' he said.

'Who's out to get you?' Petersen asked doubtfully.

'The French,' Bouchart replied, looking down at his glass.

'Oh come on Bill, the French aren't going to bump you off.'

'No Barry, I am a target.'

A few weeks later Vietnamese police told Petersen that Bouchart had been murdered. 'They found Bill dead in his bed, a bullet through his head,' Petersen recalls. 'He was left-handed, but he was found with his Colt .45 in his right hand. The bullet had somehow managed to go through the bed's mosquito net and into the back of his head.'

The Vietnamese police investigator was no Sherlock Holmes, but even he figured it had to be murder. However, the American Military Police took over the case. They officially ruled it a suicide. There was to be no investigation, no search for a killer, and no recriminations. Another body had been shoved under the bloody carpet of Vietnam.

According to Petersen, Bouchart was getting to know too much about what the French were doing. 'The French were trying to make sure things would go their way if the communists ever took over. They were supporting the communists, including supplying them with weapons. Bill was a popular fellow, but none of the French community seemed to miss him.'

Bouchart's death was a result of a larger agenda. In January 1964 France's President Charles de Gaulle recognised Red China, and called for the 'neutralisation' of Indo-Chinese nations where France once had colonial interests – Vietnam, Laos and Cambodia. This policy meant all foreign powers – notably the United States and Russia – should cease intervention in the affairs of these countries, and withdraw. De Gaulle hoped this might allow France to work its way back into the region, and French expatriates to retain their commercial interests. Cambodia's Prince Norodom Sihanouk supported the neutralisation policy and intervened where he could to promote it.

Back in Buon Me Thuot Petersen's informants told him a local French coffee grower, Marcel Coronel, was the French government's organiser of the neutralist movement in the Central Highlands, and he had many supporters among the French expatriates. Informants also told Petersen that Noel Mercurio, the official French 'Resident', the equivalent of consul, was also a key figure in the French secret service, along with the senior Jesuit priest in the region, Father Bianchetti. Petersen suspects many Jesuit priests in the region acted as agents for the French secret service, or assisted where they could to advance the French cause.

Petersen also suspected a French tea plantation owner, Pierre Gerardie, was the main French spy in the Darlac region. 'His tea plantation was small and could not possibly support him, but he always had plenty of money. He had a very beautiful and well-educated Eurasian wife and they were the centre of the expat social scene. They married in France and stayed there for six months for their honeymoon. It is quite possible she was also trained for the French secret service, the *Service de Documentation Extérieure et de Contre-Espionnage* (SDECE).

'Later on a young American Embassy official sent to Ban Me Thuot – about third secretary rank – confided in me that he was having an affair with Madame Gerardie. His job was to amalgamate and sift all the intelligence coming in from the various secret service agencies, so he held a crucial intelligence position. She was part Montagnard, and knowing I had close contacts with the Montagnard, he asked me to try to quash any rumours of the affair if they sprung up.

'I replied he shouldn't be worried about her husband finding out. Instead, he should be very concerned that the French might use it against him now, or in the future and that Pierre Gerardie probably knows all about the affair; in fact, he might even have put his wife up to it. I told the young diplomat he had seriously compromised himself.

'He didn't understand. I said, "Imagine you eventually rise to the position of ambassador and you are in delicate negotiations with the French. They just might whisper to you they know you once divulged information to the wife of a French secret service agent you had an affair with in Vietnam. You wouldn't even have had to have actually divulged any information. The point was the French could use the affair to put pressure on you."

'The young American was horrified and reported his indiscretion to his superiors in Saigon. He was quietly withdrawn from Vietnam and sent back to Washington.'

Such skulduggery was always a risk in the murky world of spy and counter-spy. This was the major reason Petersen deliberately kept his distance from any chance of romantic affairs while he was in Vietnam.

Petersen's position as an Australian Army captain seconded to the CIA put him in an unusual position. Some key people had intelligence they wanted to pass on to the Americans, but they did not want to be seen to be talking directly to CIA agents. Petersen proved a convenient conduit.

Following the second coup in Saigon in 1964 when General Nguyen Khanh toppled General Duong Van 'Big' Minh, all senior Vietnamese officials were replaced. Darlac Province's new chief was Major Bui Huy Gia, a man who got around far more than his predecessor and had his fingers in many pies. Gia would often find a reason to talk to Petersen. He had connections to Chinese nationalists and would casually disclose intelligence on tribal resistance movements in the border regions between Laos and North Vietnam: details of their military strengths, weapons and radio equipment. It was clear Gia intended Petersen to pass this intelligence on to the CIA. He also supplied intelligence about the French secret service operations in the region.

The CIA gave Petersen top-secret spy devices, including a tiny microphone that could be strapped to his chest and a radio transmitter that could fit into a cigarette packet. The signal from the transmitter could be picked up 5 kilometres away. Petersen would put a receiver in a house or car nearby with a tape recorder running and use it to secretly record conversations with key officials or informants he was meeting. However, sometimes it was more Inspector Clouseau than James Bond.

'One day I had both the province chief and the police chief coming to my house for an important meeting,' Petersen recalls.

'I taped the microphone and transmitter under a coffee table in the centre of the seating arrangement in the living room. The receiver was in a locked room of the house. During talks over tea and drinks I noticed from the corner of my eye that the transmitter had come loose and was dangling below the coffee table held only by part of the sticky tape. To me it looked glaringly obvious swinging there, but neither of the others spotted it from where they were sitting. Somehow I managed to distract them long enough to find an excuse to move us all to another room. If they'd seen it and caught me I would probably have been arrested. I would certainly have been expelled from the province and have some explaining to do to Colonel Serong and the CIA.'

Over the first 12 months in the province Petersen developed quite a sophisticated spy network of his own. The release of Y-Bham Enuol led to an increase in unrest among Montagnard and Petersen picked up word that Y-Bham had made contact with a senior Rhade chief who was a general with the Viet

Cong. Rumours were flying that the North Vietnamese would use Montagnard VC to launch an attack on Ban Me Thuot.

One centre of discontent in September 1964 was an American Special Forces base at Buon Sarpa, 60 kilometres southwest of Ban Me Thuot, right on the border with Cambodia. The base's 700 Montagnard troops complained that their Vietnamese commander was stealing from their pay and collaborating with the Viet Cong. Petersen got word of this and knew something big was about to happen.

Over weeks as rebellion brewed, Petersen talked with his Tiger Men. He explained that while he understood their grievances against the Vietnamese, a revolt would get them nothing but death and bloodshed.

'You cannot win,' Petersen told them. 'The Americans will side with the Vietnamese. The communists will not come to your aid. The same will happen to you as what happened to the Poles in World War Two. The Russians were advancing on the Germans who were occupying Poland. The Polish people rose up against the Germans to help the Russian advance, but the Russians just stopped. They let the Germans wipe out the Polish resistance – only then did the Russians move in. That is exactly what the communists will do to the Montagnard: they will let the South Vietnamese kill you off. They will stand back and do nothing as you are slaughtered, because that will make it easier for them when they finally invade South Vietnam.'

Petersen trusted his own men, but he knew they were under pressure from other Rhade. The Viet Cong had agents in just about every Montagnard military camp encouraging dissent. By mid-September Petersen felt it was coming to a head.

'Bevan Stokes was visiting me in Ban Me Thuot and in the morning he drove out to our base at Buon Enao with Y-Tin to check on things. He came racing back saying something strange was going on, the men in the camp were digging trenches and bunkers and avoided talking to him. It was then we knew a revolt was imminent. Y-Tin said his information was it would happen very soon.'

Petersen moved quickly. He didn't trust the telephones and an Air America plane was already at the airport delivering supplies, so he decided to send Stokes and Y-Tin to Saigon immediately to give the news directly to Colonel Serong and his CIA bosses.

He had to give Y-Tin false papers – as a Montagnard he could be arrested by Vietnamese in Saigon. If there was a round-up they would arrest anyone who was Montagnard, and possibly kill them on the spot. Petersen had a Filipino instructor helping train the Montagnard at the time, so they rigged up his spare ID card for Y-Tin.

Serong met them at the airport and they did not say a word in front of the Americans. After a short drive Serong stopped the car and Stokes told him what was going on. Y-Tin stressed to Serong that the communists were not behind the coming revolt, and that it was a result of mistreatment by the South Vietnamese authorities. Serong thought the young Rhade translator was naïve, as he was convinced communists had fomented the rebellion, and were about to use it to push an attack on Ban Me Thuot.[5]

Meanwhile, in Ban Me Thuot, Petersen faced a grilling by suspicious Vietnamese officers. First, the Director of Police, Ong Binh, dropped by to ask if Petersen knew whether there was going to be a Montagnard demonstration in the city the next day. Petersen kept his information to himself. He had not heard from Serong how he should handle the situation and knew the Vietnamese would storm the Montagnard base if he said there was about to be a revolt. This would make the situation even worse, causing outright armed rebellion.

Petersen told Ong Binh he didn't know anything about a demonstration, which was technically correct as it was to be a full-scale revolt. Binh told Petersen if there was a demonstration he would have to bring his Buon Enao troops into the city to help quell it.

Within an hour the province chief Major Gia arrived and demanded Petersen prevent his men joining a demonstration. 'If anything happens, if any demonstration occurs, you will be held entirely responsible,' Gia told Petersen.

The Australian protested he didn't control all the Montagnard in the province and besides, he, Gia, was commander-in-chief of the Tiger Men. Gia would have none of that, making it very clear to Petersen he was to be the scapegoat if the Montagnard demonstrated, let alone launched an open rebellion.

Petersen and his principal translator and fixer, Y-Jut, drove out to Buon Enao. They found Y-Bham telling a gathering of Tiger Men the Montagnard were not going to revolt. Y-Jut whispered in Petersen's ear there were Vietnamese spies in the crowd and the elderly leader was concerned he could be arrested.

Petersen got Y-Bham alone and told him he should go back to Ban Me Thuot and lock himself inside his residence. It was important the Vietnamese not suspect Y-Bham of being involved in any rebellion – if he was arrested it would spark a violent revolt. Petersen gave him a pistol to protect himself, and sent him back to the city with M'Nong guards with orders to stay at his home.

Petersen returned to his own home to prepare. He planted a demolition charge against the wall at the back of the house. He also made sure his guards were M'Nong, who were less likely to join any action. If the situation deteriorated his plan was to set the demolition off so it would appear rebels had forced their way in and abducted them against their will. That way it would look like they had nothing to do with the revolt.

That evening he had a tense but uneventful night. It was eerily quiet on the morning of Sunday 19 September; no one was on the streets. Y-Jut had scouted around the grounds, but all seemed intact. When Petersen found the radio dead he feared the worst. Normally the radio station, which was on the outskirts of the city, broadcast constant propaganda, broken only by Vietnamese music. Something had happened but he had no idea what. Petersen's house phone was not working. He was cut off. He did not know if his own force had joined the revolt and he'd heard nothing from Saigon.

Petersen and Y-Jut jumped into the jeep to check on Y-Bham. The guards were still there and Y-Bham was safe. They drove on to province headquarters, where they finally found out that Montagnard rebels had also seized the radio station overnight. Five hundred rebels had also seized a bridge on the road to Saigon, and it appeared the rebel leaders had made their headquarters at a nearby village called Buon Mbre.

Later that morning, an Air America plane buzzed several times over Petersen's house, the usual doorknock signal from the CIA, and Petersen drove out to the airstrip in response.

Colonel Serong arrived with Stuart Methven, a senior CIA agent in the Covert Action Branch. Petersen had heard Bryan Mills was being moved on and replaced by Methven, a big gangling American he had met several times at CIA headquarters in Saigon. Methven was a far more extroverted and flamboyant man than Mills. He had a large Mexican style moustache, and was known for throwing big parties at his Saigon mansion where he lived with his wife, child and assorted wildlife. But behind the bonhomie was a sharp, calculating mind, and a ruthless determination to get things done.

Petersen drove Serong and Methven back to town, telling them everything he knew, including his clash with the local Vietnamese province chief. They went to the provincial headquarters where the intelligence was that 3000 Montagnard had joined the rebellion. The region was on the edge of disaster: four large groups of heavily armed Montagnard rebels were on the outskirts of Ban Me Thuot. If the revolt succeeded it would deliver more than half of South Vietnam to the communists, and give North Vietnam free access to the Highlands. It would clear a direct route for the North right to the gates of Saigon.

The rebellion was well coordinated. At dawn that Sunday morning Montagnard troops on five US Special Forces bases in the region had rebelled, and taken over the bases to varying degrees. The Montagnard vastly outnumbered the dozen American Special Forces soldiers training them and the dozen ARVN Special Forces soldiers whose commander was officially in charge of the camp. At last the Montagnard's hatred for the Vietnamese had burst out into the open.

The Americans had some sympathy for the Montagnard, whom they regarded as independent minded and tough. They had to turn a blind eye to corruption among the Vietnamese. They also knew the communists had many secret supporters and agents among both Montagnard and Vietnamese. Everything had come to a head.

At Buon Sarpa to the southwest, the Montagnard disarmed the dozen American Special Forces soldiers and held them hostage. The rebels shot, or cut the throats, of nine of the 12 Vietnamese Special Forces troops stationed there.

Similarly, at Buon Mi Ga, 75 kilometres east of Ban Me Thuot, 500 Montagnard disarmed the dozen American Special Forces troops and held them hostage. Again the Vietnamese were not so fortunate. The rebels lined up the 12 Vietnamese troops, including the camp commander, and executed them by firing squad. The Montagnard rebels then moved on and seized Ban Me Thuot's main airport, 14 kilometres east of the town, preventing Vietnamese reinforcements flying in. The dirt strip airport that Air America used was left alone, unsuitable for large planes.

Thirty kilometres to the northwest, rebels seized and disarmed both the American and Vietnamese Special Forces troops at Ban Don base near the Cambodian border. As the Montagnard rebels prepared to march on Ban Me Thuot the American base commander there, a Captain Terry, persuaded the rebels to take him with them. During the long march Terry managed to convince the rebels not to join the revolt, and they turned back to their base.

But they still held the Special Forces troops captive.

At Buon Brieng base, about 70 kilometres north of Ban Me Thuot, the US Special Forces commander, Captain Vernon Gillespie, also persuaded the camp's Montagnard leader, Y-Jhon

Nie, not to join the rebellion. A reporter for *National Geographic*, Howard Sochurek, was visiting the base at the time and gives a vivid account of events at the base.[6]

Sochurek wrote that at 8.40am Gillespie received a radio report saying Montagnard at several other bases had overthrown their commanders. Having already wired the ammunition dump at Buon Brieng ready to explode if the Montagnard moved against them, Gillespie immediately summoned the 12 Vietnamese soldiers, including the base commander Captain Truong, to join him. He then called in Montagnard commander Y-Jhon Nie with his company commanders. Gillespie and Y-Jhon had a good relationship, and Gillespie considered him a friend. Y-Jhon was not happy with the rebellion but he had received orders to join the revolt.

Gillespie told them the situation: 'I am taking command of this camp. A Montagnard revolt has started. Y-Jhon, do not move against the Vietnamese here. They are under my protection. To kill them, you'll have to kill me first.'

He paused. Sochurek noticed the protruding vein in his right temple pulsing. Gillespie continued more softly telling Y-Jhon that his life was under threat and that the Viet Cong knew he was there. He wanted Y-Jhon to be guarded at all times.

Y-Jhon stood and thought for a while. He turned to Gillespie and told him in halting English that if Gillespie would allow him to perform a traditional ceremony of alliance with Captain Truong and invoke the protection of the spirits, it would mean the Montagnard could not harm Truong and his men.

The scenes that followed amazed Sochurek. He watched as Y-Jhon handed ceremonial garb to Gillespie and Captain Truong. 'Here we were, caught in the middle of a rebellion in a camp with 700 tough soldiers, all potential enemies. In one corner of the hall, a sergeant connected a storage battery to two wires that would blow five tons of ammunition, and maybe us, to kingdom come. In another corner his captain donned an embroidered loincloth, readying himself for a spirit sacrifice. The scene was grimly ludicrous.'

The American and Vietnamese army officers faced the Rhade rebels over seven jars of fermented rice wine. Brass gongs sounded and a chicken was ritually slaughtered. After several drinks the village shaman slipped a brass ring over their wrists. The spirits had been appeased. They were joined in alliance.

The reality of their situation was still there, however. Y-Jhon was refusing calls from other camps to join the rebellion, but he was out on a limb. Gillespie had the 700 Montagnard troops parade before him, then Y-Jhon told them what he had done, and told them to listen to Captain Gillespie.

'The United States is the father of the Rhade and we are the sons,' Y-Jhon said. 'When there is trouble between father and son, the son must listen to the father's advice.'

Gillespie stepped forward. A translator put each phrase into Rhade to make sure there would be no misunderstanding.

'The hearts of the Americans and the Rhade are as one heart . . . Our hearts are together now, but if the Rhade change heart and fight the Americans, we will fight the Rhade.'

When he dismissed the men and they marched smartly off the parade ground, Gillespie was satisfied they would not join the rebellion. He decided to fly to Ban Me Thuot in the camp's helicopter and told Y-Jhon to come with him. Sochurek hitched a ride to follow the story.

Meanwhile, back in Ban Me Thuot, Petersen was relieved his Tiger Men had so far not been sighted among the rebels. What he did not know was that only a stuff-up had kept the Tiger Men out of the fighting to that point. Rebel leaders had assigned the Buon Enao force the task of occupying the small airstrip where Serong had landed that morning, as well as the radio and telephone relay station on the northern edge of town. For some unknown reason, the pre-arranged signal of three mortars fired into the town did not occur, so the 350 men at Buon Enao did not move.

However the rebels did succeed in a daring raid to abduct their figurehead leader Y-Bham. Crashing through Vietnamese roadblocks into the town, a jeep and truck filled with hardline, heavily armed rebels from Buon Sarpa stormed Y-Bham's residence to abduct him. The M'Nong guards Petersen had placed there offered no opposition and the vehicles roared out of town with the old man before the Vietnamese knew what was going on.

By the afternoon Vietnamese forces had retaken the airport, then a full airborne regiment flew in to reinforce Ban Me Thuot's defences. Vietnamese Corp commander General Nguyen Huu Co flew in with the troops and set up his command headquarters in a large palatial mansion surrounded by elaborate gardens and high walls. The 'palace' was used by bigwigs whenever they visited from Saigon. Stu Methven, now the senior CIA man in Ban Me Thuot, sought out Petersen, telling him General Co wanted to see him.

Petersen was puzzled. He had never met General Co, and wondered why he'd want to see a humble Aussie captain. The meeting room was filled with the region's top brass, including

Colonel John Freund, Co's American adviser, and Colonel Donald Kersting, the US military adviser to the senior ARVN military staff in Ban Me Thuot. Methven was there, as well as Colonel Serong.

Co turned to Petersen. 'You know these people. Do you think you can talk these rebels into coming to talk to me?'

Petersen was not sure. He was confident his own people would listen to him, but he did not know the Montagnard from the other bases. The rebellion was up and running; dozens of Vietnamese soldiers had already been killed. Blood was flowing. Petersen wondered what he could say to the rebels to get them to agree to talks. What had they to lose? At this stage they held all the cards.

'Are you prepared to try?' Co said.

'When would you like me to try, Sir?'

'Now. Tonight. Can you do it?'

'Yes, Sir. I can try, but I will have to get past your defensive positions, and through their defensive positions. Some of the rebel leaders will be at Buon Enao. I'll go there.'

Colonel Freund interjected. He said Petersen's mission wasn't necessary as he had already arranged to meet the rebels from Buon Sarpa in a village near Ban Me Thuot in the morning.

Petersen took an immediate dislike to Colonel Freund. 'He was a real little martinet. He was a colonel telling a general what to do, and Co didn't like that.' Co ignored Freund and told Petersen to go ahead. It was already 9pm and going out in the dark during a rebellion was risky, going to a rebel base even riskier. As Petersen headed out to the jeep with Y-Jut, Serong said he would accompany them. Colonel Kersting then sidled up and said that he wasn't doing anything, so he too would join them.

The four men set off in the jeep, two colonels bouncing in the back with the much lower ranked Captain Petersen in the front with Y-Jut driving. Petersen waved the pass issued by General Co at the Vietnamese guards and they sped out of Ban Me Thuot towards Buon Enao. Heavy rain started falling, making the track slippery and impairing their vision. The jungle was pitch black and the faint lights of the jeep didn't help avoid potholes and ruts.

Colonel Serong recounts the mission differently in his memoirs, claiming he was the one General Co appealed to go out in the middle of the night and bring in the rebels. It's a claim that 40 years later still grates on Petersen, who is adamant Co asked him, not Serong, to go on the dangerous mission.

'Co knew Serong had just flown in from Saigon that day, and didn't know the Montagnard. Serong was there hanging on to my shirt tails, not me on to his.'

Petersen knew the track well. He also knew the spots on the road where his men were most likely to have put up roadblocks or set up ambushes. After all, he had trained them. Several times on the journey he told Y-Jut to stop the jeep.

Y-Jut called out in Rhade, and Petersen got out and walked ahead to stand in the headlights so any of his men waiting in ambush could see it was him. If he was a Vietnamese officer they would have opened fire.

There were many such ambush spots and roadblocks, and they went through the same procedure each time. When they got back to the jeep Petersen and Y-Jut saw Serong and Kersting had their guns ready to give covering fire. This would have been pretty pointless in Petersen's view. 'We wouldn't have stood a chance if they wanted to kill us.'

Most of the roadblocks were manned by Petersen's Tiger Men. They saluted as soon as they recognised him and even when troops were from units other than Truong Son, Petersen found they had heard of him and let the jeep through.

Finally the jeep's headlights picked up the gates of Buon Enao. They were firmly closed. Petersen could see the barrels of several guns trained on him as he got out of the jeep and walked up to the gates with Y-Jut. Serong and Kersting stayed in the jeep, guns at the ready but held out of sight. Petersen spoke to the men at the gate, who saluted. Still, Petersen had to talk for some time before they opened the gate and let the jeep through. The rebel leaders were assembled in a dirt-floored hut usually used as a lecture room.

'It was very tense,' Petersen recalls. 'Although I knew almost everyone there, they did not greet me in their normal cheerful manner. Their mood did not improve when I told them General Co wanted to see them.'

They flatly refused; gun fingers were getting twitchy. The rebel leaders had sent messages out to the other rebel bands, so more rebels arrived in the next hours. The hut was getting crowded. The only groups not represented were the Buon Sarpa hardliners, who were camped on the southern side of Buon Me Thuot. Petersen had a tough sell. The rebels held all the cards this night, and had little to gain by going to see General Co. Besides, they could be arrested or shot as soon as they entered his headquarters.

'You have already achieved a big breakthrough getting

General Co to come to Buon Me Thuot,' Petersen told them. 'General Co is prepared to hear your grievances.'

The negotiations were delicate, with guns bristling all around. Petersen outlined the proposal from General Co while Y-Jut translated. Petersen and the others then went into another room and waited while the rebels discussed the proposal. It didn't seem to be going well, and it was getting very late. Serong was losing his patience. He drew Petersen aside and whispered forcefully to him, 'Barry, you've got to make them agree to come back with us.'

'Sir, it is a decision they are going to have to make themselves,' Petersen replied. 'I cannot make them do anything. All I can do is try to persuade them.'

His reply seemed to set Serong off into a fury. The colonel leaned in very close and snarled: 'Don't you speak to me like that. I can have you out of this country in 24 hours!'

Petersen was stunned. The rebels in the next room could easily kill them; they had already killed many Vietnamese and they held a number of Americans hostage. They could be executed and their bodies would be never found. The only way these rebels would come back with them to Buon Me Thuot was if Petersen could persuade them to do so. Getting angry and threatening them would achieve exactly the opposite. Petersen's respect for Colonel Serong plummeted at that moment.

Finally, after several excruciating hours, a small group of the rebel leaders agreed to go back to Ban Me Thuot with Petersen and the others and talk to General Co.

Petersen was flabbergasted when, years later, he read Serong's account of the event in Anne Blair's book *There to the Bitter End*. Serong wrote that the Montagnard rebel leaders asked him to act as their envoy to the Vietnamese commander, and to guarantee their safe conduct in and out of town, when it was Petersen who had done all the talking.

'It was typical of Serong to dress me down for insubordination when I was in the middle of extremely delicate negotiations. Serong did not know these people. We were in an incredibly dangerous position.'

A handful of the rebels squeezed into the vehicle and drove back through the rain to the palace. As they climbed the stairs Serong made the dramatic gesture of holding his hands out from his body and then untying his gun belt and lowering his weapons by the side of the door. The rebels followed one by one, laying down their arms. Petersen acknowledges it was a good move, and it worked.

General Co listened as the rebels put forward their grievances and presented their demands. Co gave them a good hearing that lasted three hours. He did not react when some of the rebels were belligerent, slammed fists on tables and made threats. Among the rebel demands were:

- An elected Montagnard representative in the National Assembly
- Montagnard officers to command Montagnard troops
- District chiefs and possibly Highland province chiefs to be Montagnard
- Authority to fly the Montagnard flag
- Montagnard schools to teach tribal languages
- The right to own the land they cultivate
- Higher education opportunities
- US aid for Montagnard to be administered by Montagnard

General Co told the rebels that most of their requests were reasonable and that he would enact those within his power immediately. The others he would have to take to the government in Saigon.

Co then said: 'Now, do you still want to fight me?'

The rebels mumbled, and said they would go back to their colleagues and talk about it. Again Colonel Freund tried to intervene, saying the rebels should be immediately put on a plane and flown to see Prime Minister Khanh, who was currently visiting nearby Dalat.

Co abruptly rejected Freund's suggestion, stating he was the Prime Minister's representative in the region, and his word was all that was necessary. Clearly, there were tensions between the general and his American adviser.

It was three o'clock on Monday morning when the talks ended, even later by the time Petersen got the rebels back to Buon Enao. The sun rose as he watched the rebel leaders tell the waiting men how the meeting had gone. He heaved a sigh of relief when they agreed to cease hostilities and return to their bases.

Petersen, Serong and Y-Jut returned to town and told Co the good news then picked up Stu Methven and headed out of town to spread the word among the various rebel groups. They first headed south to tell the Buon Sarpa rebels of Co's compromise agreement, but by the time they arrived at their camp Colonel Freund had already been there for over an hour. Freund was telling them the rebellion was over and they were to go back to Buon Sarpa base.

Petersen was staggered that Freund was sending them back

without telling them of the compromise offered by General Co. His dislike of Freund was growing by the minute.

Freund was with American Special Forces commander Major Edwin Brooks and Captain Gillespie from the Buon Brieng base. Journalist Howard Sochurek, who had approached Petersen for an interview some days before the revolt, was also there. Petersen had said no to an interview, as he did to all journalists.

Petersen recalls the teetering balance of the situation. 'Serong said nothing when he should have spoken up. He was a colonel and Freund was a colonel. I was just a captain. The trucks were lined up to take them back and I thought, *Oh shit, this could all break out again*. These men were still showing signs of rebellion. To make matters worse the vehicles moved off with Colonel Freund leading them like a group of naughty schoolboys. I thought he was big-noting himself for the journalist who was busy taking pictures. Freund wanted to be seen as a hero, but he was humiliating these Montagnard and he risked violence breaking out again. These Montagnard had hung their Vietnamese commander from the flagpost, and executed more than a dozen other Vietnamese soldiers.

'Then a Vietnamese plane swooped down low. The warplane made several mock strafing runs over the convoy as it headed back to Buon Sarpa. I thought that was crazy as it could rekindle the violence.'

Freund certainly would have been very pleased with the coverage he received in Sochurek's *National Geographic* report. Sochurek said Freund had heard the Buon Sarpa rebels planned to resume their attack on Ban Me Thuot at 8.30am, unless their demand was met that all Vietnamese left the Highlands. This was a far more aggressive demand than that made by the Buon Enao rebels Petersen had taken to Co during the previous night.

When Freund reached the rebel camp in the morning he saw that Captain Gillespie, who had arrived with Y-Jhon late the previous day, was being held under armed guard by the rebels. The rebels had captured a dozen Vietnamese soldiers and had them securely tied and huddling squatlegged in the yard. Cool as a cucumber, Gillespie had ignored the rebel guns trained on him and despite angry protests from the rebels, walked over to the prisoners, drew his jungle knife and cut their bonds.

The rebels called on him to stop and snapped off the safety catch on their automatic rifles, but Gillespie just continued freeing the prisoners with the help of Y-Jhon, who was being abused by his fellow Rhade. Gillespie and the freed Vietnamese soldiers then spent a tense night surrounded by angry rebel gunmen. When Freund arrived Gillespie told him he had little hope of regaining control of the situation as the Buon Sarpa troops were under the command of communists and Viet Cong agents.

Freund stood in front of the Buon Sarpa men and told them in fluent French that if the United States did not give the Rhade rice, clothing and medicine, where else would they get it.

'Your cause is hopeless without US aid,' Freund told the rebels. As if to emphasise the point, two Vietnamese warplanes suddenly roared over the rebel headquarters at treetop level. The 700 rebel troops threw in the towel. Their frustrated leaders knew the rebellion was over.

After this capitulation Freund arrived at the Buon Sarpa base with the convoy. He offered himself as a hostage in return for the release of the American hostages who had been held at gunpoint since Saturday. The bodies of Vietnamese soldiers executed by the Montagnard littered the ground. Freund stayed in the camp until fresh American advisers and Vietnamese troops arrived to take control. Later, Sochurek hailed Freund, Gillespie and other American officers as heroes who successfully put down a rebellion. He made no mention of Petersen, or General Co's peace offer.

'This handful of dedicated Americans with an awesome display of personal courage had managed to halt the revolt – a revolt that could have drenched the Central Highlands in blood, and perhaps delivered this vital area to the communist Viet Cong,' Sochurek told *National Geographic* readers.

Petersen looked on the rebellion and its failure with sympathy for the Montagnard. 'Colonel Freund really rubbed their noses in their failure. He made them undergo a formal surrender ceremony at Buon Sarpa to Prime Minister Khanh. The promises of General Co were never enacted; the result was that thousands of Rhade, especially those at Buon Sarpa, defected and joined the Viet Cong or walked over the border to join Montagnard independence forces in Cambodia. The base was eventually abandoned and the few Montagnard left were absorbed into a Vietnamese camp close to Ban Me Thuot.'

The Montagnard defectors took arms and supplies with them over the border into Cambodia. They also took Y-Bham Enuol. The old man, who still had Petersen's pistol, became head of a new Montagnard independence movement, FULRO – the *Front Unifié de Libération des Races Opprimees* (Front for the Liberation of Oppressed Races).

Petersen did not agree with Colonel Serong that the Viet Cong were behind the revolt, viewing it as very much Montagnard driven. In his opinion those behind it were the Cham tribe backed by Prince Sihanouk in Cambodia. The French had also given it tacit support.

Despite the danger of being shot at a roadblock in their midnight dash to speak to the rebels, Petersen felt safer doing that than staying inside his house in Ban Me Thuot.

'If I had not left town to go to the rebels I think I would have been attacked by the Vietnamese. I had my enemies among them and this would have been a good time to get me. I thought I was safest with the Montagnard.'

After spending time in the Highlands, Barry Petersen knew the challenges the Montagnard faced and the threat their traditional ways were under. Because of this he was sympathetic to the Montagnard cause during the revolt. Some of their demands were basic human rights: for their children to have access to higher education; a degree of autonomy at the village and district level; they wanted representatives in parliament. Others Petersen felt were unreasonable, like wanting their own flag. He knew the Vietnamese would never tolerate that.

The Montagnard rebellion failed because they missed their opportunity on that Saturday night and early Sunday morning, Petersen states, when they failed to press their attack on Ban Me Thuot.

'The Vietnamese did not have a strong infantry battalion in Ban Me Thuot. They had an artillery battalion, and that would not have held out 3000 well-armed and well-trained Montagnard fighters. By midday on Sunday the Vietnamese had regained control of the airport without much of a fight and started flying in reinforcements. If either side had attacked on that Sunday it would have been a bloodbath.'

Bevan Stokes and the translator Y-Tin flew from Saigon back to Ban Me Thuot on the Tuesday. Colonel Serong and Stu Methven were satisfied the revolt was over and caught the same plane back to Saigon. Stokes found the Vietnamese troops were still extremely nervous.

'Y-Tin wanted to see if his family was OK, but on the way to his village we stumbled into a Vietnamese paratrooper roadblock,' Stokes recalls. 'They were very pissed off, and wanted to kill us on the spot. They had seen Montagnard kill their comrades and throw bodies down the pit latrine. These soldiers were ready to kill anyone. Y-Tin pretended he was Vietnamese and I backed him up.

'I was in uniform, but despite that they poked me in the belly with an automatic gun. One paratrooper put a pistol to my head and cocked it. They thought I might be helping the Montagnard. They were just about out of control, real vicious bastards.

'Y-Tin told them in Vietnamese that I was Australian, but it wasn't doing any good. They knew we were training the Montagnard, and probably thought we were part of the rebellion. A sergeant came over and stopped them from killing us, then they took us back to their base and threw us in a cell. I managed to get on to Barry by phone and after a while he turned up and they released us. It was touch and go for a second.'

That afternoon Petersen and Stokes, with their two invaluable interpreters, drove out to the Tiger Men camp at Buon Enao.

A newly recruited Rhade, Y-To Nie, was haranguing the men, speaking to them like he was the one in charge. As Petersen approached he could hear the rebel leader telling the crowd only Montagnard had the right to decide who should lead them.

'Not the Vietnamese!' The crowd roared in approval.

'Not the French!' A loud cheer went up.

'Not the Americans!' There was less of a cheer at this.

'And not the Australians!' By this time Petersen had reached the assembly and could be seen by his men. They murmured their approval of what Y-To was saying, glancing uncomfortably at their Aussie captain. Petersen was armed only with a side arm, while the 400 Montagnard were carrying automatic weapons. He didn't know if these men, who had been ready to kill just a day earlier, would turn on him. Y-To snarled at Petersen and called for a show of hands for a new Montagnard leader in the camp. Hands went up electing Y-To. The rabblerouser was now the man Petersen would have to deal with in the camp.

For several days it was an uneasy arrangement. Petersen made some checks with intelligence and it was clear Y-To was a Viet Cong agent. He had been imprisoned in Hue for spreading communist propaganda before arriving in Buon Enao asking to join up.

Petersen resumed patrols. It was quickly obvious Y-To was not going to fight the Viet Cong as he spent most of his time campaigning for FULRO and advocating peace with the Viet Cong. The Tiger Men were getting fed up with his endless speeches, so Petersen decided it was time to move. Gathering a few of his trusty fighters, he confronted Y-To at gunpoint. He pointed his pistol at Y-To's head as he disarmed him, saying, 'That's it. You are out. Take your followers and leave now. If I see you again, I will kill you.' Y-To left, and crossed the border into Cambodia.

Colonel Serong might have clashed with Petersen in the heat of the negotiations, but once he got back to Saigon he did what he could to reward Petersen for his efforts. 'The hours of negotiations were a tribute to Petersen's language skills and to his tact,' Serong wrote in his report for Canberra. 'He smoothed every explosive statement and opened up a new tack at each impasse. He persuaded the Montagnard leaders to go before the Vietnamese commander, conscious of the penalties they faced. They had, after all, been killing Vietnamese soldiers over the previous 24 hours. A single misplaced word might have signalled the end to the government presence in the Highlands.'

On Serong's recommendation, Captain Barry Petersen was awarded the Military Cross for his brave efforts in helping quell the Montagnard rebellion. Howard Sochurek may not have acknowledged Barry Petersen's crucial role in bringing peace but his superiors certainly did. For a military man like Barry that was worth more than newsprint any day.

7

THE JOHNNIE WALKER MIRACLE

By the beginning of 1965 Petersen was one of the most experienced Australian officers in Vietnam. He had been conducting his mission for the CIA on his own in Ban Me Thuot for 16 months, and had built up an intricate network of informants, strategically placed friends and officials who owed him favours. His Montagnard guerilla force had grown to more than 1000 and his influence in the Central Highlands was extensive.

He had allies in the most senior positions in the Montagnard leadership, and had won the grudging respect of his CIA paymasters. He had also won the admiration of some of the top commanders among the Vietnamese army officers, but there was ongoing suspicion from others that he was being too successful.

In September 1964 he'd been given a 12-month extension to his mission and as far as he was concerned his only fear was that some day it would all come to an end. He loved the independence of his post and felt he was achieving important results with the Montagnard force in the fight against the Viet Cong in a strategically vital region. He relished the cloak-and-dagger thrills of his CIA mission and some of the crazy characters with whom he came into contact.

Sometimes being secretive led Barry Petersen to very strange situations, even the dead rising up and walking – with the miracle of Johnnie Walker whisky.

The CIA asked Petersen to create a secure zone in a remote backwoods area, far from prying eyes, especially of the Viet Cong variety, for a Vietnamese Special Forces team to practise parachuting into the jungle at night. It was all very hush-hush. The men were jumping from unmarked Air America carrier planes, they wore unmarked clothes, and were under strict orders not to talk to anybody.

But after more than 12 months of surviving nefarious intrigues, political skulduggery and shifty spooks of all types, Petersen knew there was more to it than that. He also knew how to find things out that he wasn't supposed to know.

Sidling up to the parachutists, he listened carefully to their accents and comments. He could tell they were all originally from North Vietnam. They were young, fit and had been well trained at a Special Forces base called Long Thanh, 20 kilometres east of Saigon. Petersen chatted to the drivers and instructors, and put together enough pieces of information to learn the training was part of the Delta Program, a top-secret operation designed to infiltrate former North Vietnamese back into the

North to spread propaganda, commit sabotage and eliminate key North Vietnamese officials.

'I thought security was pretty slack if I could learn all that simply by chatting to a few people around the drop area,' Petersen recalls. 'On the third drop, one of the paratroopers came down heavily in tall trees and broke his neck. I was already back in Ban Me Thuot and was horrified to learn that the American captain who was in charge had simply sent the body to the hospital, still in his suspiciously unmarked clothes.

'Anyone with an experienced eye could tell by the bruises and snapped neck that the man must have been killed in a parachute fall. It was late at night and the body was dumped in the morgue until the morning when hospital officials would do the paperwork.'

Petersen knew the VC had eyes and ears everywhere. If they learned a mysterious body with a broken neck had turned up in the Ban Me Thuot morgue, they might be alerted to a possible paratroop mission into North Vietnam.

'I had to do something. I found the captain in charge of the training in a town bar frequented by foreigners. There he was, manning the drums on the bandstand – smashing and crashing away, still dressed in military greens with his pistol on his hip. He couldn't have done more to advertise himself if he had hung a sign around his neck declaring "American Trainer for Secret Mission".'

Petersen managed to get the captain away from the drums and suggested it was not a great idea to leave the body of his dead soldier in the hospital morgue where the living would take an interest.

'Oh wow! I hadn't thought of that,' said the American. 'What can we do about it?'

Thus began what must have been one of the strangest operations of the Vietnam War – stealing a body from a morgue.

When Petersen asked his fixer, Y-Tin, for ideas, he replied, 'I know the old man who looks after the morgue at night. He is Montagnard. He puts the bodies away until the doctor comes by in the morning to look at them and do the paperwork.'

'Will he take a bribe to look the other way if we take the body out?'

'I don't think you'll need to do that. He likes a drink or two, whisky. You sit with all those dead bodies all night and you'd drink too.'

So Y-Tin headed off to the morgue armed with a couple of bottles of CIA-supplied Johnnie Walker whisky. The old morgue attendant was delighted. Together they knocked off half a bottle while swapping yarns, then Y-Tin good-naturedly gave the old man the other bottle and said he'd mind the store while the old fellow ducked out to finish off the bottle with a mate.

As soon as he was gone, Y-Tin whistled up a couple of Petersen's guards waiting nearby with a jeep. They found the body of the dead paratrooper easily – he was the only one in jungle greens with his neck in an impossible position. They loaded the body into the jeep, sitting the corpse up between them so it would not arouse suspicion with any guards they encountered, and drove quietly across town to Petersen's house where he was waiting with the anxious American captain.

The American was delighted to get the body back. They dragged the body into a spare room until the morning, then stuffed it into a hessian bag and drove it out to the airstrip where it was loaded on to the Air America plane taking the captain back to the paratrooper base near Saigon.

'The strange thing was the hungover morgue attendant never asked where the missing body had gone; nobody on the morgue staff wondered why a dead body had seemingly got up and just walked out of the morgue,' Petersen says with a laugh.

Flying a dead body in a hessian bag was nothing unusual for the pilots of Air America, a ragtag airline financed by, and exclusively run, for the CIA. Its civilian pilots flew a wide assortment of planes with no markings and went wherever they were told, carried whatever was put on the plane, no questions asked. Petersen got to know a few of the pilots.

'They were an incredible assortment of people from all parts of the world – a lot were nationalist Chinese, but there were many from Europe, Philippines and, of course, America.'

The Air America pilots flew a range of planes, from large transports to smaller aircraft for short, dirt strip landings. Petersen found the men friendly enough, but they rarely talked about what they were doing or why they were working with the CIA. Essentially they did it for the money – they could earn in one week what would take a month as a regular commercial pilot.

Petersen recalls how Air America pilots often flew by the seat of their pants. 'One time I was taking some senior Vietnamese officials on a Dornier plane to a meeting. The pilot had made a mistake and gone to the wrong airport before flying to Ban Me Thuot, and he hadn't refuelled. We were flying over the mountains when suddenly an alarm went off. It sounded like a car horn. I knew from experience it meant the fuel tank was critically low and it was time to switch over to the emergency tank. I wasn't worried as I saw the pilot reach down and switch over to the other tank, but the alarmed Vietnamese officials got up and cried, "What was that?" One of the Americans, very relaxed, just drawled "Ah, he's just blowing the horn at another plane." So the Vietnamese looked out the windows trying to see how close this other plane was.'

It was not all laughs, though. Air America planes and helicopters were unarmed and limited to transport and parachute drops, but they often flew over hostile territory and were shot at many times. A total of 87 Air America pilots were killed flying missions for the CIA over Vietnam, Laos, Cambodia and elsewhere. The famous helicopter perched on the roof of the US Embassy evacuating the last people from Vietnam was an Air America chopper.

Petersen heard from one Chinese pilot a story that showed the danger often came from within. 'I heard Air America lost a plane dropping paratroopers over North Vietnam. It was top secret so no one was supposed to know they were dropping squads of troops into the North to infiltrate and sabotage communist forces. They were northerners who had come South during partition, and were sent back as spies. The bloke in the morgue would have been one of them. In this case the pilots dropped the troops over the right spot, but the last man to leave the plane pulled a grenade out of his pocket and threw it back into the plane before he jumped. The plane exploded and it went down, killing the pilot and the crew. The grenade thrower might have been the only traitor in the group, but there were many secret Viet Cong hidden among the northerners that the South recruited. It was all hushed up.

'I did hear of Air America carrying drugs in Laos, but not in Vietnam. I understand the reasons for it. They were working with private armies who were commanding Montagnard mercenaries. The CIA were paying them and, to keep them onside, were flying their opium out for them. I was told the CIA were raising their own funds by selling opium in Hong Kong, but I don't know if that was true.'

The name Air America is often linked to the shadowy side of war and there were many mysterious crashes that the company tried to hush up. One particular story was of a Beechcraft flying a US Embassy official, widely accepted as a CIA man, as its sole passenger when it crashed on its final approach into Cu Chi Province. The small plane was found riddled with bullets. The strange thing was that all the bullets had been fired from inside the plane.[1]

Petersen had no other choice but to fly Air America when he flew to Saigon every six weeks or so to pick up the cash he needed for his Montagnard operation. He'd order the plane by phone. It would arrive in the morning, fly over his house to let him know it had arrived, and then he'd meet it out at the airstrip.

'When I landed in Saigon I'd go to the CIA section of the US Embassy and see the Air America booking officer, United States Air Force Sergeant Jim Wood, and book a plane to fly back to Ban Me Thuot the next morning. Jim was on loan to the CIA to run the booking for Air America planes. He also ran airplane maintenance and things like that.

'One time he asked me if I could get him half a dozen Luger pistols. Apparently the CIA had boxes of them, German World War Two vintage pistols. Jim told me the pilots liked them much better than the American military-issue pistols.

'I said I couldn't as they wouldn't be accounted for my operation. Jim just laughed. "Barry, everything that goes out of the warehouse is written off the moment it leaves." Well, I owed the pilots, so I put in an order for half a dozen Lugers on top of my regular weapons request.

'Two days later a shipment of weapons arrived. Among them were half a dozen boxes of freshly reconditioned Lugers, along with a couple of spare magazines. I handed them over to Jim on my next trip to Saigon. He was very pleased. Lord knows what rackets he was running, but I had made a friend in a very key position.

'Another time, when I was sitting next to one of the pilots flying down to Saigon, I looked at his watch and I thought his time must be wrong. Then I realised it was a 24-hour watch. I had never seen one before. The pilot showed it to me and it was a good Swiss watch issued to all the Air America pilots. I thought if I could get Lugers for the pilots, maybe I could get watches for my own operation – they would be extremely useful for my radio operators. So I ordered a few. They came, so I ordered them by the dozens. I had one, Bevan Stokes had one and I gave one to all the radio operators. They were wonderful watches. The CIA seemed to have everything.'

Petersen usually stayed in Saigon for a day and a half, putting his orders in, submitting his latest report and handing in receipts for expenses. He'd occasionally be invited to have lunch or dinner with Stu Methven who lived with his wife, Joy, and their children in an old mansion on the outskirts of Saigon.

'Stu was a colourful character and he'd collect an interesting group of people at his parties. There would be CIA people, embassy people and sometimes journalists. For the CIA and people like Methven, journalists can be a good source of information, as they go to places and talk to people they can't get to. Journalists also see things differently, trying to work out the truth of what's going on. They're also useful for deliberate leaking of information – stories you want to get home or misinformation to mislead the enemy.

'The parties always started with liberal doses of Salty Dog, a mix of half gin and half grapefruit juice. Stu filled a large hand crafted solid silver Thai punchbowl with the potent mix, glasses dipped in salt to give them a salty rim. It certainly kicked off a party.'

During one of those sessions, one of the CIA bosses said to Petersen, 'Barry, you are not ordering any operational grog. You're letting the team down. You should be giving bottles of whisky to the province chief and others.'

Petersen replied that he did, but that he bought the grog out of his own operation fund.

The CIA men were mortified. 'Barry, don't do that. Just put it on your order form along with the ammunition and everything else.' So he started ordering crates of whisky, cognac and wine from the CIA. The bottles were clearly marked across the neck of the bottle 'Expressly for the Diplomatic Corps'. The alcohol certainly oiled the wheels of his diplomacy.

At one of Methven's parties Petersen met the legendary Lucien Conein, the former US lieutenant colonel who parachuted into Vietnam in World War Two to help organise the Viet Minh fighting the Japanese. He stayed on, training Montagnard to fight the Viet Minh who were battling the French. Their experiences with the Montagnard gave Conein and Petersen a common interest and they got on well.

'Lou Conein was a very good friend of General Nguyen Khanh, who became prime minister after the coup against Minh,' Petersen recalls. 'Conein told me that Khanh wanted a bulletproof limousine just like the US president. Lou got the CIA workshop to armourplate the limo and presented it to Khanh at his palace.

'"But how can I tell if it is really bulletproof?" Khanh asked.

'Conein told Khanh to order his driver to sit behind the steering wheel. The nervous driver got in and closed the door. Conein promptly pulled out his pistol and at point-blank range shot all six bullets at the window and door.

'"The driver looked shit scared, his face had gone white," Conein laughed. "But Khanh was impressed, and he was very grateful for the bulletproof car."'

After the parties and lunches with such colourful characters, Petersen would pick up his money supply the next morning as he headed to the airport. 'It was in bags full of bundles of piasters, the Vietnamese currency. I had a revolving fund of 50 000 piasters (US$625) a month, and I would be down to about 3000 at the end of the month when I went to Saigon. I would be carrying up to 48 000 piasters (US$600) in bundled-up notes and it took several canvas carry bags to carry it all. I'd jump in a taxi with the bags and my overnight bag and throw it into an Air America aircraft. I was usually alone on the plane unless I had taken one of my offsiders with me.'

CIA accountants were like accountants anywhere – so long as they had a piece of paper as a receipt they were happy, regardless of where it came from.

One highly suspect receipt involved the hiring of a Frenchman who had a service station to deliver converted troop trucks to the Highlands.

The Frenchman seemed to be able to get through Viet Cong roadblocks without any problems – another sign the French were cooperating with the VC. He'd simply pay the toll the Viet Cong demanded at their checkpoints. It was like a tax. When he arrived he'd give Petersen the receipt the VC had given him, and he'd be reimbursed. Petersen would then pass the VC tax receipts on to the CIA accountants. A lot of CIA money went directly to the enemy that way, but it didn't matter, no one seemed to care so long as there were receipts to balance the accounts.

Viet Cong and North Vietnamese regular troops stepped up their operations after the collapse of the Montagnard rebellion. More and more men and supplies pushed down the Ho Chi Minh Trail and the number of ambushes of South Vietnamese troops on the roads increased, even attacking large convoys in hit-and-run operations. Elsewhere, the VC intensified assaults on US bases, launching attacks on the massive US base at the central Vietnamese town of Pleiku. Tactics were brutal. A suicide bomber walked into US soldiers' quarters disguised as a cleaner and blew himself up, killing 29 American soldiers. A massive 135-kilogram car bomb exploded outside the US Embassy in Saigon, killing two Americans and 20 Vietnamese. It was a turning point. The US started flying in combat troops to protect their installations.

The VC were showing their intent on bringing the war right into the town of Ban Me Thuot. Many foreign servicemen regularly frequented a bar opposite the Darlac Hotel. Petersen was one of these servicemen and he'd become friendly with one of the bar girls called Co Than, a widow and mother who worked there to support her child. One busy evening, when Petersen was not there, an orphan shoeshine boy called Ngoc walked in. A familiar sight at the bar, polishing shoes of patrons, regulars liked Ngoc because he always had a smile and went about his work cheerfully. The boy entered quietly through a side entrance, a grenade hidden in each hand. The pins on the grenades had been removed, so he had to hold the safety levers down to stop them going off. Walking to the centre of the crowded dance floor he opened his hands, releasing the firing pins. The blast from the two grenades killed him and many others, including Co Than.

Barry Petersen was stunned by the attack. He could not comprehend how a nice kid like Ngoc could be persuaded to do that; he didn't believe the boy had been political enough at that age to become a suicide bomber. One possible explanation in Petersen's mind was that the VC were holding a hostage somewhere and Ngoc had been forced to do it.

Rattled, Petersen intensified his operations. He was convinced his best tactic was to stick to small teams of eight-men patrols, keeping them less visible, easier to melt into the jungle, easier to make fast hit-and-run raids, easier to melt into Montagnard villages for the night. The VC responded to his sniping tactics by forming ever larger units.

'This was exactly what I hoped for,' Petersen said. 'They were making themselves bigger and easier targets. We'd copied the successful early VC guerilla strategy, and it was working.

'In one incident two of our teams were patrolling in the southeast of Darlac Province and discovered one end of a Viet Cong ambush set up alongside a road a large South Vietnamese convoy was due to travel along. The well-hidden VC were waiting until the convoy was well and truly spread along the line of foxholes before they opened fire. The road was so swampy that elephants had to pull the vehicles through the mud, delaying the convoy.'

The VC were looking expectantly up the road waiting for the convoy when Petersen's two teams sneaked up on the last ambush pits at the far end. The teams suddenly attacked the first pit in the line, wiping out the five or six VC. In a fierce, swift engagement, the two teams on either side of the road ran from one pit to the next, firing automatic weapons and lobbing grenades. They wiped out more than half a dozen pits before the VC fled, their element of surprise gone. None of Petersen's men were injured.

Petersen's men were loyal and up for any fight but sometimes they were too keen, and took on more than they could chew. In another incident an eight-man patrol was keeping an eye on a North Vietnamese battalion fortification which had around 400 troops inside. One night they crawled up to a machine gun post and attacked, killing everyone they could, and taking away a Russian 62-millimetre belt-fed machine gun. It was a brave action, but seven of the eight men were wounded. It wasn't an action Petersen approved of, but it was difficult to tell them they had done wrong. They received medals for bravery from the Saigon government, as did many others in the Truong Son Force.

Petersen himself was given a gallantry award by the South Vietnamese High Command which said: 'The Truong Son Force has attained one of the best combat records in Vietnam by inflicting heavy casualties and equipment losses on the Viet Cong while sustaining a minimum of friendly losses.'

Just like their leader, the Truong Son Force were proving to be a formidable enemy and a powerful asset for the South Vietnamese.

8
MEETING MENZIES

In March 1965 Petersen was shocked to learn Colonel Serong was on his last days as commander of the Training Team and he was resigning from the army. Serong had been tipped for big things in the army, certainly he'd been expected to reach the rank of general, maybe even chief of the army. In 1963, before the Montagnard revolt, he'd been summoned to Washington to impress on senior American officials the importance of counter-insurgency programs such as those being used with the Highland tribes. Invited to address the US President's Special Committee on Counter-Insurgency, the White House's planning group for the Vietnam War, Serong sat with key people such as Attorney General Bobby Kennedy, CIA Director John McCone and assorted top brass for 40 minutes, pressing the need for more units like those run by Petersen and US Special Forces in the Highlands.

But Serong had also irritated a lot of people in the Australian government and defence hierarchy. Perhaps his greatest black mark was that he was seen as being far too close to the Diem regime. The Australian government's primary interest was not in propping up a corrupt dictatorial regime, but persuading the United States to become more heavily involved in the South East Asian region.

When Petersen heard Serong was to take a post in Saigon with the United States Operations Mission he knew the Australian was jumping ship to his friends in the CIA.

Petersen flew to Saigon to say goodbye. He had had his differences with the man, and he thought Serong had an enormous ego, but he acknowledged Serong had done a lot for him and the Training Team, and had pursued excellent and appropriate military tactics for Vietnam.

'Barry, you have to take a break,' Serong told him. 'You've been out on your own in the Highlands for a year and a half and you need to get away for a while.'

Petersen protested. 'I'm fine, Sir, and there's lots to do.'

But Serong was intent on sending Petersen back to Australia for two weeks, not on leave, but to give briefings to senior Australian officials.

'You'll have time to unwind, but there will be an official debrief. Many top people want to talk to you – ASIS, External Affairs, Army chief, Military Intelligence.'

Barry Petersen did not want to leave Vietnam but Serong was still his commander so he did what he was told.

Soon afterwards Petersen landed in Brisbane, but he had no time to see his family in Queensland. His orders were to fly straight on to Melbourne where ASIS wanted to talk to him.

'It was a strange feeling, coming back to Australia after so long in Vietnam. I was not in uniform coming into Customs. Australia had not decided to send combat troops to Vietnam at that stage, and the Training Team's mission was still very secret, especially mine with the CIA. It was best to keep a low profile.'

The low profile disappeared when Petersen dutifully declared a couple of odd items in his baggage. He pulled out a kris, a ceremonial dagger, given to him by a friend in Malaya. Also wrapped up was a tiger skin the Montagnards had presented to him. He'd planned to leave both items with his family.

'Customs were very excited. They took the tiger skin for fumigation, but they confiscated the kris saying it was a dangerous weapon. I said it was only a ceremonial sword, and wasn't used for fighting, but it met the bureaucratic definition of a weapon, and they kept it.'

As usual, Petersen had good connections. A few strategic calls to intelligence people, and the kris was returned to him by Customs a few days later.

His return was no holiday. Dressed in civilian clothes, Petersen met a group of senior ASIS officers at Melbourne's Victoria Barracks, well away from prying eyes. He had a box of goodies with him for the spooks.

'It was equipment I had picked up that the VC were using. Some of it was surveillance stuff like eavesdropping devices, ID cards and propaganda they distributed. The ASIS guys said that was useful, but what they really wanted to know was how effective Australian training was to prepare for the mission in Vietnam. They didn't ask how the war was going. They wanted to know the differences in the way the Australian Army Training

Team did things from the US Special Forces. They wanted to know what our relations were with the CIA on the ground, how we handled the Montagnard compared to the Americans.'

Petersen told them that, overall, things were going well, that the system of keeping to small units was more effective than the US approach of using large forces. The US strategy of strategic hamlets was not working as their army did not put defensive patrols out beyond the heavily fortified villages, and the VC found the hamlets to be a convenient way of picking up American weapons.

After several hours being debriefed by ASIS officers, one told Petersen casually: 'Oh, by the way, the DG [Director General] Sir Walter Cawthorn would like to take you to lunch if you are free.'

'Er, yes, certainly,' said Petersen.

Petersen felt it was rather extraordinary that a mere captain would be invited to lunch by a former general and head of Australia's equivalent of the CIA and MI6. He didn't know it was about to get even more extraordinary.

'I thought maybe as an ex-soldier he wanted to hear the situation direct from a soldier. I thought it would be low key, just a chat.'

Petersen was ushered into Cawthorn's office. The tall, ramrod-backed former general, armed with the regulation white military moustache, greeted the captain wholeheartedly. Cawthorn had been a distinguished soldier; a regimental sergeant major at Gallipoli, he was put in charge of military intelligence in India during World War Two. After a polite chat, they went to Cawthorn's waiting car and were driven to the exclusive Melbourne Club. Nothing could be further from Petersen's rather basic digs in Ban Me Thuot, or guzzling maggot-ridden rice wine in the thatched longhouses of the Montagnard.

The Melbourne Club is the heart of Australia's snobbish, old-school establishment. It has been the men-only home away from home for business and military leaders, conservative politicians and landed gentry since 1839. No nouveau riche are found here, no Jews and definitely no women. It is England Upper Class transported to the colony. The unwritten law of the Melbourne Club is that no one talks about whatever happens inside its hallowed halls. No working class, apart from the discreet waiters, are ever allowed through its thick oak doors.

Petersen was awed being in the old Victorian building with its thick leather seats. He couldn't help but wonder how these crusty old men would react if he brought some of his Montagnard friends into their rarefied world.

As they took their seats at a table reserved for just the two of them, Petersen looked up at the next table and was stunned to see silver-haired Prime Minister Sir Robert Menzies sitting with two other men. Menzies had been prime minister since 1949, a legend in conservative Australia, and the country's longest serving leader. The jowled Menzies nodded a greeting to Cawthorn.

Cawthorn leaned forward. 'Barry, have you met the Prime Minister?' he asked quietly.

'No, Sir,' said Petersen.

'Come on then. I'm sure he'd like to meet you.'

Cawthorn got up and went over to Menzies' table, had a short talk with him, then beckoned Petersen over.

'Prime Minister, I'd like to introduce Captain Barry Petersen.

He's just back from Vietnam where he is doing very valuable work in the Highlands with the Montagnard.'

Menzies stuck out his hand. 'Well done young man,' he said. 'Keep up the good work.'

Petersen shook Menzies' hand, muttered his thanks, and they returned to their table.

Petersen thought it was a fortunate coincidence that Cawthorn had the table next to Menzies for the lunch. Later, he thought, bearing in mind the question Cawthorn was about to ask, maybe it wasn't such a coincidence. Menzies might have had a good reason to get a look at this junior army officer doing extraordinary things in Vietnam.

Over an oyster entree and a main course of roast beef, potatoes and gravy, Petersen and Cawthorn chatted about life in the Highlands. Cawthorn had already done a tour of the Training Team's operations and had stopped briefly in Ban Me Thuot. Petersen had met him and taken him out to Buon Enao to see the Tiger Men and witness exactly what was going on.

Cawthorn was pleased at what he saw in Ban Me Thuot and the information Petersen had gathered. The first two Australian officers to work with the CIA, John Healy and Peter Young, had not been given much access to CIA programs or intelligence.

'The CIA was doing its best to ensure we Australians did not find out too much about their operations,' Petersen recalls. 'Australia was still much closer to British intelligence at the time, having worked with them in Malaya. Cawthorn wanted ASIS to get much closer to the CIA.'

Petersen saw his opening, and put to Cawthorn something that had been on his mind for some time. His mission at Ban

Me Thuot had involved a lot of secret service work and he'd found it was something he enjoyed.

'General,' he began, 'I have been thinking for some time that I would like to join ASIS and do intelligence work full time.'

Cawthorn heard Petersen out, then put his knife and fork down. By this time Menzies had left and they were almost alone in the dining room.

'The truth is Barry, after what you have been doing, you would probably find it rather boring,' Cawthorn replied. 'There's a lot of desk work, sifting through intelligence reports, listening to phone taps, dealing with different agencies and so on, rather than being out in the field. Look, think about it. But if you still want to apply you will have my backing.'

After the plates were taken away, and they were settling down to a pleasant glass of port, Cawthorn very casually asked: 'By the way, Barry, going on your experience in the field, what are your feelings about Australia putting combat troops into Vietnam? How do you think they would go? Would they be effective?'

The question took Petersen by surprise. Nothing official had ever been said about sending combat troops to Vietnam, although there had been discussion in the press. At the time most of the Australian public seemed to be in favour of it. The Menzies government had been talking for years about the Domino Theory, and the dangers of complacency.

Petersen's mind was on full alert. 'I immediately twigged something was up. Top people don't ask questions like that unless they already have a plan. I knew Cawthorn was asking me because I'd been there longer than anyone, and I'd been working independently with Vietnamese and Americans.'

The young captain picked his words carefully. 'I don't think there would be a problem, Sir. I think the Australian troops would not have any difficulty. They are well trained for jungle warfare.'

A day later Petersen was in Canberra seeing Chief of the General Staff, Lieutenant General Sir John Wilton. 'They used to call him Smiley, because he never did. He was friendly with me and very curious about the Montagnard and the difference between my approach and that of the American Special Forces. At the end of our talk Wilton asked me exactly the same question as Cawthorn – how would Australian combat troops go in Vietnam? I told him exactly the same as I told Cawthorn, that they were well trained and would do well. I left that meeting in no doubt whatsoever that the government had already made up its mind to send combat troops to Vietnam.'

Next stop for Barry was the Department of External Affairs and a meeting with the head of the South East Asian desk, Arthur Malcolm Morris. Petersen was chuffed at seeing so many senior people, who were seeking his opinion, so he was unprepared for what was coming.

Petersen walked into Morris's office. The bureaucrat was sitting behind his large desk, flanked by two grim-looking Department officials armed with files. Petersen was motioned to sit in a chair placed on its own, two metres in front of Morris's desk. There were no smiles, no offers of cups of tea. Petersen's battle instincts kicked in. He braced himself.

Morris launched into Petersen. 'What are you doing up there,' he blasted. 'You are running your own show, things are getting out of hand. You've been fomenting rebellion among the Montagnard. The Vietnamese government is furious. They have evidence you supported the uprising and assisted the Montagnard in their revolt.'

As Morris rapped out his accusations like a machine gun spitting bullets, his sidekicks handed him documents which he waved at Petersen.

'The Vietnamese prime minister has demanded you be withdrawn. He says you are a known sympathiser with Montagnard independence and you are undermining the government of South Vietnam.'

Petersen was reeling. Having just been praised by ASIS and Defence, he had not expected this attack from foreign affairs officials. But as every good military man knows, the best defence is offence. Petersen hit back.

'That is not true, Sir. If the Vietnamese government is claiming they have evidence I supported the rebellion, then that evidence is wrong. I had nothing to do with the rebellion except to help end it. My unit stayed out of it, and I helped broker a peace deal with the province chief.

'The last thing I would want is a Montagnard revolt. For my force to be effective they need the cooperation of the Vietnamese authorities. I made sure the province chief was appointed the commander-in-chief of the Truong Son Force. We could not operate without money and supplies from the United States. Why would I encourage their independence?'

Petersen told the stony-faced bureaucrats that everyone knew the Montagnard wanted autonomy, and that he was constantly treading a fine line – keeping their support by being sympathetic to their grievances, but never giving outright support to their campaign for autonomy.

'I say to them we have a problem on our hands right now with the communists. Let's get that sorted out, and then you can worry about autonomy. Yes, I do admire and like the Montagnard. They have put up with a lot throughout their history, but they have survived with their culture intact. They are brave and fearless fighters, and they fight with us much like the Gurkhas fight for the British.

'I do sympathise with their aspiration for a degree of autonomy. But total autonomy is foolish as there are too many tribes and they are cut off in the mountains with no raw materials, no economy, no access to the sea. It's a pipedream. First they have to stop the communists taking control.'

After an hour of grilling Petersen, and not getting an admission from the young army captain, Morris settled back in his chair and became more friendly. He seemed satisfied Petersen had not 'gone native' and was not running his own private army rebelling against the war machine.

When he left Petersen was furious. 'What a hide these bloody bureaucrats had to sit in Canberra questioning me, an officer risking his life on the front line for foreign policies they put in place. I knew then that I had enemies in high places. I wasn't sure why. I had just done what was asked of me and done it the way I thought best. It was Bryan Mills and the CIA who told me to set up this Montagnard force. It was Stu Methven who threw money at me to keep it going and told me to keep making it bigger.'

The heated meeting with Morris had ended on cautiously amicable terms. Morris accepted Petersen had not turned rogue, and was not running his own private war in the remote jungle highlands. But even though things seemed pleasant enough the young captain knew he was a marked man in the jungle of political bureaucrats. He would have to watch his back.

He was then ushered to the office of the head of the Department of External Affairs, Sir James Plimsoll, where he was finally offered a cup of tea. Plimsoll was friendly, and made no accusations. That dirty work had clearly been handled by his underling. After an amiable chat about quaint Montagnard customs, Plimsoll casually asked the same question about combat troops he'd been asked twice before. Petersen used exactly the same response he had given Cawthorn and Wilton. The three most senior men in the three most crucial government departments regarding Vietnam had asked an identical question. Petersen knew the Australian troops were going.

After a quick stopover in Queensland to see his parents, he returned to Vietnam. Once back in Saigon he met Serong's successor, Colonel David Jackson.

'Sir, the Australian government is about to send combat troops to Vietnam,' Petersen told him.

'Really, that's news to me,' said Jackson, genuinely surprised.

'Everything I heard points to it, Sir.'

At the time Petersen thought sending combat troops and widening the war would be a positive development, even though he thought the best way to fight the war was with advisers. He was later to regret his optimistic advice to the bigwigs in Australia.

In true military fashion Captain Petersen had answered only the question his superiors put to him: how would combat troops fare in Vietnam. He had not been asked if it was the right military move, so he did not volunteer his opinion. There was no suggestion of sending conscripts at that point, and Petersen believed professional and well-trained Australian soldiers would cope well in Vietnam. Besides, after top level defence and political decision makers had all put exactly the same question to him he surmised the decision to send combat troops had already been well and truly made and that anything he did say would not change what was to come.

9

FIRED

One month later, at 8pm on 29 April 1965, Prime Minister Sir Robert Menzies rose to his feet in Parliament. The chamber was almost empty as no one was expecting a major announcement at that late hour, long after newspaper deadlines had passed. Without drama, Menzies announced he had received a request from the government of South Vietnam for further military assistance.

'We have decided, and this has been in close consultation with the government of the United States, to provide an infantry battalion for service in Vietnam . . . the takeover of South Vietnam would be a direct military threat to Australia and all the countries of South East Asia. It must be seen as part of a thrust by Communist China between the Indian and Pacific oceans.'

This was not exactly true. Australia actually invited itself to the war in Vietnam. Menzies and the hawks in his administration were anxious to involve the United States ever more deeply in South East Asia, and they saw a war in Vietnam as the best way to do it.

As far back as 17 December 1964, Menzies, along with Foreign Minister Sir Paul Hasluck and Defence Minister Shane Paltridge, told Cabinet they had decided to send combat troops to Vietnam. This was, however, Menzies' decision, regardless of how it was presented. The prime minister said it was decided on the recommendation of the defence chiefs of staff. What he didn't say was that many senior defence chiefs disagreed, as did several of his foreign affairs advisers.

Four months after that decision to send troops, Menzies was still hunting for a hook on which to hang a reason to send young Australian men to war. In early 1965 the South Vietnamese government did not want to give the rampant North Vietnamese another excuse to say the South was opening the door for yet more foreign soldiers to fight on Vietnamese land. So far, American and Australian advisers had had little success in routing Viet Cong communists and their sympathisers from among the 14 million people living in South Vietnam.

But what the Vietnamese wanted was irrelevant. 'The Australian government was totally indifferent to the aims and expectations of the South Vietnamese government,' wrote Michael Sexton in his book *War for the Asking*. 'Not only was a South Vietnamese "invitation" not sought until the last minute, but the Australian government was determined that troops should go even if the South Vietnamese did not want them and had to be coerced into taking them by the Americans.'

Menzies twisted the truth. South Vietnam never did formally request a battalion of Australian troops to defend their country against communists. Instead, the South Vietnamese government belatedly accepted Menzies' offer of a battalion. Three hours before he rose to speak in Parliament that night, Menzies received a cable from the Australian Embassy in Saigon saying South Vietnam's Prime Minister Phan Huy Quat had verbally accepted Menzies' announcement to be made the next day 'of the decision to provide a battalion at Vietnamese request'.

At the time it didn't matter whether Menzies had deceived Australia. Public opinion had been whipped into an anti-communist frenzy by a pro-war press. A Morgan Gallup poll found 64 per cent believed communism would drive on to Australia if not stopped in Vietnam, and another 72 per cent believed China was a direct threat to the country. Prominent newspapers said the 'red scourge' was heading inexorably southwards towards Australia (a repeat of the 'yellow peril' fears of Japan in World War Two) and it was best to stop them in Vietnam rather than Darwin. Only Rupert Murdoch's new national newspaper, *The Australian*, branded the decision as wrong and reckless. The Australian Labor Party warned the war would inevitably require conscripts to be sent to Vietnam, 20-year-olds who were not old enough to vote or allowed to have a drink in a bar until they were 21.

All that was far from the immediate concerns of Captain Barry Petersen when he returned to Ban Me Thuot with orders from Stu Methven to add several hundred more troops to his Tiger Men force. The Viet Cong were stepping up their operations, and the volume of men and arms coming down the Ho Chi Minh Trail continued to increase.

'We need to turn up the heat, Barry,' Methven said one day over drinks at Petersen's house. 'I want you to set up a couple of counter-terror teams. We have to take the war right up to the VC.'

Petersen hesitated. He wasn't sure what Methven meant. He hadn't heard the term before. 'What are counter-terror teams?' he asked.

Methven was surprised at Petersen's question. He thought someone in his position would know already.

'They are our hit men,' Methven said unabashed. 'They play the game the same way the VC do. They carry out reprisals. They go in and knock off Viet Cong agents, the higher up the better. They hunt them down and take them out. They put the squeeze on communist sympathisers.'

Petersen was taken aback. He'd been told of a bizarre plan for an assassination squad when he first came to the Highlands using deaf mutes. He'd been horrified then and helped bring the idea to a halt. He hadn't changed his mind down the track. Petersen thought it was sick and he was dead against it.

'You mean assassination squads?'

'Yes, if you like. We need to train a couple of squads to sneak into villages, kill VC or their sympathisers, and get out. We've got to take terror to the VC, use their own tactics against them.'

Petersen didn't like it. It was a gut reaction, he explained later, a matter of morals. 'If anyone has to be got rid of I already have the men who can do that,' he told Methven. 'I don't need to train professional assassins.'

Seeing anger rise in Methven's face, Petersen quickly explained: 'Stu, you'll have a Frankenstein monster in the making if you do that sort of thing. You would be training Montagnard to be assassins, not soldiers. Many Montagnard hate the Vietnamese so much they would kill them whether they were from North or South. My task is to train militia who obey orders, who fight as soldiers. No, I won't be in it.'

Methven was furious. He had not expected this Australian captain to refuse a CIA request. After all, the CIA supplied him with everything he had. This officer had been sent by the Australian Army to operate under CIA control, but he was still an Australian Army officer. Could he refuse a CIA order? Methven must have decided persuasion would be better than putting that to the test.

'Barry, we are doing this in every province. It is very successful,' he argued.

'No, I won't be part of it,' Petersen snapped back. Once he took a stand that was it. He was stubborn and pressure would only make him dig in his feet even further. If the CIA's idea was to copy Viet Cong terror tactics, Petersen would not help them. He'd seen Viet Cong chop off the head of a village chief, murder his entire family and then display their bodies so the rest of the villagers would be terrorised into obeying them. He'd come to fight communist terrorism, not to commit the same atrocities on the Vietnamese people. To do so would be against every military code of conduct and rules of engagement Petersen could think of.

What he did not know was that an Australian Army mate of his, Captain Ian Teague, had actually devised this plan. Petersen and Teague had spent more than nine years in the army together, including jungle fighting in Malaya. In 1964 Teague had visited Petersen for a few days to look over his Montagnard force and had slept cuddled up with Barry's pet leopard cub. In 1964 Teague was seconded by Colonel Serong to the CIA's

Combined Studies Division, and posted to beleaguered Quang Ngai province, halfway up the coast between Saigon and the demilitarised zone.

Serong told Teague that Quang Ngai was the third most VC infiltrated province of South Vietnam at that time. Out of 660 000 people in the province, around 150 000 were VC or sympathisers.[1]

Teague was to make a considerable impression with his efforts at Quang Ngai, and his contribution was to have long-term consequences. He saw much the same problems as Petersen, but he came to a markedly different conclusion on how to deal with them.

Dressed in civilian clothes, he spent six weeks touring the province in an civilian jeep with a interpreter, talking to everyone from regional chiefs to bottom-of-the-pile troopers and villagers. He quickly found there were two Vietnams – by day the villagers were loyal to the government, by night the Viet Cong ruled the countryside. The villagers received no protection from VC infiltrators, and to survive they had to bend with the wind.

Teague found the VC were well organised, with a solid hierarchy of regional commanders, tax collectors, propaganda experts, political officers and fighters. They were ruthless, torturing and killing villagers who resisted. For more than 15 years they had been using the villages as places to hide and taking their supplies and food.

Teague thought one anti-VC program showed promise. His AATTV predecessor in the province, Captain Guy Boileau, had trained around 40 men from one village to defend their own village area. The scheme had been set up by two US advisers with close links to the CIA – Frank Scotton and Bob Kelly. The units also conducted goodwill programs such as medical checks and road construction.

Teague expanded the program and within a few months had the units, called People's Action Teams (PATs), operating in several districts. The core of their success was that the recruits were protecting their own people.

He drew up a 10-point plan for the units, which included taking the best fighters and forming five-men assassination squads to go out and kill key members of the VC infrastructure. Called Counter Terror units (CT), the assassination squads acted on intelligence gathered by the PATs and sent to a regional intelligence committee supervised by the CIA.

'We grew to have 25 CTs,' Teague recounted in a 2008 interview. 'Their mission was to ferret out VC infrastructure and destroy it. They operated in exactly the same way as the Viet Cong – tight teams of just five men, slip in, do the deed, and slip out.'

When the first PATs were successful, the CIA told Teague to extend them across the province. 'After less than a year the Combined Studies Division was pouring 10 million piasters a month into the program – around US$120 000 at that time. Each PAT member was taking home 400 piasters (US$4.70) a month. For the Vietnamese that was a hell of a lot of money being pumped directly into each village.'

The PATs earned every cent. In one village they spotted a large force of several hundred VC. They called up regular army reinforcements and attacked at dawn, killing 79 VC. 'My problem was holding the young blokes back,' Teague recalls.

'They wanted to tear in with machine guns and keep on going. But their job was to stay and protect the villagers.'

By the end of the first 12 months of CT operations 379 Viet Cong had been recorded killed, 214 captured, and 187 weapons taken, good odds for a loss of 32 PAT members and 118 wounded. Only one deserted.[2]

Teague believed it was just as important to win the hearts and minds of the villagers, so he drew up a simple set of rules by which his PATs had to operate: respect the people, help the people, protect the people and obey orders. He made no secret these principles were pinched from the VC themselves.

He also laid down a code of conduct, written on one side of a card PAT members had to carry with them at all times.

- Always be polite
- Pay the right price for anything you want
- Return what you borrow
- Pay for anything you lose or damage
- Do not be overbearing
- Do not destroy crops
- Do not molest women
- Treat prisoners fairly but firmly

On the other side of the card was the PAT emblem – a dragon over a map of Vietnam.

Colonel Serong and the Combined Studies Division were so impressed with Teague's program they decided to introduce it to provinces across South Vietnam. Teague ended up with 310 PAT units comprising 13 500 personnel across the country. Keen for Australian Training Team officers to remain at the forefront of the program, Serong sent Captain Jim Devitt, Captain Allan Thompson and Lieutenant David Brockett to learn from Teague and get PATs operating in other provinces.

In March 1965, 12 months after working on the program, Teague was ordered to hand over his Quang Ngai operation to a CIA officer and base himself in Saigon to coordinate the PAT programs, and the assassination teams that went with them. The CIA wanted to take the program national.

It was this drive that brought Stu Methven to Ban Me Thuot to ask Barry Petersen to get with the program. Teague was not surprised when he learned Petersen had refused to be part of the assassination squads. Petersen had made his aversion to CIA assissination tactics very clear when Teague visited Buon Me Thuot in 1964. He acknowledges his fellow Australian had a different moral standpoint on how to fight the war, but he has no doubts assassination squads were needed, and that they worked. Vietnam was, after all, a very different war to previous conflicts – there was no front line, no easily identifiable enemy and no clear end result. Teague felt Petersen was 'walking a tightrope' with the Montagnard, trying to do what was right for them, and had allowed himself to identify too closely with his indigenous troops. Teague said Petersen was 'too sympathetic'.

The irony is that Petersen had no objection to his Tiger Men carrying out missions that amounted to cold-blooded assassinations. He describes one mission he ordered that had all the hallmarks of the CIA's assassination squads. 'It was in Lac Thien district,' he recalls. 'Bevan Stokes told me there was a Vietnamese man who had a little coffee shop and restaurant built out over the paddy fields next to the road to the town. After VC attacked a village they would sometimes rendezvous there. They would relax, laugh and joke and have a few coffees and so on.

'When we got word of that, I said, "Right, we'll give him a big scare, but we will make it look like the VC did it."

'We got our guys dressed in VC-style black pyjamas, and they threw a hand grenade into the place. The owner was wounded as well as one or two of his family. It would make the shop owner wonder what he had done wrong, and then he might turn against the VC. They did it at night, and left something behind that belonged to the VC to make it look like it was them.'

To a non-military person, the difference between having your men do this type of operation and being classified as an assassination squad might be a matter of semantics, but Petersen was adamant that carrying out this type of operation was not the same as an assassination squad.

'The difference is that it was just a one-off effort. It was better than having a team professionally trained to do this all the time. Instead, I sent two or three of the men just to frighten the guy who was sympathetic to the Viet Cong. The purpose was to make him lose his absolute support of the communists. But when you create a hit man who is trained to kill anyone who is fingered, that is something I don't support at all.'

This stand made Petersen a marked man as far as Methven and his superiors at the CIA were concerned. Methven was peeved that the Australian had flatly refused the order. A few weeks later Methven told him he wanted to send a new young CIA agent to join him for a while in Ban Me Thuot. It was so he could learn the ropes, he explained. Methven said the man's name was Bill Smith, and he had just been transferred from the CIA station in Laos where he had been working with the Montagnard there. Smith was to examine the Truong Son Force and see if he could assist Petersen with what he had learned in Laos.

Alarm bells immediately rang for Barry. The CIA was running its own secret war in Laos, but he had heard enough to know it was a dirty campaign using a Montagnard army to fight North Vietnamese coming down the Ho Chi Minh Trail. The CIA mainly used the Hmong, fierce jungle fighters, and Air America kept them supplied with weapons.

When Bill Smith landed in Ban Me Thuot Petersen took an immediate dislike to the young American. Cocky, brash and overflowing with confidence, Smith instantly started pointing out to Petersen dozens of faults he saw in the Truong Son operation.

'What you need here, Barry,' said Smith, 'is to get these tribesmen to go out and hunt down the Viet Cong and kill them. You need to raise a counter-terror team to take the war up to the communists, use their own terror tactics against them... give them a taste of their own medicine.'

Petersen bristled but held his temper. He knew Methven had foisted this young agent on him to try to push him into creating assassination squads. He told Smith it would not work in this area, and explained why.

'Smith moved into my house and always seemed to have a beer in his hand. He struck me as a lazy bastard, always lying around the house telling me what I was doing wrong. He never went out on any patrols with me.'

Petersen had to go to Saigon for the monthly money run and other chores, reluctantly leaving Smith alone for almost a week. On his return he was summoned to see the province chief Colonel Vinh and told to bring Bill Smith with him.

'Colonel Vinh was polite but obviously angry. He told me that while I was away Smith had recruited 100 Muong tribesmen, enticing some of them away from the province chief's own forces by offering them higher pay. Vinh said Smith had also been pressing his staff to agree to setting up assassination squads. I had already discussed these killer squads with Vinh, and he agreed they were not right for this province. Vinh turned to Smith and told him he wanted the Muong tribesmen back, that he had exceeded his authority, and that he had a lot to learn about Vietnam and the Highlands.

'Then, just as we were leaving the room, Smith turned to me and said in a voice loud enough for Colonel Vinh to hear, "He's like all the other Vietnamese. He can be bought."

'I was aghast at his sheer rudeness and furious that he had said it loudly enough for Vinh to hear. I turned to Smith, got right in his face and said firmly: "Shut up," and walked him out of there.'

Petersen immediately rang the CIA Covert Action Branch. He got deputy chief Wynn Oliver on the phone and told him what had happened. Petersen demanded Smith be recalled immediately to Saigon.

He then marched up to Smith, who was in an armchair, beer in hand. 'I have called an aircraft to take you back to Saigon. You are out of here.'

Petersen admits that in reality he had no authority over the young CIA agent. 'I was Australian Army and he was CIA. I was working for them, but he was on my turf and it was my program.'

Smith flew out on the first Air America plane the next day.

To follow up, Petersen wrote a strong report condemning Smith for his actions, in particular for his lack of respect for the Vietnamese province chief. The reaction from Methven and the Covert Action Branch chief, Tom Donahue, was cool. They urged Petersen to write another, milder, report as they said it would damage the young agent's career. Petersen thought about it and relented, submitting a second, less damning report, so long as Smith would not come near Ban Me Thuot again.

'I did not see Smith as a threat to me personally, but I did see him as damaging to what I had built up in Ban Me Thuot, and damaging to relations with the Vietnamese command in the area. Maybe Smith was operating under orders from Tom Donahue to go around me and set up assassination teams with the Vietnamese, thinking I would just have to go along with it. Sure, it was CIA funded and a CIA program, but he was interfering in something I had worked hard to build up. Worse still, he had insulted the province chief. I knew it would worsen the already frosty relations I had with Donahue, but so be it.'

Sending a CIA agent packing from a base that was, after all, financed and part of a CIA program must have infuriated Methven and Donahue. Their concerns about Petersen's behaviour had intensified and their fears the Australian Army officer seemed to be involving himself even more deeply in Montagnard affairs seemed justified.

Despite the new CIA agenda Petersen focused on what he had been doing well. His rapidly expanding force was fast outgrowing the camp he had built at Buon Enao. His monthly revolving fund had risen to five million piasters (US$62 000) and he needed to establish a new, larger base east of Ban Me Thuot. He chose the location carefully, making sure it was out of range of the artillery of the Vietnamese 23rd Division based inside the city. He did not want the Vietnamese suddenly bombarding his Tiger Men in the event of another rebellion.

When the base was almost completed, one of the Rhade commanders, Nie Tren, dropped by to let Petersen know he was going out to the base later that day.

'I have to go to Dam San base,' Nie Tren said.

Petersen had not heard the name before.

'Dam San? You've given the base a name have you?'

'Oh yes, Sir. That is your name. We name the base after you.'

Petersen was puzzled. This was news to him.

'What does Dam San mean?'

'Ah Sir, Dam San was a legendary Rhade warrior. He could beat anyone. No one could beat Dam San, except the Spirit of the Sun. You know that big rock just off the road down toward Lac Thien district? Legend says Dam San decided to challenge the Sun, and one day he ran up that rock and threw his spear at the Sun. But the Sun struck him dead.'

Petersen was surprised. He was honoured the Rhade thought so much of him that they would give him the name of a mythical demi-god warrior, even if it was a warrior who overstretched himself and died taking on the Sun. To name the new base after him was a rare honour in Montagnard culture.

'I had planned to name the new base after the Vietnamese provincial chief. That would have been the smart politics. But it was the Rhade choice.' Petersen could have over-ruled his men but chose not to. He was obviously impressed with his new status.

However, he decided it would be best not to tell Methven or his Australian Army commander about it. He knew Methven and his superiors in the CIA thought he was getting far too close to the Rhade, and that he was already far too big for his own boots.

'There was irony in the name – was I challenging the greatest power only to be struck down dead, like Icarus and Dam San?' Petersen asked himself. Quite frankly, by this point he didn't care. His belief that the Americans were destroying the country and the Vietnamese people in the way they were running things was growing stronger all the time.

Two months after completion of the Dam San base, the small village nearby was wiped out during a US Air Force napalm air strike. It was yet another case of destroying a village to save it from communism and further fuelled Petersen's belief that the Americans were doing it all wrong.

Petersen's devotion to the Montagnard was clearly starting to blind him to the realities of his situation with the CIA. The Vietnamese were still wary of Petersen's close connections with the Montagnard leadership and their ongoing suspicions about his role in the rebellion were mounting. They had good reason.

'I had a deepening affection for the Rhade,' Petersen wrote in his memoirs. 'I did not feel like a transient, someone who was just here for a short time to do a job and move on. I felt myself a partner with the Highlands and the Montagnard. I was coming to understand them and to sympathise deeply with them.'[3]

Stu Methven certainly noticed these developments. Around Saigon he started referring to Petersen derisively as 'Lawrence of the Highlands'. He didn't mean it as a compliment, but when Petersen heard it he wasn't upset. On the contrary, he was quite flattered to be compared to the eccentric British officer TE Lawrence who rallied the Arabs to fight the Turks in World War One.

'I didn't model myself on Lawrence of Arabia. He wasn't even in my thoughts as I worked with the Montagnard. If anything, I saw a model in Orde Wingate and the Chindits in Burma who lived in the jungle behind Japanese lines and fought an ongoing guerilla war.'

Captain Barry Petersen ignored the irony in Methven's name calling. More and more Montagnard chiefs were coming from far and wide to pay homage to this new incarnation of their demi-god, Dam San, and plead with him to send Tiger Men to protect their village.

In one such procession the Montagnard village chiefs came dressed in traditional handwoven black and red costumes bearing gifts of metal bracelets. Winding their way into Buon Enao and to Petersen's house in Ban Me Thuot, the chiefs carried a woven bamboo bowl of brown rice with an egg or two perched on top. Eggs are valuable to Highland village people and the gift of food was a rare honour. Many walked long distances out of the jungle on foot until they could get some sort of transport to the town.

In each case Petersen accepted the gifts and went through a traditional welcoming ceremony. This meant more rice wine. 'I will send men to protect your village, but first you must send me fit young men to train and join the Tiger Men,' Petersen would tell them.

Back they would come a few weeks later with a dozen young men in tow. Overwhelmed with recruits, he had visions of his force continuing to expand beyond 1200.

The problem was many of these new recruits came from villages far outside the area the Truong Son Force was supposed to be looking after. But Petersen took the young men anyway, rationalising that if they were with the Tiger Men, they could not be conscripted by the Viet Cong.

The Montagnard began to regard Petersen as chief provider to the Highland people. One major tribal chief presented him with an extremely fine handwoven loincloth and shirt that must have taken dozens of people months to make. Made from locally grown spun and dyed cotton embroidered in intricate patterns, the black woven shirt had long sleeves with red piping across the chest overlaid with silver embroidery and small spherical brass buttons. The loincloth was a long, broad, scarf-like strip of cloth about 30 centimetres wide and 5 metres long. This was wrapped between the thighs and then around the waist a number of times. The sides of the legs to the hips were left bare.

Petersen felt he was increasingly regarded as a paramount chief by the Montagnard rather than an Australian military adviser. His interpreters continually reminded him of his new-found status. There had been no announcement, no ceremony, no fanfare – it had happened before he was made aware of it, and he was unable to prevent it. But then, he didn't really want to.

Petersen felt, quite simply, on top of the world. His operation was going well, and his Tiger Men had become a significant force in the Central Highlands. He was an Australian Army captain in a unique position in the Western involvement in

Vietnam, leading a force of 1200 men virtually on his own, without senior officers looking over his shoulder. His advice was sought by the top levels of his government and he had been introduced to the prime minister. He had established his independence from his CIA masters by refusing to follow their edict to introduce assassination squads and sent one of their agents packing. He was fighting the war against the communists in the manner he believed it should be fought, winning the hearts and minds of the local people, a phrase that 40 years later would become used and abused by US strategists in wars in Iraq and Afghanistan.

Petersen was proud he had won the trust of the Montagnard, and flattered with his new status as demi-god. The Vietnamese were largely leaving him alone, and he had managed to build his new camp out of range of their guns. The CIA had bottomless pockets to fund his force, even delivering valuable watches, alcohol and collectable guns as payola.

'No other Australian, American or any other Caucasian had quite the same free hand,' he later wrote. 'Maybe I was only a minor monarch but I was as close as anyone got to being the absolute ruler of his own little cabbage patch.'

Just when it seemed it couldn't get any better, Stu Methven told Petersen the new US ambassador, General Maxwell Taylor, wanted a briefing on CIA programs in the Central Highlands. Petersen prepared a briefing paper for Methven, giving the history of the Truong Son operation, its successes and the future plans. Petersen was careful that credit for the program went to the CIA, skimming over his own role in the success of the program. He had heard relations between the CIA and members of the Australian Army Training Team were starting to sour: Captain Adrian Nesbitt had told him during a visit that Australians were no longer allowed to go into the field officers' case room at CIA headquarters in Saigon.

Australian officers attached to the CIA's Combined Studies Division had long used the room along with American field officers to write up their reports. Now the CIA made the Australians use a neighbouring room – Serong's old office – and even glued up the keyhole in the door that led to the field officers' room. The small office had a safe where Australians could leave their paperwork, but the Americans had the lock's combination. Petersen could understand the Americans' need to get into the safe if an Australian officer went missing or was killed, but he heard the CIA officers were frequently opening the safe and taking whatever they wanted.

Serong had left the army but was still heavily involved with the CIA. Petersen had heard the CIA were getting tired of his former commander, who was contradicting the optimistic forecasts of the war from top US officials. With the high turnover of CIA staff, Petersen felt the new arrivals were not aware of the contribution Serong and the Australian Army officers had made over the years. 'They resented our experience and our success,' Petersen said.

He should have known things could not go on as they were – the CIA would not allow it. And things were changing.

General Maxwell Taylor had been a fierce hawk in the early days of Vietnam, urging President John F Kennedy to send increasing numbers of US troops to Vietnam. In 1964 he succeeded Henry Cabot Lodge as ambassador, and had orders from new president Lyndon Johnson for the US military to take control in Vietnam. Taylor was to shake up the Vietnamese government, which Johnson felt was not doing enough to bring the war to a decisive victory. The new ambassador was told to ensure the US was heavily integrated into every anti-communist program run by Vietnamese authorities and pushed strongly for the US to commence the massive aerial bombing of North Vietnam in 1965.[4]

Taylor was enthusiastic about counterinsurgency operations, particularly if they involved locals such as the Montagnard. He wanted a closer look at this Central Highlands program which seemed to be producing good results. When he asked his CIA briefers about the field case officer handling the operation at Ban Me Thuot, and Methven reluctantly told him it was an Australian Army captain who had been in the Highlands for almost two years, Taylor was surprised. On the spot he decided to fly to Ban Me Thuot to see for himself the Truong Son Force and meet this mysterious Australian officer.

Methven told Petersen the ambassador was coming the next day and that he was to report to the Bungalow at midday to give him a personal briefing on the Tiger Men. Petersen was confused, there was nothing he could add that was not in the briefing note he had given to Methven a day earlier, but he said he would be there.

The moving of an American ambassador in a war zone is a mammoth event. One transport plane after another flew in carrying armoured vehicles, armed guards, 20 to 30 American top brass and advisers, and several Vietnamese generals. Petersen had on his best Australian Army uniform, which he had not worn for some time. At the appointed hour he fronted the meeting in the heavily fortified and soundproofed headquarters.

'The briefing took only about 30 minutes. I didn't tell the ambassador that I was doing this and I was doing that. I very clearly said the program "*WE*" had in Ban Me Thuot was running very successfully with small groups of Montagnard. I described the patrols we did; that the program was successful because the eight-man teams included people from about three villages, and they would patrol from village to village so that wherever they went, there were always a couple of members of the patrol from the village they stopped at. The patrols never stayed more than one night in each village and kept moving to keep the VC offguard.'

Ambassador Taylor and the Vietnamese generals seemed impressed. When Petersen finished Taylor thanked him and turned to the rest, saying: 'This is the type of operation we should be conducting throughout the whole of South Vietnam.'

Petersen was pleased to hear this but he didn't think his Highlands model with the Montagnard would work all over Vietnam, particularly not in the more heavily populated Delta region. But he kept his thoughts to himself. Taylor congratulated Petersen on his efforts, an endorsement Petersen thought might keep the CIA off his back over the assassination squads and vindicate his stand against Stu Methven and Methven's boss, Tom Donahue.

As General Taylor and his brass were leaving, one of the ambassador's aides leaned over to Petersen and said: 'Did you hear what the ambassador just said?'

'No,' replied Petersen.

'He asked why the CIA had to use an Australian to run this sort of program. He wanted to know why an American was not capable of doing it.'

Taylor might, at a stretch, have meant it as a compliment to the Australian Army captain. But to the CIA men who financed and ran the agency's covert programs it was a red rag to a bull. There was already a large element of resentment among CIA officials towards the military, both Australian and American. The CIA station chief, Peer de Silva, had argued against a military intensification of the war and the North Vietnam bombing campaign. The CIA felt it was more worthwhile fighting the communists on a small, more focused scale, with more counter-insurgency teams taking out the Viet Cong infrastructure, but lost the argument to Ambassador Taylor and the American commander, General Westmoreland. The generals saw the Vietnam War as another version of the Korean War, and visualised massed armies facing off against each other.

The Vietnamese themselves had little say in all this. By mid-1965 the Americans were simply paying lip service to the wishes of the Vietnamese government. Top US officials were treating the Vietnamese leaders with open contempt, constantly humiliating them, and Vietnamese generals could see the US was prepared to fight the communists to the last Vietnamese. The death toll was steadily rising on both sides, but the Viet Cong were more powerful than ever. At the beginning of 1965 a total of 417 Americans had been killed in Vietnam. By the end of 1965, as US combat troops poured in, the US death toll rose to 2379.

Petersen's relations with his CIA masters were worsening, but on his next trip to CIA HQ in Saigon he discovered just how bad it had become, the agency was now spying on him. When he called in at the field case officers' room, which Australians were not supposed to enter, he noticed a bunch of papers on one of the desks addressed to him. Some had been opened and obviously read.

Scooping them up, he took them and went to the senior Australian military officer, Brigadier David Jackson, to tell him his mail was being intercepted and inspected by CIA case officers.

'The CIA always thought we were ASIS agents using a military cover so they excluded us from information about what they were up to. They didn't want me to know about Operation Delta, the secret dropping of Special Forces inside North Vietnam; I only found out about it when they wanted to use our base for night practice for parachute drops. I also learned my phone was being tapped. A line ran from my house to the US signals office in Ban Me Thuot. The signals officer in the Bungalow was Colonel Laurence E Browne, whom the other Americans disliked. I was tipped off by one of the Americans that Browne listened in on calls going through his signals switchboard and taped them.'

For that reason Petersen was always extra careful about what he said on the phone, and from then on he always assumed his mail was being intercepted and read by the CIA.

He was especially wary when, in early July 1965, he was approached by Y-We Eban, an agent for his old friend Y-Bham Enuol, president of the Montagnard independence movement FULRO. Now based on the other side of the border in Cambodia, Y-Bham had amassed a force of several thousand

Montagnard, causing great concern to both North and South Vietnamese governments.

While it had close links with the communists, FULRO was desperate and took aid wherever they could get it. Some FULRO Montagnard still worked with the US, but Petersen was concerned that any sign he was associating with FULRO would be the last straw for his crumbling relationship with the CIA and South Vietnamese leaders.

Y-We gave Petersen the stunning news that 1000 FULRO fighters had crossed the border and were waiting outside Ban Me Thuot. He said they wanted to join the Truong Son Force and fight against the Viet Cong. Y-Bham had judged the VC were doing his people great harm in their push south along the Ho Chi Minh Trail. Y-We wanted Petersen to come and meet the FULRO force leaders.

'If this FULRO force were to join my Truong Son Force it would double their numbers to more than 2200. It would be a resounding political shift for the South Vietnamese government in the Highlands. But I knew I had to tread carefully as the Vietnamese would be furious if they found I was dealing with FULRO on my own.'

Petersen told the CIA what had happened, and Tom Donahue agreed it was too good an opportunity to miss. But Petersen insisted the Vietnamese provincial government would have to handle the negotiations.

Y-We took Petersen, a translator, and senior CIA operative Dorsey Anderson to meet the FULRO force. Anderson was keen on building assassin training camps and perhaps saw his chance with this new force wanting to be signed up. When the trio arrived at the meeting place, four FULRO chiefs strode out to meet them.

'They were dressed in an assortment of uniforms – American, South Vietnamese and black pyjamas, and were poorly armed,' Petersen recalls. 'I thought they looked very much the worse for wear, and obviously needed the wages and food they expected to get if they tossed in their lot with our side.'

The FULRO leaders said they would talk only to Petersen, which annoyed Anderson – he did not like to be left kicking dust outside while an Australian army captain was inside doing all the talking. Petersen figured the FULRO leaders needed him more than he needed them, so told them bluntly they would have to negotiate with the South Vietnamese authorities. Eventually the FULRO leaders agreed to see General Lu Lan, commander of the 23rd ARVN Division based in Ban Me Thuot. Petersen stressed they were not to raise any demands with General Lan, only offer their services. He did not want to be seen as an advocate for FULRO's campaign for Montagnard autonomy.

As soon as the meeting with Lan began, the FULRO leaders slammed down a list of demands for autonomy before they would agree to fight the Viet Cong and the meeting broke up in disarray. Petersen was furious. As they left, he berated the FULRO leaders for breaking their word. The FULRO men apologised, asked for another meeting and promised they would not present demands. When General Lan reluctantly agreed, Petersen stressed this was for Vietnamese and Montagnard to sort out between themselves, and that he would not take part in the meeting.

To help get things moving Petersen gave the FULRO leaders a list of points they might agree to, including Vietnamese officers being in charge of their units. At a meeting with senior American advisers he helped draw up maps where FULRO could be deployed.

The next day's proceedings between Lan and FULRO were an improvement, but Petersen was upset when he heard Colonel Laurence Browne had marched in and placed maps on Lan's table, telling him where the FULRO forces could be deployed. Lan said any decision would have to go further up the ARVN chain of command.

When the top military man in the region, General Vinh Loc, flew in to look over the agreement, he immediately sent for Stu Methven and Petersen. Loc was a hard-line Vietnamese nationalist who resented foreign influence in Vietnamese affairs. He was close to Air Marshal Ky, the corrupt head of the Vietnamese Air Force and now prime minister. Ky had a special interest in the Highlands as for years he had used the remote area for air drops of raw opium from Laos.[5] Loc launched into Methven and Petersen, accusing them of interfering in Vietnamese affairs. Lan tried to point out these were the first talks with FULRO in the ten months since the rebellion and Petersen had helped bring them about. General Loc was not impressed.

Methven was seething that he and the CIA had been dressed down by a Vietnamese general. As he was about to get on the plane to Saigon the next day, he turned to Petersen and said curtly: 'I think this might be the end of your Truong Son Force, Barry.'

'Oh, I don't think so,' Petersen replied. He was confident he had insulated Truong Son from the dealings with FULRO. He felt he had played it by the book as far as American and Vietnamese authorities were concerned.

'You could see General Loc was not very happy. He's got influence.'

'Oh, I reckon the Truong Son Force has made a good enough name for itself to survive any bullshit like this.'

The next day Barry Petersen was summoned to Saigon, and fired.

10

FAREWELL

Petersen was aghast. He had suspected that at some time in the future the CIA would move to replace him, but when the hammer blow came and he was told he was gone, he couldn't believe it.

He had turned up at CIA HQ, which had moved into the US Embassy building in Saigon, expecting to give a briefing on how the FULRO recruits could best be used. The first person he ran into was Bill Evans, the Covert Action Branch's chief of programs. Petersen got on well with Evans. When he asked the American what was going on, Evans took him aside and said Tom Donahue and Stu Methven wanted him out of the Highlands. Petersen asked when he was supposed to go.

'Now, immediately,' said Evans.

Petersen's heart sank. He thought he had at least until the FULRO matter was settled. He asked who was supposed to replace him.

'They have Jack Benefield in mind. He's a career CIA man. He was meant to go to South America but he was sent here instead.'

Evans told Petersen he thought the decision was crazy as he had done a good job, but Methven seemed determined to put his own man in the post. Evans told Petersen he should fight against being removed and get Brigadier Jackson to support him.[1]

Petersen then bumped into Wynn Oliver, the CIA deputy branch chief, who had carried out his earlier demand to remove Bill Smith. Thinking he had an ally in Oliver, Petersen asked him what could be done. While Oliver was sympathetic, he told the Australian it was the Vietnamese government that wanted him out of the Highlands. Petersen strongly doubted this and said he wanted to see branch chief Tom Donahue.

Donahue had the pasty look of a desk man who knew how to fight bureaucratic battles rather than the dirty war going on in the jungle. In fact, Petersen had never seen him outside Saigon. 'The Darlac officials are starting to resent your presence,' Donahue told him.

Petersen knew this was untrue. He had good relationships with the provincial officials, including General Lan. He felt relations were particularly positive after he had helped arrange the FULRO meetings. Petersen pressed Donahue for details.

'We have feedback,' he replied vaguely. 'From American sources ... Look, we have a fellow called Jack Benefield we want to send up there to replace you.'

Petersen went straight to Brigadier Jackson, his commanding officer in Vietnam, and told him what had happened.

Jackson seemed surprised the Americans were saying it was the Vietnamese who wanted him removed.

'They told me they felt two years was more than enough time in a hostile station and that you deserved a well-earned break,' Jackson said. 'I told them you were the best judge of that, and it would be up to you whether it was time to take a break.'

Jackson was even more surprised when Petersen told him the CIA had already decided to send one of their own to replace him.

'If anyone is to replace you it should be an Australian. I'll talk to Donahue about it.'

Jackson returned from his talk with the CIA chief somewhat humbled. He told Petersen ominously: 'Look Barry, it's probably in your best interests to leave the Highlands rather than try to fight it out.'

Any chance of support from Australian authorities was gone. Petersen went to talk to Donahue and Methven about the handover and asked if he could at least go back to clean out his house and say farewell to his troops and friends among the Montagnard. They reluctantly agreed, but told Petersen he was to tell the Montagnard he was returning to Australia. They insisted that once he said goodbye he was to sever all contact with the Highland people.

Then Donahue said to him: 'You've developed far too much influence with the Montagnard. This makes it very difficult for anyone else to take over from you. You have developed a personality cult in the Highlands.'

Petersen protested that he had been careful not to encourage this. While he had not encouraged it, the fact was that the Montagnard had made him the focus of a cult-like hero-worship. Maybe the CIA chiefs had heard he was being called Dam San, the mythical warrior demi-god. They certainly thought Petersen had gone native, that he was far too close to the Montagnard and sympathised too much with their independence cause.

The CIA had also been deeply embarrassed by the US ambassador questioning why an American wasn't capable of running the program an Australian captain was carrying out successfully. Many who served in Vietnam at the time took the view that the agency was not only envious of other services, but also paranoid about maintaining control. They fought turf wars with the army and their allies as though CIA control was what the war was really all about.

Even more ominous for Petersen was the CIA's admission that they felt they had lost control of him, that he was refusing CIA orders to set up assassination squads in the belief if was not in the interests of 'his' Montagnard. This had been the last straw.

Petersen had been with the Montagnard for two years, twice as long as the normal posting to Vietnam, although many in the Australian Army Training Team stayed more than the required 12 months. Still, Petersen was angry as he did not want to leave the Highlands. He had built his Tiger Men force up to 1200 soldiers and had developed good relations with the Montagnard leaders, and most of the Vietnamese commanders in the region. He also had plans to build the force up to more than 2000 to secure additional areas of the province from Viet Cong attacks and North Vietnamese infiltration through the Ho Chi Minh Trail.

'Our system of mobile patrols was working. We were expanding, and it was going well – we had found a successful formula to hold back the Viet Cong in the province, when other provinces were losing against them. Most other groups went out and did one patrol, then hurried back to camp thinking the work was done, claiming their area was clear of VC. Our Tiger Men continued patrolling over and over, they carried out ambushes and they knew their area like the back of their hand. That's why Ambassador Taylor thought it was a good idea.

'We had frequent clashes with the VC, but our casualties were low compared to theirs. We had the highest kill ratio to casualties of any force in Vietnam. It was always hard to keep an accurate record of the deaths of Viet Cong. For instance, in that one attack where I was not present, my troops must have killed at least 130 people to get so many weapons, but kept no prisoners. You did not stop to count bodies, it was too dangerous. The larger the group, the more switched off the men are: subconsciously they feel more secure, making them easier targets.

'Our hit-and-run tactics made the VC enlarge their forces to groups of 20 to 30 and even 40 so it became easier for us to keep track of them and inflict more casualties. We had turned the tables on them by doing exactly what they had been doing successfully for years.'

Petersen believes that if his Tiger Force had kept operating in this manner they would have detected the large North

Vietnamese force that came down years later and surrounded Ban Me Thuot before the South Vietnamese had any clue they were there.

'Our intelligence was better – I don't think they would have been able to get their forces down in such large numbers undetected and overrun Ban Me Thuot. When the town eventually fell, the Vietnamese fled with everything they could carry. They were attacked by the Montagnard as they left and I have no doubt that some of my men, if not most of them, would have been involved in those attacks.'

A year before he was fired from his post Petersen had drawn up plans for his Montagnard force and other dissident groups to act as an underground resistance if the communists won the war. In a formal paper to his Australian commanding officer in June 1964, he suggested preparing anti-communist guerilla units operating behind enemy lines and that the best potential for a resistance movement was among strong religious sects and the ethnic minorities in the Central Highlands.

Petersen didn't say so but he was clearly nominating himself as an underground resistance leader, saying the force would need to have trust and confidence in the foreign liaison personnel. It would require six to 12 months of work in advance of the communist takeover.

Petersen knew his Tiger Men were ideal for such an underground resistance movement. He had already, 'purely for information', started collecting a record of all Montagnard in the area who could be wireless operators, medics and leaders of resistance units. US Special Forces could not do it, he insisted, as they worked from forts in big units relying on air power and did not live and work with the local people.[2]

Petersen's report went down like a lead balloon. 'I gave a copy to the Americans and they blasted me for being defeatist. They did not want to hear anything suggesting the US was not going to win the war. The Australians were simply not interested. It got put on a shelf somewhere and gathered dust.'

When the CIA ordered him out of Ban Me Thuot, Petersen's grand vision to become the great white resistance leader of Vietnam came to an abrupt end.

Before returning to Ban Me Thuot to pack his bags and say his farewells, Petersen did a bit of spying of his own. He checked out his replacement, Jack Benefield, and to his disgust he found the man was a complete amateur. A bulldozer driver in the US before he joined the CIA, he spoke a bit of Spanish so the CIA marked him for the South American office. However, at this time the CIA was expanding so fast in Vietnam that they were pulling new recruits in from everywhere. He wasn't much use in Saigon, so Benefield was being sent to the Highlands to take over an existing operation.

When Petersen returned to his house in Ban Me Thuot he found the local CIA agent, under orders from Saigon, had already taken away all the files and records from his safe. Donahue rang to tell Petersen the agent had found Vietnamese army code books in the safe and demanded to know what they were doing there.

'What are you talking about? Why the hell would I want to listen in to Vietnamese army radio communications trying to decode them?' a furious Petersen replied. 'I am flat out with my own force. You think I would have time for that? What the hell are you playing at?'

Donahue dropped it. Petersen guessed the code books had been planted by the CIA to try to compromise him with the Vietnamese. Petersen also believes the CIA took his financial records in case they needed to forge evidence that he was pinching CIA funds. By the end of his stint Petersen's monthly fund of five million piasters, about US$62 000, was a small fortune. He let the CIA know he had sent duplicates of all his records to the Australian Embassy. The CIA never made a complaint about his accounts.

He then began his round of farewells. It was an emotional time for him; over two years in the Highlands Barry Petersen had made many trusted friends. The feeling was mutual for some, it seemed. General Lan pinned the Vietnamese Cross of Gallantry with Silver Star on the Australian's chest, saying how much better it was to deal with a professional soldier than a civilian from the CIA.

The citation read in part:

'The outstanding success which the Truong Son Force has attained in combat actions against the Viet Cong is attributed directly to [Petersen's] vast knowledge of military operations and his wealth of military experience. Captain Petersen has on numerous occasions accompanied the Truong Son Forces on combat operations and without exception, the influence of his presence, advice and leadership, ensured complete and total success of these operations. The Truong Son Force has attained one of the best combat records in Vietnam by inflicting heavy casualties and equipment losses on the Viet Cong while sustaining a minimum of friendly losses.'

General Lan wrote to the Saigon government detailing Petersen's achievements in the region and his efforts in bringing FULRO to the South Vietnamese. In their private talk Lan revealed to Petersen that General Vinh Loc wanted him out of the country. 'He believes you are behind the Montagnard uprising and their forces coming in from Cambodia. I told him you were not responsible for the FULRO forces coming over the border and I explained in detail what happened and he believed me. But he wants you out. Then the Americans started using that as an excuse.'

Lan then launched into an extraordinary tirade against the CIA, saying their officers were everywhere and most Vietnamese government and military leaders 'distrust and hate them'.

General Lan told him he would never accept a CIA man in charge of the Truong Son Force.

'You are a soldier like us. We will accept a soldier, but we will not accept a civilian operative of the CIA.'

Petersen would relay General Lan's thoughts to Donahue when he returned to Saigon. It was met with a stony silence.

When Jack Benefield arrived to take over Petersen's operation he turned his nose up at the native way the Australian ran his household with its dirt kitchen and hand washing in the backyard. Benefield rang the CIA stores to order an electric stove for the Vietnamese cook, and an electric washing machine for the housekeeper. Neither woman had the faintest idea how to use them, and were quite distressed. Ultimately, it didn't matter as the local Vietnamese authorities suddenly decreed Benefield was not to live in Ban Me Thuot, he was to fly in for day trips only. The decision infuriated Donahue and Methven, and there was further suspicion that Petersen had organised the snub.

Petersen was not permitted to stay in Ban Me Thuot long and was flown back to cool his heels in Saigon. The CIA put him up in pleasant accommodation, a villa in the city which he shared with other Australians working with the CIA's Combined Studies Division. He was provided with a jeep, and told by the CIA he was free to travel anywhere he wanted in Vietnam, or even outside the country. But he was not to go back to Darlac Province.

Unsurprisingly, Petersen discovered that his mail from Ban Me Thuot, from the Montagnard as well as that of his current Australian deputy, Warrant Officer John Roy, who was at Buon Enao camp, was being intercepted and read by the CIA. Petersen was furious. He protested to the Australian Embassy, and warned other Australian Army officers. He is not sure he ever got all his letters back.

One development in particular confirmed for the CIA every notion they had that Petersen was too close to the Montagnard. They were not pleased when General Nguyen Van Thieu, who had become President of South Vietnam after yet another coup in June 1965, asked the US Embassy if Petersen could go back to the Highlands to help relations with the Montagnard.

On 9 August, the FULRO president Y-Bham Enuol, a personal friend of Petersen, wrote to President Thieu, appealing to him to send Petersen back to the Highlands. Y-Bham wrote that Petersen had helped reunite the FULRO Montagnard with the South Vietnamese, and he was needed in the Highlands.

President Thieu sent a copy of Y-Bham's letter to the US ambassador. A high-ranking Vietnamese government official also asked the Americans if Petersen would be returned to the region. The US Embassy told President Thieu's office in no uncertain terms that the Australian was definitely not going anywhere near the Highlands.

One of the CIA officers who supported the beleaguered Australian captain slipped him a copy of the letter. Petersen seemed to have some supporters among the CIA officers, but not at the top where he needed it.

Over dinner in Saigon, deputy chief of the CIA's covert branch Wynn Oliver personally apologised to Petersen for his treatment by CIA officers. However, Oliver said, he was not in a position to support him publicly.

A few of the Australian journalists based in Saigon started to get a whisper of the story that a decorated Australian hero had been treated very shabbily by the Americans. Petersen had met several reporters during his time in Vietnam, mostly during his trips to Saigon. He studiously avoided giving any hint of what he was doing and certainly never mentioned that he was working for the CIA. His mission was still top secret: few Australians knew a handful of their best soldiers were working for the CIA.

Petersen had met the veteran newspaper reporters Denis Warner and Pat Burgess at various functions. They were smart enough not to press the mysterious army captain on what he was doing or who he was working with. The discretion paid off for Burgess, one of Australia's most experienced war correspondents.

It was a stinking hot night in mid-August and the wide veranda of Saigon's Continental Palace Hotel was the place for journalists, spies, embassy people and off-duty military to gather for drinks and discreetly pass on information. Pat Burgess persuaded Barry Petersen to sit down for a drink. He'd heard Petersen had been shafted by the Americans, but he also knew he couldn't write a word of it. Petersen trusted Burgess would not write anything that would breach his confidence, and he needed to talk to an unbiased Australian without a political agenda.

A young, ambitious American-born journalist called Gerald Stone was also looking for Petersen. Stone had migrated to Australia three years earlier and had been sent to cover the Vietnam War for News Limited. He'd heard something of Petersen's isolated post in the Highlands and it sounded like a good story. Stone didn't know what Petersen looked like. That night at the hotel he walked up to Burgess and his unknown drinking partner to talk about another matter. When Burgess deliberately did not introduce Petersen, Stone took the hint and left. But Stone was on the trail of a good story, and wasn't about to give up.

In September 1965 the CIA finally gave permission for Petersen to return to Ban Me Thuot for two weeks of formal farewells with the Montagnard. The farewells stretched into three weeks of endless rounds of feasts, rice wine jugs and ceremonies as he said goodbye and thanks – not only to Vietnamese and American officials he had dealt with, but also his personal staff and the Montagnard warriors.

The main farewell ceremony, appropriately, was at Dam San base. With the agreement of Brigadier Jackson, Petersen invited an Australian journalist trusted by the military, former soldier Denis Gibbons, to come to the ceremony and record it for posterity.

It was a spectacular sight. The longhouse, which was 10 metres high and almost 50 metres long, was decorated with palm fronds and wild banana trees. More than 30 rice wine jars were lined up in the middle of the hall and big buffalo-hide drums sat along the walls. Down one side of the hall there was a long row of bronze gongs lying on a thick plank of teak wood. Brightly coloured woven mats marked the place of honour where Petersen was to recline like some Oriental potentate.

On really big occasions the Montagnard sacrifice a buffalo along with pigs and chickens which would be blessed and eaten during the feast. Petersen's ceremonial farewell was so big an occasion that dozens of chickens, several pigs and three buffalo were to be sacrificed. Montagnard life is centred on a belief in spirits that govern events and good or bad fortune; sacrificing beasts placates the forest spirits and wins favour. Even after all his years in the Highlands, Petersen admits the sacrifice of a buffalo is not a pleasant sight to Western eyes.

'The beast is tethered to a pole and a Montagnard elder moves in from behind and hamstrings it. The rear of the poor beast slumps but its forelegs remain extended. In this way its vulnerable breast is offered, and a second elder approaches with a spear and drives it into the heart. The buffalo drops to its side and dies very quickly.'[3]

The blood is collected and mostly drunk raw. Huge chunks of the beast are carved off, and, with the hide still attached, buried in the embers of a large wood fire along with the pigs and chickens.

While the meat was cooking, Petersen, dressed in traditional costume, mingled with the hundreds of guests. When it came time for the speeches the Australian captain stood straight and tall at attention in front of the seated dignitaries as Montagnard chiefs sang his praises.

More than 300 of his Tiger Men Force paraded past their departing leader as he saluted them. He then walked slowly along the ranks of men standing to attention, shaking every soldier's hand and saying goodbye. Petersen was deeply moved as he saw tears in the eyes of many of them. 'By then I had tears in my eyes too.'

He then moved to recline in the place of honour on the woven mats. One of the buffalo heads was placed at his feet and a sorcerer hovered over the head, chanting spells and pleas to the spirits to protect and smile on the honoured guest for the rest of his life.

When the sorcerer was finished and Petersen moved to sit in a chair, an axe head was placed at his bare feet. The Australian slowly lifted one foot and put it on top of the axe head. Blood and rice wine was poured over the foot and a live chicken, squawking and flapping its wings, waved in circles over his head. Now it was time to drink the dreaded rice wine. A high-ranking Rhade woman beckoned Petersen to sit beside the largest of the jars. She had sampled the brew and found it good. Petersen was not to drink from it, but simply hold the long bamboo straw while lines of Montagnard came forward bearing gifts and tributes. Most presented bracelets, thin brass rods twisted into circles that were then clamped around his wrist as he continued to hold the straw. By the end of the ceremony Petersen had 220 bracelets around his wrists and ten necklaces of amber beads around his neck. For the Montagnard these were extremely valuable gifts.

The gongs started ringing and Montagnard warriors beat the drums, which were so big they reached up to their chests. It was time to drink the wine. The drum beating got louder and the gongs picked up their rhythm as more and more of the potent rice wine went down. Montagnard groups broke into popular songs and Petersen smiled and laughed contentedly. He really did love these people and was sorry he was leaving them. The drinking and singing went on late into the night until just about everybody collapsed. That was also part of Montagnard tradition.

Denis Gibbons took photos of the amazing ceremony deep in the Highland jungle, a ceremony few outsiders would ever see. Gibbons laughs and recalls he didn't remember much after he started drinking the rice wine.

'It was like rocket fuel. It tasted magnificent but I had a terribly sore head the next day.'

But Gibbons was disturbed by the meaning of what he had witnessed. Because he'd been in the army before becoming a journalist, he had an entree to soldiers few journalists could ever hope to achieve.

He was one of the most experienced war correspondents in Vietnam; he had seen action all over the country. He'd been wounded seven times in the years he was there. As a down-to-earth bloke Gibbons had a strong bullshit meter, and he was struck by how Petersen had so completely become absorbed in Montagnard life. 'I knew he was being kicked out of the Highlands, and I wasn't surprised after I saw him all dressed up in the native clothes,' Gibbons remembered.

Sitting in his Sydney home surrounded by his Vietnam War photos, Gibbons recalls, 'Petersen had lost the plot, he'd gone feral. He had committed the worst thing an army officer working behind the lines could commit. He'd gone native. The Australian generals would not tolerate that no matter how good a job he was doing.'

Petersen had one more task to complete before he left the Highlands for what he thought would be the last time. He had hoped to take his pet tiger, Sunny, back to Australia and donate it to Sydney's Taronga Zoo. The captain of HMAS *Sydney* had agreed to take the animal back with him on his run between South Vietnam and Australia. Sunny had grown to the size of a small Bengal tiger and had to be handled very carefully. The ship's workmen built a special steel cage for him and the captain had even sent a message home that they were coming back 'with a tiger in the tank' – a well known advertising slogan for a petrol brand at the time. Everything was all ready to go until the last minute, when a bureaucrat in the Defence Department in Canberra put his red pen through it. Petersen had to give Sunny to the Saigon Zoo instead, where the tiger lived for another 23 years before dying of pneumonia.

Once back in Saigon Petersen was congratulated and thanked by Australian command. Brigadier Jackson wrote a glowing official report that said in part:

'Captain Petersen's achievements in Vietnam have been outstanding. He has been responsible for the initiation and the building of an extensive para-military, political and civic action program in a critical area of Vietnam. The success of his program is a tribute to his courage, determination, good sense and practical ability. No officer of his age and experience, I am sure, has been faced with more responsible, diverse, difficult and dangerous tasks and handled them with such outstanding success. His work in Vietnam and his unusual environment has been such that it will take a deliberate effort on his part to settle down to a "normal" military appointment. He is recommended for accelerated promotion.'

For Barry, the greatest compliment was still to come. Shortly after returning to Saigon, he got word from a senior Vietnamese government official that the head of the Vietnamese Prime Minister's Department, Ong Bui Diem, wanted to see him. It was to be an off-the-record meeting, and the Americans were not to know about it. The Australian Embassy charge d'affaires, Roy Fernandez, was aware of it and had given it the green light.

The meeting was to be at the office of the Vietnamese Prime Minister, Air Marshal Nguyen Cao Ky. A flashy dresser with a pencil thin moustache, Ky had come to power in a coup with General Thieu four months earlier. Petersen knew the front entrance to the French colonial building was bound to be watched by the CIA, so he decided to engage in a bit of cloak-and-dagger activity. He cased the area the day before, and found the prime minister's grounds backed on to the Saigon Zoo. On the day of the meeting Petersen pretended he was visiting the zoo, and when he was satisfied he was not being followed, ducked down a back alley where he had spotted a loose fencepost. He squeezed through and found himself in the shady, tree-filled garden behind the grand old French colonial building that housed the prime minister's offices.

Ong Bui Diem greeted Petersen courteously, offered him tea and said he had heard so much of him that he wanted to meet personally. For more than an hour the top Vietnamese government official quizzed Petersen on the problems the South Vietnamese faced in the Highlands, the best way to handle the Montagnard and the situation with FULRO. At the end of the long talk and after many cups of tea, Ong Bui Diem told Petersen he was sorry to see him leave South Vietnam as he had a great understanding of the situation and people of South Vietnam. He said the Vietnamese government was 'not altogether happy' with the way the Americans mounted many of its operations in their country. He asked Petersen not to tell the Americans of their meeting. Despite the satisfaction he would have had telling the likes of Donahue what the Vietnamese government thought of them, he kept the discussion secret for decades.

Petersen was being kicked out of the Highlands at a time when the Viet Cong were clearly winning the war. In 1965 the VC stepped up attacks and controlled just about all the rural areas of South Vietnam, along with several regional towns. South Vietnamese brigades composed of several hundred troops were being ambushed and wiped out almost every week. Dozens of American advisers were being killed alongside the South Vietnamese forces. In that year the Viet Cong went on a rampage, assassinating almost 2000 villagers and officials, and kidnapping another 12 800. Viet Cong agents successfully infiltrated the South Vietnamese militia and army, including those within US bases and forts. Many Vietnamese workers inside US bases and offices such as cleaners, cooks and clerks were secret

VC, and female VC agents often worked in brothels, bars and restaurants.

When the Australian Prime Minister Sir Robert Menzies announced he would send combat troops to Vietnam in April 1965, there were already 50 000 US combat troops in the country. The American troops had started arriving just a month earlier. By the end of 1965 the American combat force rose to 150 000. The US Air Force commenced heavy bombing of North Vietnam after a Viet Cong raid in February on a US base near Pleiku, about 200 kilometres north of Ban Me Thuot, which killed eight Americans.

The first Australian battalion of 600 combat troops was attached to the US 173rd Airborne Brigade and was operating under US command in the province of Phuoc Tuy, 80 kilometres east of Saigon. Eighty members of the Army Training Team were scattered across the country on various missions and the Royal Australian Air Force had 73 crewmen and ground staff with six Caribou transport planes.

The Australian Army found itself facing the same problem as Petersen: the Americans' reliance on massive firepower to beat the communists into submission and never mind 'collateral damage' of innocent civilians caught in the crossfire. Australians preferred a much more targeted approach, getting out in the jungle to take the VC on hand to hand and trying to win the hearts and minds of the uncommitted villagers.

Against this background of a steadily worsening military situation, Gerald Stone had gone up to Ban Me Thuot chasing the news story of the mysterious Australian hero of the Highlands. He found Petersen had already left, but that did not deter him. He travelled around the area talking to Americans, Vietnamese and Montagnard, piecing together the puzzle. His full-page article appeared in Sydney's afternoon tabloid newspaper the *Daily Mirror* on 7 September under the headline 'Vietcong enemy No. 1 – Australian was the Tiger Man of Vietnam'. It was the first the Australian public had heard of this Australian war hero. Without mentioning that Petersen was on a secret mission for the CIA, Stone set the scene of his extraordinary heroic mission training Montagnard in the remote Highlands, opening the story with the stirring words: 'One man can't win a war alone, but he can try like hell.'

Stone reported that for two years Petersen had battled native superstition, prejudice, rebellions and the Viet Cong to produce one of the toughest anti-guerilla forces in the country. He breathlessly told his readers Petersen had kept a tiger at his villa, gave his native fighters a tiger emblem for their caps and trained them to patrol the jungle and fight the Viet Cong in small teams, beating the VC at their own game. His report then said ominously: 'Until now the activities of the Brisbane-born officer have been a closely guarded secret and many of the details are still classified. Last month, however, Captain Petersen was reassigned to Saigon without official explanation.'

Stone had met an American officer in the area, Captain Donald Canaday, who knew Petersen. 'There are a lot of things about his operation we can't talk about,' Canaday told him. 'We Americans like to think we are tops in everything but I think every American here is willing to admit he was the best soldier in the sector.'

Another American, Captain James Dottle, added: 'Barry could think like a VC. He fought this war the way it should be fought with small units of six to eight men. He had a ton of guts and led many of the patrols himself, not telling anybody where he was going except to put out the word that if he wasn't back by a certain time we should go looking for him.'

Even though Petersen insists he never spoke to Stone, the reporter's article was remarkably accurate and contained information only someone very close to Petersen could have known. Interviewed in 2008, Stone said he had been given a background briefing by Ted Serong, and much of the information for the article probably came from the former colonel. Serong would have wanted his Training Team men to get the recognition they deserved. It was also in line with Serong's long-held views that Australians knew how to fight the Vietnam War better than the Americans.

Stone's glowing article reported that it was Petersen who thought up calling his force Tiger Men and getting the tiger badges made, then diplomatically arranging for the Vietnamese commander to present them to the men.

Stone also reported the VC had put a hefty reward on Petersen's head. The VC spread the word that 'they would rather take him than the US colonel who served in Ban Me Thuot as adviser to a division'. This was probably Colonel Laurence Browne, a man Petersen detested because he thought the American was damaging relations with the Vietnamese.

Stone's article must have gone off like a bomb when it filtered back to the CIA office in Saigon. It was obvious that even if Petersen had not briefed the reporter for the article, someone close to him did. This gave the CIA another big concern about Petersen. Would he start talking to the press about what he was doing under CIA orders in the Highlands? Would he go public with the methods being used by them, such as the assassination squads he had refused to be part of? Could Petersen be trusted to keep his mouth shut?

It was enough of a concern for some members of the CIA to want to kill Petersen.

Peter Young, one of the first members of the Australian Army Training Team in 1962, had retained many contacts from that time when he had been part of the CIA station at Da Nang. In 1965 he was the military attaché at the Australian Embassy, and well plugged into the clandestine American intelligence community. He'd been keeping an ear on the Petersen story for several months. It wasn't really in his area of interest, though, his focus was more military intelligence and the progress of the war.

But Young had been picking up worrying whispers about Petersen, and knew he had upset some serious people. He'd known Petersen from their earlier army days and regarded him as a thoroughly professional soldier. Young bumped into him in Saigon as he was being forced out of the Highlands. 'You are making a big mistake getting above your CIA controllers,' he told Petersen. 'You've alienated yourself from the Agency by sending back one of their agents in disgrace and you defied your controller. You do that to an organisation like the CIA and they see you getting too big for your britches. You need to remember who is paying the bills. They see you pursuing political agendas which are not conducive to the political agendas of the CIA, the American military and the South Vietnamese.' Young continued to tell Petersen he had got into realms of policy that were above him. He had mightily offended the Vietnamese in his work with the Montagnard 'I said you had done all that, and it's no wonder they want to get rid of you.'

A few weeks later Peter Young was in Singapore on R&R with an American army friend, Jack Fitzgerald, who was in American military intelligence.

'Fitz was there with a mate of his called Thayer,' said Young. 'I can't remember Thayer's first name, but he was also in military intelligence. They were mostly majors and half colonels. We were talking over a few beers and I asked them what was going on with Barry Petersen.

'They said "Don't be surprised if Petersen falls under a bus." They said he was to be "gotten rid of". This was a war in which the CIA ran its own war, and things did happen. The implication was they would do anything to get him out of the way.'

At first Young thought the American intelligence men were kidding. However, the fact was the CIA men were a law unto themselves in Vietnam. They were untouchable. Young still found it hard to believe they would actually kill an allied army officer if he got in their way. He joked to his American friends that there were no buses in Vietnam for Petersen to fall under.

'They didn't laugh or back down. They had made their point. Petersen would meet with an accident if there was trouble removing him from the Highlands. He would be made to look like a hero, but it would happen. There'd be salutes and tributes all round. No one would ever know the CIA were behind it.

'The CIA were going to get rid of Barry one way or another,' Young said. 'When you move in those circles where they were targeting all sorts of people, it was nothing to send someone in to assassinate and carve someone up. They'd make it look like an accident, or a robbery, or an attack by the enemy. Petersen was all by himself out at Ban Me Thuot. It would have been easily done. I have no doubt they would have done it if Petersen had not left when he did.'

Young did not pass a warning on to Petersen at the time. 'It was outside my bailiwick,' he said. In fact, Young did not tell Petersen of what he had heard until 1988, after Petersen had published his memoirs.

'Petersen was already leaving and I thought the reason to have him eliminated was over. I did bump into him again in Saigon and told him to watch his flank. He had put a lot of people offside so had good reason to keep a low profile. I felt at the time it wasn't so much the CIA who would bump him off, but the Vietnamese. There was little doubt that the Saigon police chief, General Loan, would have been very interested in Petersen's movements,' Young said.

General Loan was a corrupt killer. He was said to have been running Saigon's booming drug trade, collecting raw opium flown in on Vietnamese C-47 transport planes from Laos and selling it to Chinese crime syndicates. Loan's secret police then took a cut as the illegal drug was distributed around the city for American GIs.[4] Years later Loan became infamous around the world thanks to photos and film of him holding a pistol to the head of a prisoner in a Saigon street, then executing him in cold blood.

Loan, like some in the CIA, clearly let nothing get in the way of his own agenda. If the warning passed on to Peter Young was accurate, Barry Petersen left the Central Highlands just in time. There certainly were elements in the CIA and their covert operators who were prepared to do it. Others doubt the CIA would have taken the drastic action of killing an allied officer. It is not something the CIA will admit to, and there are no written reports available to confirm it one way or the other. The fact remains Petersen did not put it to the test. He left the Highlands reluctantly, but as ordered, and lived to tell the tale.

11
A PAIN IN THE ASS

Retired from the CIA and living in Europe, in 2008 Stu Methven roared with laughter when asked if there had been people in the CIA planning to kill Barry Petersen.

'Barry was a pain in the ass, and there were people who would have been pleased to see him gone, but to say that he would have been killed if he had not left the Highlands is so off the wall it is unbelievable. Nobody was thinking of trying to eliminate him. That is so far out. The things they attribute to the Agency are often way out. I deny that categorically.'

Aged in his early 80s, Methven was still anxious to distance himself from Petersen and his operation.

Methven insists he was not Petersen's handler in the CIA, that he could not give Petersen orders as that was not his role. 'I was in charge of Montagnard affairs and that sometimes brought me into contact with Barry. I thought we had got on well, and I was surprised when I heard many years later that he was claiming the CIA had plans to bump him off.'

Methven said he had no idea why Petersen would make such a claim. 'I found Petersen to be a fabulist, a teller of fables. Look, I don't want to get into a pissing match with Barry Petersen. I would rather just ignore the whole thing. I spoke to a few others and they were very surprised at what he said.

'Sure, we always called him Barry of the Montagnard, Barry of the Highlands. But the only similarity he had to Lawrence of Arabia was in his own mind. There were other Australians in teams who were very reliable and very good.'

Methven denied telling Petersen to form counter-terror teams or assassination squads. 'No, I didn't ask him to do that. I was just visiting up there in Ban Me Thuot. He did not work for me. I was not his handler and had no involvement in directing him in operations or stuff like that.'

Methven said that when he first met Petersen he thought he was a very affable Australian. 'He was very intelligent and keen to do the job. But I have no doubt he formed an opinion he was much more than he was. Petersen built on something that had been started by someone else, and there were others in the area working with the Montagnard. He was not as alone as he made out. He said they saw him as some sort of demi-god. Well I never talked to the Montagnard, but I never saw that.'

Methven was keen to dismiss Petersen as 'a bit of a megalomaniac' who fancied himself as another Lawrence of Arabia. 'He was an oddball who was very impressed with himself,' Methven fired off, still annoyed more than 40 years later that Petersen had rubbished the CIA.

'It was a difficult situation up there with the Vietnamese and the Montagnard. Barry might have had something to do with smoothing that over, but the Vietnamese commanders were very pissed off at all of us, the Americans, for working with the Montagnard, arming and training them. General Vinh Loc would blame us any time there was trouble from the Montagnard.'

Methven said the CIA did take note of what Petersen wrote in his 1988 memoirs and Peter Young's claim he had been told by US military intelligence officers that the CIA had plans to kill Petersen if he did not leave the Highlands quietly.

'We thought that was just Petersen getting carried away with himself,' Methven said. 'We did not take it seriously.'

Methven played down his role in Vietnam, insisting he had only been the liaison between the Agency and programs with the Montagnard. At this point he made it clear he had said enough, saying he was 'a bit gun shy' as he lived on a CIA pension. 'The Agency does not take kindly to its employees talking about what they did in that era,' he said, then terminated the interview.

Methven was being a little modest in belittling his role in the CIA. He was at the heart of the CIA dirty tricks teams and paramilitary operations for decades. After Vietnam he was appointed deputy CIA station chief in Indonesia when the Soviets were trying to get a toehold there for a military base. His assignment was to try to recruit Soviet KGB agents to turn informers for the CIA.

Methven was then made CIA station chief in the Congo when the Agency was secretly supplying weapons to anti-communist guerillas in neighbouring Angola, as well as propping up the cruel and ruthless dictator Joseph Mobutu. Mobutu was the CIA's favourite ally in Africa, and his country was the clearinghouse for US covert action throughout the continent during the Cold War.[1]

Despite his claim he worked only in the background in Vietnam, Methven was no desk soldier. He is reputed to have led secret raids into North Vietnam in bids to rescue American prisoners of war. He was deep into assassination squads and counter-terror teams long before Barry Petersen arrived in the Highlands.

While Stu Methven disparages Petersen and dismisses reports the CIA had plans to have him eliminated if he did not leave quietly, others close to the action do not.

The veteran Australian war correspondent Denis Warner, who had close ties to the secret world of spies, knew something strange was going on behind the scenes. In a letter to Petersen in 1978, Warner wrote: 'You may not have been aware of them, but all sorts of rumours floated around Saigon in the mid-1960s. One I remember was that you were hiding from the CIA.'

Warner was Stu Methven's close personal friend. When Methven was in Jakarta as deputy CIA station chief, he asked Warner to act as his son's guardian while he was at Timbertop, the isolated bush campus attended by students of the exclusive Geelong Grammar School in their third year of high school. Prince Charles made Timbertop famous when he spent a year there.

Petersen said he approached Warner in 1988 after hearing of the assassination plan from Peter Young. 'When I told Denis what Peter Young had told me, he said he would not be surprised if it was right.' Warner told Petersen that Stu Methven had been eventually eased out of the CIA for pushing the boundaries too far.

When approached for comment on this statement in 2008, Warner said his memory had gone, that he was nearly blind and did not feel up to discussing the subject.

Ian Teague, the Australian Army captain who drew up plans that included assassination squads and worked closely with the CIA in Vietnam, said it was possible some in the CIA would have planned to eliminate Petersen if he caused them trouble.

'Anything is possible with the CIA,' Teague said. 'I never heard anything about them preparing to have him killed, but they certainly wanted him to leave the country. Barry got too full of his own importance.'

Teague said the CIA would be especially concerned at the time that the public might hear through the media that they were carrying out secret unsavoury operations in Vietnam with the assassination squads. In 1965 press coverage was still predominantly favourable to the war and the way it was progressing. Public opinion did not really turn against Vietnam until news footage showed bodies coming home in bags and stories of atrocities committed by US and allied troops began to leak out.

'I guess in mid-1965 the CIA would be concerned that one of us involved in forming assassination squads would talk to the press about it. In 1966 a source of mine in the CIA told me that a memo was produced in Saigon for the Combined Studies Division that no Australian was to be allowed to rise to the status and position that Barry and I achieved while we were there.'

Captain Don McDowell, who trained Vietnamese villagers for propaganda teams in Vung Tao Province during the war, said Australian Army officers were quietly excluded from the hard edge of CIA covert operations after mid-1965. He later saw intelligence reports indicating that the CIA were distrustful of Australian Army officers after their experience with Petersen. On his return from Vietnam, McDowell ran the army headquarters desk handling intelligence coming from Vietnam, Laos and Cambodia and was surprised to discover the Australian Army top brass were also wary of Petersen.

'Barry Petersen was regarded as a thorn in the side of the Australian Army,' McDowell said. 'He was a non-conformist, he was a thinker and he was not a team player. He knew things that other, more senior, people in the army did not know. He had an inside track they did not expect mere captains to have. Barry Petersen looked good until he started to look too independent. That was frowned upon by the army.'

McDowell said top ranks in the army also distrusted members of the AATTV once they returned to Australia. 'Colonel Serong was on the outer. For years he had run his own operation in Vietnam with little control from HQ, and then he'd gone over to the CIA. Officers he'd taken with him on the AATTV were tainted, they were seen as Serong's boys. They had been operating with too much independence, they had been on their own under the CIA with all the money and equipment the Australian Army could only dream about.

'Several of my colleagues from the Training Team were buried in backwaters after they returned from Vietnam and it took years before their talent and skills were recognised. The Australian Army had the attitude that officers should live by the book, do their time in headquarters, know their place, and do the right thing by the army. Only then would you get ahead. The army disapproved of individuality and independent thinking.'

McDowell said many CIA operatives were envious of the far better trained Australian Army advisers with jungle warfare experience who, through their easygoing manner, got on far better with the Montagnard and the Vietnamese. The Americans were frustrated they could not penetrate the Viet Cong and had trouble getting the Vietnamese army to fight. Then they were confronted with Barry Petersen who ran a successful Montagnard force, but refused to do what the CIA wanted with assassination teams. McDowell said it was no wonder some in the CIA could have been furious enough to put Petersen away.

Warren Reed served in Vietnam as a soldier and was later an ASIS agent for a decade working alongside CIA agents in Asia and the Middle East. He is certain there would have been elements within the Agency prepared to eliminate Petersen if he was blocking their plans. 'They would have arranged an accident,' he says. 'It would not be official or on paper anywhere. It probably wouldn't even be organised by anyone who dealt with Petersen. There are factions within the CIA who are absolutely ideological and ruthless. At the time of Vietnam the US command was demanding results and body counts. If they saw Petersen getting in their way I have no doubt some enthusiastic operatives were prepared to get one of their hired heavies to bump him off if he didn't leave.'

Colonel Le Van Thanh, who had two terms as Darlac province chief over the two years Petersen was operating out of Ban Me Thuot, trusted the Australian and the two became friends. In 1973, two years before Saigon fell, Thanh managed to get himself appointed defence attaché in South Vietnam's embassy in Canberra. When Saigon fell he was accepted as a refugee and stayed. He now calls himself Peter and lives in a quiet Canberra suburb, his home filled with Vietnamese and Roman Catholic memorabilia. His family is scattered around the globe – in Australia, America, France and South Korea. He has five children and 11 grandchildren.

'Barry is a good man and at first I thought it was a good idea to train the Montagnard,' he recalls. 'But later I realised it was a mistake. Imagine if I came to Australia and gave Aborigines military training. It is the same with the Montagnard. The Montagnard are not intelligent people. They want freedom in the jungle like the Aborigines here. Then came America and they taught them how to conquer the Central Highlands. The Vietnamese government did not want that. The Montagnard wanted to kill me as a province chief, they wanted to kill all Vietnamese.

'Barry got too powerful. The Montagnard followed him as he gave them money, gave them clothes, gave them weapons. They will follow whoever gives them something. Barry was an effective force for training and patrolling, but there were not many Viet Cong in the province while he was there.'

Thanh says that in a way Petersen was his own worst enemy because he was too successful. 'The Montagnard followed him too closely. The Vietnamese government saw this and wanted him out. I know Barry says the Americans wanted to kill him, but many, many people were killed in the war. Too many.'

The Australian diplomat in charge of the Australian Embassy when Petersen was sacked was more sceptical about his achievement. Charge d'affaire at the time as the ambassador was away, Roy Fernandez met Petersen only briefly after he'd been dismissed from the Highlands. Fernandez remembered Petersen looked like he'd 'gone native'.

'Petersen had Montagnard bracelets all the way up his arms after his farewell and was obviously very fond of them. He was upset and a bit worried about the impact the removal would have on his career, but I would not say he looked angry. He was a bit anti-CIA at the time, but I did not get the impression he was worried about what they might do to him. The CIA did not talk to me about his removal.'

He doubts Peter Young's story that the CIA was prepared to kill Petersen. Fernandez says he always took what Peter Young said 'with a grain of salt'. Young was military attaché at the embassy, but Fernandez felt he was an army officer who was always trying to impress others with his supposed insider knowledge. 'I am sure Peter Young was reporting what people told him, but you have to ask whether that information was accurate. Low-level intelligence types may have told Peter Young that story, but they all tend to think they are James Bond. It was probably just loose talk. It certainly did not come up in my talks with senior CIA officials.

'Senior American people would have been very concerned about our reaction [to Petersen being killed]. They knew we were looking after Barry Petersen, that is, we at the embassy and Brigadier Jackson. Petersen left the Highlands, and that was the end of it.

'The Vietnamese saw Petersen as getting too much influence with a group that was potentially hostile to them. They wanted him out. If anything was to happen to Petersen it would have happened up in the Highlands, not in Saigon. Once he was out of the Highlands the matter was over.'

Fernandez said Teague's information that the CIA ordered a clampdown on Australians getting too high in their covert operations was probably accurate. 'It does not surprise me. The CIA always wanted more control over people.'

Despite Fernandez's view that Peter Young was an ambitious officer with an inclination to exaggerate, Young had very good sources in US military intelligence and had his nose far closer to the real situation than diplomats in the Australian Embassy. Peter Young was the sole military officer to predict the Tet Offensive six months before it happened. Young had managed to get accepted into the American military's top-secret intelligence unit (SIGINT) and even to the innermost sanctum of the Current Intelligence and Indications Branch (CIIB), the highest level analytical area at General Westmoreland's HQ.

Even inside that top-secret sanctum there were some papers marked NOFORN, meaning 'no foreigners', and they were put away before Young could see them. He was banned from taking any papers or notes to the Australian Embassy that the US did not regard as secure.

Young's greatest asset was his American friend Major Jack Fitzgerald. The pair studied enemy transmissions and troop movements, and agreed all the intelligence they had seen indicated that the Viet Cong were gearing up for a major nationwide attack in 1968. Young was convinced it would take place during the Tet holiday in January 1968. He was the only intelligence officer who dared to make this forecast. His warning was dismissed by the generals and more senior intelligence officials. Young was proved to be absolutely correct.

Although the Tet Offensive happened a little more than two years after Petersen was dismissed from the Highlands, it does demonstrate that Young had extremely good sources in military intelligence. It shows his American friend, Major Fitzgerald, was well plugged into what was going on. So when Fitzgerald told Young the CIA were prepared to assassinate Petersen if he did not leave the Highlands quietly, it had a high degree of credibility.

Gerald Stone acknowledges his 1965 article could have had a major impact on Petersen's CIA handlers. 'There were rumours around Saigon at the time that Petersen was on a CIA list,' Stone said. 'It was in the context of him being on a Vietnamese army hate list which would certainly muddy him in the eyes of some sections of the CIA.'

Stone said there were many illegal drug rackets going on between the Vietnamese army and some sections of the CIA at the time, so a lot of the dealings were based on arrangements well outside official policy.

This is one of the reasons Stone was determined to do a story on Petersen. He was a man of mystery. He was surrounded in secrecy. Nobody could get near him, and those who did, like Pat Burgess, did not write about him. Journalists and military people in Saigon were divided on the man. Some saw him as a Walter Mitty character, a strange solitary man who had fantasies about himself as a great hero. Others saw him as a genuine military genius and fearless character who was fighting the war the way it should be fought.

Serong could have been playing a strategic card by tipping Stone into writing the flattering article on Petersen. Stone had only been in Vietnam for a few months, arriving with the first

Australian combat troops in June 1965. He had few contacts in the country and was keen to get a good story. Serong was virtually a part of the CIA by this time and may have heard Petersen was in danger. Stone had been an officer in the US army at the time of the Korean War, and Serong would have respected that military link. He probably thought a flattering article on Petersen might just save his bacon. It certainly would have been more difficult to assassinate Petersen once he was revealed to the Australian public as a hero, no matter how well his death might be disguised as an accident or an attack by the Viet Cong.

Stone is in no doubt that if some extremists in the CIA wanted to kill Petersen, they would have done it if the Australian had kicked up a stink about leaving the Highlands.

'I'm sure there were certain elements within the CIA who did not want the public back home knowing what they were up to in Vietnam. The assassination squads were just part of their dirty tricks. They were killing lots of people who they felt got in their way. The more they did it, the easier it became for them to kill. It didn't matter if it was someone on their side or the enemy,' Stone said.

Petersen was surprised at what Young told him in 1988. It was certainly the greatest act of betrayal he could imagine. He had done his best at Ban Me Thuot, and he felt he had succeeded despite overwhelming odds. Everything he did in relation to the Montagnard was to make his mission and the CIA-funded operation a success.

'I knew the people in the CIA were capable of assassinating me if they decided to do it. I was capable of assassinating someone myself. It is what we do in war. But you have to ask why they would want to eliminate someone who was succeeding in their mission. That I can't understand. It had to be something else.'

When Brigadier Jackson was interviewed in 1972 by historians at the Australian War Memorial he backed away from explaining how Petersen had caused a problem for himself in the Highlands.

'Barry had been in country with the Montagnard living with them most of the time in very dangerous circumstances for two years. In my mind he was tired. He was under very great nervous strain and I felt in his own interest that if he was going to live a useful life in the future it was necessary that he come out as an individual.'[2]

He also said he had his own reasons for not replacing Petersen with another Australian in the Highlands.

'There was pressure both from the Vietnamese government and the US MACV [Military Assistance Command Vietnam, the command unit managing the US military in Vietnam] headquarters . . . to get the Australian effort divorced from the Montagnard in the Highlands. There was also pressure from international channels into Australia itself. The Australian ambassador was most concerned [about what Petersen was doing]. It was causing a great deal of suspicion even though Petersen's activities were successful from a military point of view.'

Jackson was determined to send Petersen as far away as he could from inquisitive journalists, and vindictive American intelligence operatives. He told Petersen that despite his lengthy posting to Vietnam it would be best if he did not return to Australia for a while – there were too many people still trying to get a story on him. And due to the classified nature of his work in the Highlands he should stay out of circulation for a few months until things died down. He asked Petersen where he would like to go.

Petersen asked to go to Singapore. It was relatively quiet there and he could keep a low profile while he compiled the comprehensive report he'd intended to submit to the Australian Army command on his two years with the Montagnard. He said if it was possible he'd also like to visit Borneo where some British, Australian and Malaysian forces were resisting incursions from Indonesian forces.

His departure from Vietnam was much quieter than his farewell from the Highlands. After a few handshakes with his fellow Australian AATTV officers, Petersen slipped out of Vietnam on 14 October 1965, flying in a commercial plane to Singapore.

12

ACTION IN EXILE

Petersen was surprised by the hostility of his reception when he arrived in Singapore. The Australian officer in charge, Brigadier FR Evans, immediately demanded to know why the captain was in his base and accused him of being a 'political outcast'. Word had got around that he had committed some major sin and was a marked man. Evans did not want him around, and even went to the extreme of barring him from the Australian officers' mess. Normally an officer would have had to be caught doing something very ungentlemanly to receive such a ban. Petersen was mystified. He picked up his bags and moved to a British officers' mess on the outskirts of the city where he was made welcome.

Barry spent a few quiet months in Singapore recuperating and writing up his report on his time in the Central Highlands. In it he made a prescient conclusion:

'The people who can best counter an insurgency effort, whether it is communist or otherwise, are the indigenous population themselves. Foreign troops cannot effectively do it operating as a conventional force unless they have the popular support of the population in that area, and I do not mean the government officials and intellectuals in the major cities. Do we have this popular support in Vietnam?

'Care must be taken in motivating the indigenous population to resist insurgency. Poorly applied motivation can "backfire". Offensive action at all times is a principle of successful counter-insurgency efforts. If the offensive action is applied by the indigenous forces it is more acceptable to the population than if it is applied by a foreign army.'

Petersen warned that 'blind' cooperation among allies could drag one ally far too deeply into mistakes made by the other ally. Perhaps with a touch of irony he added: 'It is imperative at all costs that an assisting foreign national *NOT* become involved in the internal politics of a country. It is difficult at times to remain aloof from internal politics, but involved mediation, support for one faction, excess liaison with any particular faction and the passing of opinions can, and should, be avoided.'

Petersen wrote that when acting as an adviser it was best to make them think they had the original idea and allow them to take credit for it. It was important for advisers to be acutely aware of the internal politics of the people they were dealing with.

He laid out the enormous challenge facing Western nations in trying to convince Asian people to adopt Western nationalist values and an aversion to communism.

'How can we Caucasian foreigners . . . hope to imbue a cosmopolitan population with a sense of nationalism and a will to fight fellow Vietnamese (misguided as they might be) in a fight for survival against communism (which the majority do not even understand)? ... All we can hope to do, as an emergency measure, in stemming the tide of communism, is to exploit ... those things dear to humans – their racial traits, customs and religion if any.'[1]

After completing his report, Petersen was given a brief posting to Borneo where he was taken under the wing of the British secret service, MI6. He was given the cover of a liaison officer with a British Special Air Service Regiment squadron based in the former British colonies of Sabah and Sarawak in north-eastern Borneo. The provinces were aiming to join the new nation of Malaysia. But Indonesia, which had most of the island of Borneo in its province of Kalimantan, was trying to seize Sabah and Sarawak. The British were trying to stop them, using local ethnic native forces to patrol the jungle border. MI6 had heard of Petersen's experience in Vietnam and wanted him to look over their operation.

As Petersen studied the MI6 operation in Borneo, he discovered something that surprised him, something that would also surprise most Australians and Britons.

Britain had a bizarre and rather shameful involvement in Vietnam immediately after the Japanese surrender in 1945. The Viet Minh under Ho Chi Minh fought the Japanese occupiers throughout the war with some support in arms and assistance from the US. The Japanese had installed a puppet Vietnamese government and let French collaborators run the administration.

When the Japanese surrendered, Ho hoped for US support in helping Vietnam become independent. He even copied the

US Declaration of Independence in framing his own claim of independence for Vietnam from its French and Japanese colonial rulers.

But the US, along with Britain, had promised at the Potsdam Conference of July 1945 that France could restore its pre-war colonial rule over Vietnam. The US regarded nationalist desires in Indochina as a minor side issue to the larger issue of containing communism in the Soviet Union and China. To help with disarming Japanese troops, the Allies decided to divide Vietnam at the 16th Parallel – cutting the country in half at the port city of Da Nang. The British would take responsibility for the south and the Chinese Nationalists of Chiang Kai-shek, who opposed communism in China, would be responsible for the north. As Stanley Karnow says in his definitive history, *Vietnam*: 'It was a formula for catastrophe.'[2]

Vietnam was in chaos as warring factions leapt into action to try to gain control of the country. Ho's Viet Minh found itself battling Trotskyites, criminal gangs and religious fanatics as much as French colonialists trying to regain control. Violence intensified in the power vacuum left by Japanese troops, who stood idly by waiting to be disarmed by the British. Viet Minh occupied key government buildings in Saigon and Hanoi, and proclaimed they were the new government.

The British officer in charge in the south was General Douglas Gracey, very much an imperialist who believed 'natives' should know their place, and that place was well below Europeans. During the war he'd commanded an Indian Army Corps which fought creditably in Burma. In September 1945 he arrived in Saigon with 20 000 seasoned Indian troops.

He immediately armed 5000 French soldiers who had been released from Japanese prisoner-of-war camps. He allowed the French to launch attacks on Viet Minh-controlled buildings. As the violence escalated, General Gracey even rearmed the former enemy, handing guns back to surrendered Japanese marines. Gracey asked the Japanese troops to help put down the Viet Minh. French civilians joined them, fighting to regain their plantations and businesses from Vietnamese.

Angered at the sight of fully armed Japanese troops once again marching in their streets the Viet Minh hit back, attacking a European residential enclave, slaughtering 150 French civilians in their Saigon homes and shutting down electricity and water plants. Gracey feared losing control to the Vietnamese so he used his American-supplied ships and planes to bring in thousands of French troops.

By December 1945 Gracey was able to hand Vietnam back to its old colonial masters, the French. He had exceeded his orders. He had given weapons back to the defeated enemy, Japan, even though he was sent there to disarm them. It was not the first time the people of Vietnam were betrayed, and it would not be the last.

History records that Gracey's action was the last Britain had to do with the Indochina wars. The French went on to betray Ho Chi Minh, seizing the northern part of his country while he was in France negotiating peace. The Viet Minh then began its long war against the French colonialists, who were heavily backed by money, equipment and military advisers from the United States. President Harry Truman ignored opinions from his experts that Ho Chi Minh, despite being a communist, was a nationalist first and a pragmatist second. Truman saw only

Ho's red flag, and believed him therefore an agent of Moscow. Washington decreed France had to be supported in its colonial war in Vietnam because it was a stand against Soviet expansionism. France eventually lost, and the United States stepped in to continue the fight against the communists.

But while in Borneo, Petersen was shocked to discover the official history was wrong. Britain was still involved in the Vietnam War, albeit in the most secretive and covert manner. One of the MI6 men he met in Sabah was a colourful character called Dick Noone. When World War Two broke out Noone was an anthropologist studying the tribal natives of Malaya. Asked by the British to set up secret reconnaissance units using small groups of indigenous people to spy on the Japanese and monitor their movements, Noone expanded the spy units to Thailand. As Singapore fell he escaped to Australia and joined the Australian Intelligence Department, the forerunner of ASIS. In 1952 he was back with MI6 in Malaya, running an operation using natives to spy on the communists.

Like Petersen, Noone was an intensely private person guarding many secrets. The two hit it off immediately with their mutual interest in anthropology and admiration for the indigenous people of South East Asia. Then Noone surprised Petersen by casually dropping in to the conversation that he had also worked with the Montagnard.

'I wasn't allowed to deal with them directly. I was saddled with a Vietnamese Special Forces team,' Noone told him.

'Have you been to Vietnam, Dick?' Petersen asked him, barely believing what he had just heard.

'Yes . . . about the same time you were there.'

Petersen was staggered. Britain was not supposed to have been involved in the Vietnam War, but here was an experienced MI6 officer saying he had fought there. Noone went on to tell Petersen he had taken a Special Forces team of Malays and natives from Borneo to Vietnam's Central Highlands north of Darlac Province. Noone's team joined a Vietnamese Special Forces team, and they worked with US Special Forces. Noone said his Malay unit got on well with the Montagnard as they speak a similar language and have common cultural roots. However the Vietnamese grew suspicious of the Malay troops, and tension between them turned into open hostility. Noone told Petersen the situation became so bad he had to ask for his unit to be withdrawn.

There is no doubt that approval for Noone and his Malay unit to be deployed to Vietnam would have had to come from the highest levels in the British government. Petersen should not have been surprised to hear of Noone's mission – in Vietnam anything was possible.

Petersen's time in exile came to an end late in 1965 and he was recalled to Australia. He was promoted to Major and put in charge of tactical training at Ingleburn, west of Sydney. Petersen could not stand army officers who stood over and bullied those below them in the ranks and quickly won a reputation among the troops as a 'soldier's soldier'. He saw one young lieutenant berate and abuse privates. Petersen had a quiet word with the commanding officer that the bullying lieutenant had better not go to Vietnam. Despite the warning, the lieutenant was sent to Vietnam and ended up being 'fragged' (killed) by one of his own men in the camp. Petersen reckoned the arrogant officer had probably been put in charge of a platoon that had already seen a lot of combat and his men simply rebelled.

One of the soldiers under Petersen's charge during jungle training, Glen Barry, recalled that during the jungle course they had been pushed very hard by a bullying lieutenant. When the lieutenant ordered him and another soldier to stay in icy-cold water for an unnecessarily long time, they refused the order. 'It was unsafe. We were to wait in the water while trainees jumped from a high platform into the river. We were to make sure they surfaced and got to shore, but we couldn't do the job as we were freezing. We told the lieutenant it was too dangerous and refused to stay in the bitterly cold water.'

The lieutenant reported them to Petersen, who duly called the privates in and bawled them out for refusing an order. Petersen then ordered the privates to stand right outside the door to his office while he had the bullying lieutenant stand to attention in front of his desk. Barry could hear Petersen tearing strips off the lieutenant, telling him he should have listened to his men and not put their lives in unnecessary danger.

'Petersen knew we could hear everything he said as we stood outside his door. He wanted us to know that although he had to punish us, the lieutenant was the one at fault and he had dressed him down for it. That is the mark of a great officer.'

Petersen covered a lot of ground once he was pulled out of Vietnam. A man of many talents, he also did a short stint as aide-de-camp to the Governor of New South Wales, Sir Roden Cutler, a widely respected and admired hero of World War Two who had won a Victoria Cross fighting the Vichy French.

Then, in the first half of 1968, he was sent to study at a psychological warfare course at Fort Bragg in North Carolina, home to many of the US Special Forces Petersen had come across in Vietnam. Also at the course were military officers from Vietnam, the Philippines, South Korea and Malaysia.

'I got in touch with the defence attaché at the Australian Embassy in Washington as a courtesy call,' Petersen said. 'He said Stu Methven had heard I was on the course and wanted to invite me to a party when I came up to Washington. I don't know how Stu would have heard I was at Fort Bragg. Maybe the CIA circulated the information to those who might have been interested. I didn't have a clue at that time that I was supposed to have been targeted for elimination by the CIA. I only knew that I had left on a sour note with Methven and others in the Agency.

'Anyway I accepted Stu's invitation and when the study group was taken on a trip to Washington I broke off and went to his house. I met Stu and his wife, Joy, and it was as though nothing untoward had happened between us in the Highlands. They were both very friendly. We talked about old friends, and what had happened to them. That was it. We did not discuss the mission or why I was pulled out. I never heard from him again. It was only in 1988 when Peter Young told me the CIA was ready to have me eliminated that I thought again of Stu Methven.'

A man with Petersen's knowledge and training was too valuable to the army to ignore. In 1970 Petersen was sent back to Vietnam in command of Charlie Company, 2nd Battalion Royal Australian Regiment, otherwise known as 2RAR. Unlike many with the rank of major and above, Petersen was to be a front-line soldier going out on patrol with his troops and leading from the front. His unit was stationed with the bulk of the Australian deployment in Vietnam at Nui Dat in Phuoc Tuy Province, east of Saigon. Eighty-five per cent of his 140 troops had not been to Vietnam before, and had never seen action. Petersen had spent more time fighting in Vietnam than nearly all other Australian officers, but it was his first time commanding a large number of Australian soldiers in combat. He was intent on getting as many as he could back home alive.

13
RETURN TO VIETNAM

In April 1970, Major Barry Petersen found a very different war from the one he had left five years earlier. The US was cutting the size of its forces as the conflict became steadily more unpopular at home and anti-war demonstrations grew. Revelations of atrocities such as the massacre at My Lai added to the growing pressure on President Richard Nixon to find a way out of the quagmire.

By 1970 the size of the US presence in Vietnam had shrunk to about 300 000, well down from the peak of 540 000 in 1969. Although US forces openly attacked VC bases in Cambodia, widening the war, their fatality rate in Vietnam had fallen as they stepped back from engaging the enemy, handing defensive positions in the provinces to South Vietnamese troops, part of the 'Vietnamization' policy. Morale was low among US troops, with 200 reported incidents of 'fragging'[1] and an estimated 60 000

US soldiers using drugs.[2] During the five years Petersen had been away, official US figures[3] cited a total of 53 448 American servicemen and at least 100 000 South Vietnamese killed in action. An estimated 631 000 North Vietnamese troops and Viet Cong were dead.

The Tet Offensive of 1968 decimated Viet Cong ranks, but they kept on coming. Shortly before Petersen arrived, Viet Cong terrorists killed 450 Vietnamese in a series of terror raids in Saigon.

Over their five years in Phuoc Tuy the Australians had largely forced Viet Cong out of the province through constant jungle patrols. But North Vietnamese troops were hidden 25 kilometres away in the jungles of the northern neighbouring province of Long Khanh. Stretched for supplies and numbers, they were hanging back, waiting for the well-armed US and Australian forces to go home. The commander of Australian forces at that time, Major General Colin Fraser, said communist forces 'avoided any major contact' with the Australians because their main targets were South Vietnamese troops and officials who were taking over posts from the Americans and Australians as part of the US 'Vietnamization' policy.[4]

'I was going back to a war I knew we were going to lose,' Petersen reflected years later. 'I was determined to keep as many of my men alive as possible as I thought it was a pointless cause, and that we shouldn't be there.

'If you asked most of the informed military experts at that time they would have privately admitted the same thing. Publicly, nobody from the military would say it. The Vietnamese people had had enough. They didn't want the South to win if it meant the war would just go on and on. You have to see it from their point of view. Vietnamese villagers had been in a state of war for almost a hundred years – first the French, then the Japanese, then the French again, the Viet Cong and the Americans. All of them bombing and killing and torturing the peasants who were just trying to survive.

'I think it would have been far better if the Americans had supported Ho Chi Minh right from the beginning when he copied the American Declaration of Independence to announce his claim of an independent Vietnam. They would have had a friend and a foot in the door. But the Americans saw only a communist, and communists had to be fought even if it meant backing France into its old colony.'

These were not sentiments Petersen expressed at the time. Like the many other doubters in the military, he knuckled down and did his job as best he could. The two years he had spent with the Montagnard were still shrouded in secrecy and mystique, but enough was known to make him a legend among his troops. Rumours circulated among them that Petersen had been on some sort of CIA hit list because he had told them to get stuffed. Petersen, as a good commander does, kept his mouth shut, which only added to his air of mystery.

'There was no question I would refuse an order or resign from the army and join the protesters. I had watched with some disgust as the anti-Vietnam protesters took out their anger on the soldiers returning from the war. I was horrified when a woman covered in red paint or blood threw herself at the soldiers marching up George Street returning from Vietnam and covered them in red. I heard some protesters were sending money to North Vietnam. That was abhorrent to me as they were supporting the enemy of our soldiers. The anti-war protesters shouldn't have focused on the soldiers who were just doing what they were told – they should have focused on the politicians who sent them there.'

Petersen felt the Vietnamese themselves were forgotten in the way the rest of the world saw the war. 'I was in the US on the psychological warfare course when the North Vietnamese attacked in the Tet Offensive in 1968. I was watching the war on TV like millions of Americans, and I noticed there was no mention of the Vietnamese fighting the war. It was all America, America. They talked about Americans holding out in Khe Sanh. I thought, You bloody fools, it is another Dien Bien Phu. The Americans had made the same mistake as the French of building themselves into huge forts which the North could attack.

'I did read one report of a young Vietnamese lieutenant leading a patrol out of the camp which was caught in a machine gun ambush. They fled back to the camp, but the lieutenant lay wounded about 20 metres out from the wire. A few of his men ran out to try to drag him back in, but they got shot. This was an old tactic of the VC – leave one wounded and then shoot those who try to rescue him. The lieutenant pleaded with his men not to try to rescue him, but they were just about to make another dash for him so he shot himself in the head. He killed himself so no more of his men would die.

'Yet at the same time all you heard on American TV was that the American troops despised the South Vietnamese soldiers for not fighting. They moaned and complained they had to fight the war for the Vietnamese. How many Americans would have done what that young Vietnamese officer did?'

Petersen knew only too well that in war the Americans looked after themselves first and foremost. They had a rule that US medical calls to their helicopters rated far higher than assisting their Vietnamese allies. In one incident in the Highlands a village was under attack by VC and a helicopter was on its way to them to drop ammunition and supplies. But at the last moment it was diverted to pick up an American soldier who had cut his hand while handling a knife. By the time the chopper got to the village it had been overrun and set on fire.

Petersen tried to instil in his troops an understanding of the Vietnamese predicament. 'I told them that if the villagers don't join the VC they get tortured and have their heads chopped off. If they do join the VC they get attacked by South Vietnamese units or bombed by Americans. My aim was to get my troops to fight fairly and to treat the people on both sides fairly. I still thought that the best way to fight this war was the way I had been fighting with the Montagnard – to assist the local people to defend themselves. I knew what I had done in the Central Highlands would not work everywhere because of all the different ethnic and religious groups of Vietnam. But I thought we should spend time exploring what works best, rather than just impose our system on them. The Vietnamese had been fighting for several generations and it was their country. I could see how they resented having young West Point graduates coming straight into their first conflict, telling these veterans who had been fighting all their lives how they should be doing things. It was sheer arrogance of the Americans to think they knew better, and I could see it was pissing off the Vietnamese.'

Petersen noticed a sad deterioration in the life of Saigon. The old-world charm he found when he first set foot in the city in 1963 was long gone; in its place were brassy honky-tonk bars. The Vietnamese women dressed in elegant *ao dais* had largely vanished; in their place were sleazy girls in hot pants trying to hook a bit of Yankee dollar. The girls could earn more from lusty GIs in one week than the farmers outside town could earn in a year. Drugs were rampant and street crime was as big a danger as the Viet Cong. Instead of the hustle and bustle of bicycles and cyclo taxis, the streets were filled with traffic jams, big American cars belching fumes, jeeps racing round corners bearing trigger-happy gun-toting soldiers.

When Petersen arrived at the Australian forces base at Nui Dat, 60 kilometres east of Saigon, he was greeted with a warning from his battalion commander, Lieutenant Colonel John Church.

'Barry, don't get any ideas about getting back to the Highlands. We have a directive that you are to stay away from there.'

Petersen was taken aback. Once again he was being treated as though he had committed some crime. Petersen thought the directive probably came from the then Australian ambassador, Arthur Malcolm Morris. It was Morris, a desk officer in Canberra when Petersen returned for his round of briefings in 1965, who accused Petersen of supporting the Montagnard rebellion. Petersen was annoyed, but shrugged it off. There was no point dwelling on it, as far as he was concerned his immediate task was returning to the traditional role of soldier, putting all his skills to leading his men in the face of the enemy.

Petersen led Charlie Company on their first patrol in the jungle some distance from the base. He had lots of experience on this type of patrol, having done them in both Malaya and Vietnam's Central Highlands and he had trained his Tiger Men how to spot booby traps and mines. The safest place to walk was right down the centre of the path where it is well trodden. The VC and villagers use these paths too. Any sign of disturbance just off the path or in the bushes nearby could be exploding mines that blast off limbs or kill you outright.

Petersen picked a well-used path to set up an ambush. He checked for mines and booby traps before placing his men in good spots on either side of the path. They settled down to wait in absolute silence. They didn't have to wait long. A few hours into their vigil two men walked into their ambush, walking silently. His men opened fire and killed them. They were identified by their Vietnamese army interpreter as political officers from North Vietnam, senior men in the North Vietnamese army charged with spreading propaganda among the southerners and keeping their own men in line.

A few days later one of Petersen's Charlie Company patrols ran out of luck. They discovered a VC bunker and were setting up a machine gun post to cover the bunker system and set up an ambush when one of the men rested on a log. The log disguised a mine hidden underneath it. The mine blew up, chopping the young soldier in half and killing his offsider. Another three men were wounded.

When the Australians searched the bunker they found an American-issue pack holding Claymore mines. Journalist Keith Willey was with the troops at the time. In his account of his experiences with Charlie Company he wrote that the troops were furious when they discovered the US mines in the North Vietnamese camp.

In his book *Tales of the Big Country*, Willey said a US armoured unit had been through the area several months before, leaving behind rations, ammunition and even three automatic rifles. 'This would have meant a court martial if Australians had been responsible, but the Americans had a casual attitude towards their materials even when these would obviously be invaluable to an enemy starved of supplies.'

Petersen was devastated. He had warned his men about mines and done countless practice runs, but the VC were cunning in disguising their booby traps. The Australians found other mines in the area, some only centimetres from the side of the path on which they had been walking. The VC had left the bunker as bait, and for a fraction of a second the excited soldiers had dropped their focus.

Petersen looked into the eyes of his men after this first encounter with death and recognised that they needed a lift to get them going again.

He immediately took the position of forward scout to continue the patrol. It was an extraordinary sight for the troops to see a major taking that role, the most dangerous spot in the jungle patrol. But it worked. The young soldiers got back to their job.

A few months later Petersen's company was again out patrolling the northern edge of Phuoc Tuy province when he noticed a small set of tracks going across the path from the jungle. His scouts thought they were pig tracks, but Petersen's experienced eye saw more.

'Pig's arse they're pigs,' Petersen said and ordered his scouts to follow the tracks.

The tracks led to signs of humans, about five of them, in what had once been a camp. For four long days they followed the trails left by the Viet Cong, who appeared to be meeting up and gathering with larger units. Petersen and the scouts estimated they had grown to more than 150 troops, and were about 24 hours ahead. The VC kept backtracking and crisscrossing to try to confuse anybody following them. Their trail would vanish every evening as they crossed a creek or river, but Petersen doggedly kept after them, picking up their trail in the morning.

On the fifth hot and sticky day, when their rations were about to run out, Petersen heard machine gun fire in the distance. One of his patrols had finally run into the enemy. Seconds later gunfire broke out in another direction. Petersen immediately radioed for helicopter gunships and the artillery forward commander, Lieutenant David McPherson, had artillery fire support ready to hit the enemy positions.

But instead of taking cover and fighting from their dug-in bunker system, the VC chose to scatter and withdraw. Some were killed by helicopter gunships, others by the artillery shells that landed with incredible accuracy. Petersen ordered in tracker dogs and they joined up with a platoon tracking one of the larger breakaway enemy groups. The group zigzagged across a field and hid in forest on the other side, waiting for their pursuers. The platoon commander spotted the trap and called in helicopter gunships and artillery fire.

Petersen's company spent the day tracking down individuals who had escaped the choppers and artillery. Many were captured wounded, many surrendered. It was a bloody day, but a good one for Charlie Company. Altogether the enemy was estimated to have lost 32 dead, dozens more wounded and surrendered. The force included the enemy district chief and his protection unit. The enemy headquarters in the district had suffered a major blow and did not reform while Petersen's battalion was in Vietnam. For his bravery in the action Major Petersen was awarded a Mention in Dispatches. A friend back at headquarters told him he was initially recommended for a bar to the Military Cross he was awarded in 1965, but due to a bureaucratic quota system of medals, his award was downgraded to the Mention in Dispatches which was depicted by an oak leaf on the campaign medal.

Petersen's next mission was almost his last. With his company keeping watch over a creek junction the enemy was suspected of using as a crossing, he had positioned himself on a little hill away from the hidden soldiers where radio reception was good and helicopters could drop supplies. After several hours the Viet Cong walked into an ambush set up by one of the forward patrols. The firing was furious but the enemy quickly dispersed, again not wanting a full-on confrontation with the Australians. The Australians had not been in anything like a battle for the past four years, ever since the Battle of Long Tan when a vastly outnumbered company of Australians beat a North Vietnamese Regiment just north of the Nui Dat base.

Half an hour later, the machine gunner covering Petersen's little command centre signalled to him he could hear the enemy coming. Petersen was hooked up to the radio, calling in chopper support and artillery. He whispered down the line for silence as they were about to have contact, then clasped his hands over the earpieces, holding them tight to his head to cut any sound. He lay down, burrowing himself into the sparse undergrowth. Then he saw the enemy soldiers edging their way into the clearing – coming straight towards him. His artillery officer was a metre from him also desperately trying to look invisible. Their rifles lay beside them, but neither dared try to reach for them for fear the movement would give their vulnerable position away. Petersen could see three North Vietnamese soldiers, then five metres away. He could not believe they had not spotted him with radio gear all around him and a pile of packs a short distance away. Inside his head he was screaming the order to the machine gunner and the handful of soldiers guarding the command post to open fire.

Just when it seemed inevitable the NVA soldiers had to see him, the machine gunner finally opened fire, taking down the lead man and the one behind him. The third soldier dropped to his knees and opened fire but was killed within seconds. Petersen breathed again, and got back on the radio to order strikes on the enemy.

Petersen's final jungle mission was to find an enemy outpost in the mountains in the north of the province which had been detected making radio broadcasts. The area was known VC country which had been heavily bombed by the Americans. Still the radio kept up its broadcast, giving details of Australian and American troop movements. Charlie Company would have to go in on foot to find it and destroy it. After some time moving silently through the hills, a patrol spotted an enemy sentry on a far hill. They did not open fire but watched to see where he would go when he was relieved. When they tracked the sentry returning to a hilltop where the bunker system had to be, Petersen organised his troops for an assault. He ordered artillery fire on the rear of the hill to stop the enemy escape, then his men moved up the hill to assault the bunker, leaping from one bit of cover to another as they advanced.

Petersen positioned himself in the centre and a bit to the rear so he could see how his troops on either side were advancing, the same as he had done six years earlier as he led his Montagnard troops in the attack on the Viet Cong village in the Central Highlands. Suddenly heavy fire from the bunker poured down on the troops to his right. The men dived to the ground, taking cover. Petersen could see two of his troops, both young conscripts, edging away from the bullets whizzing around their heads. They leaped, crawled and dashed from one rock or log to another, and they were fast approaching Petersen's own position in the centre of the line. As they got closer and closer and were almost on top of him, Petersen yelled out: 'Hey, you blokes, the war's that way!' and pointed directly up the hill.

'You should have seen the expression on those young blokes' faces,' Petersen recalls. 'They weren't retreating, just trying to get to a better position, but they suddenly found themselves on top of this old man, the bloody major. I can imagine them thinking, "Crikey, we're almost as far back as that old bastard." Anyway they grinned and headed straight up that hill.

'Unfortunately the effect of shouting is that it draws all the enemy fire on you. The enemy, correctly in this case, assume the one doing the shouting must be the commander, so best shoot the bugger. That is exactly what happened. They stopped shooting at the right wing and the two young troopers, and concentrated their fire on me. It shut me up.

'I tried to dig myself into the hill, but one of the bullets smashed into a rock just in front of me and the next thing I knew I had blood in my mouth. I wasn't sure if I had been shot or just bitten my tongue. It must have been the former as months later two small pieces of shrapnel worked their way out of the bottom of my tongue. Until then I hadn't realised they were there.'

Charlie Company took the bunker to find it was controlled by the dregs of the NVA. These were poorly trained peasants who had been given a gun and told to hold their position. It was another sign that the Australians were preventing the bulk of the North Vietnamese army from taking control of Phuoc Tuy province.

Towards the end of his posting in 1971 Petersen was asked to lecture at the Vietnamese Armed Forces Command in Dalat in the Central Highlands. Several other Australian and New Zealand officers were to give talks, but the star attraction was US Colonel David Hackworth, the most highly decorated US soldier at the time. Hackworth was of much the same opinion as Petersen – the Americans were using the wrong tactics to combat the guerilla warfare run by the communists and that American soldiers were woefully inadequately trained for their task in Vietnam.[5]

When Petersen got back to his base after the lecture he was battered and bruised, having been involved in a car accident on his way to the airport in Dalat. He had no time for injury as he was immediately called to attend an official military ceremony. He really looked the part of the war hero as he was handed a medal awarded by the Vietnamese government, the Cross of Gallantry with Silver Star. It was his second, the first was from the Vietnamese, too, as he left his first posting in 1965. The Americans had claimed it was the Vietnamese who wanted him out of the Highlands, but here they were, presenting him with another medal.

The Australian ambassador, Arthur Malcolm Morris, the same foreign affairs bureaucrat who had grilled Petersen during his briefing tour of Australia in 1965, was at the ceremony. Morris called Petersen over and quietly asked him if he would be prepared to go back to the Highlands to do some intelligence work: the Australian government wanted to know how things had changed since he had left. Petersen was surprised. This was the man he believed had ordered him never to return to the Highlands. Something must have happened to make him change his mind. Petersen left the ceremony and ended up spending a week in hospital recovering from his car crash. On his release, he flew back into Ban Me Thuot for the first time in six years.

He was travelling unarmed with his army batman (personal aide) Private Graham Nelson. His cover story was that he was on leave, visiting old friends in the Highlands. It wouldn't have convinced the CIA, but he didn't intend running into them.

Petersen was shocked at the change in Ban Me Thuot. 'It had gone downhill – the old charm had disappeared. It was filled with American and Vietnamese soldiers and the bars blared loud American music. The old French colonial buildings were still damaged from the Tet Offensive in 1968; nothing had been repaired.'

Some old business friends he had dealt with six years earlier greeted him with open arms, but what he heard from them filled him with despair. Ordered to leave the villages they had lived in for hundreds of years, the Montagnard had been forcibly resettled in big camps closer to the city. Supposedly it was for their own safety, but the move destroyed their lives. The Vietnamese military commander, General Ngo Dzu, ordered the Montagnard villages and everything in them be destroyed as soon as they left so the Viet Cong could not use them. This also meant the Montagnard would not be tempted to return. The longhouses Petersen had spent so many happy hours in, getting thoroughly drunk on rice wine, were all burned to the ground. Heavy brass cymbals and drums that the villagers could not carry with them had been thrown into the bonfires. One hundred Montagnard villages were burned to the ground and 40 000 Montagnard people forced out. Even their livestock had been slaughtered so the Viet Cong could not benefit from them. Montagnard culture was being systematically wiped out.

The Truong Son Force was gone. Remnants of the Tiger Men had been absorbed into the South Vietnamese militia, but many had defected to the FULRO independence movement over the border in Cambodia.

'I was told that six months after I left in '65 the Americans bombed a Montagnard village that I had under protection with the Tiger Men. I had sat with these people, drinking rice wine. They were good people who didn't want a bar of the war. They just wanted to be left alone.'

Petersen says today, 'The Americans were probably told the village had been taken over by the Viet Cong. They are prepared to accept civilian casualties to achieve their aim, which might be to destroy the enemy hiding in a village putting it as the casualty of war, collateral damage. They did it time and time again in

Vietnam, Laos, Cambodia and they are still doing it now in Iraq and Afghanistan. But all it did was drive more people into the hands of the communists or the jihadists. They hammer the life out of something before they go in and have a look.'

Back then, Petersen knew the Ban Me Thuot secret police had put a tail on him as soon as he arrived at the main airport. He borrowed a car from one of his friends and lost the police as he sped out of town to see for himself how the Montagnard villagers were coping and whether his old Truong Son Force camps still existed.

'It was heartbreaking. The Montagnard had been dumped in overcrowded camps with little or no water supply.

'In the Pleiku region to the north, many tribespeople were dying of starvation because they had such poor land and the Vietnamese hadn't given them enough food to survive on. They would run away but their villages had been destroyed.

'Ironically the Montagnard were less secure in their new camps than in their old villages because the Viet Cong could target them more easily, so the temptation to defect to the VC must have been strong.'

Petersen managed to track down some of his old Montagnard friends in the camps. 'They were much poorer than when I last saw them and totally demoralised. But still they welcomed me with smiles and the sacrifice of a chicken. They even insisted on opening a jar of rice wine.'

It took the Americans three days to discover Petersen was in town. The US adviser to the province chief, Lieutenant Colonel Wayne Smith, was not pleased to see him and demanded to know what he was doing. Petersen gave his story of being on leave, but Smith didn't buy it. This was his turf and no Australian should be there. Petersen did what he had done many times before with bumptious colonels. He steeled his eyes, stood straight and said bluntly: 'I am an Australian major travelling with my general's permission, and that is all I need.'

It was a stalemate. The US colonel could not order this ally out of the Highlands without good reason. No doubt he immediately sent cables back to his commander in Saigon and at some point Petersen's name would pop up in the CIA office. Petersen knew the way the US intelligence system worked, and reckoned he had a few days yet to complete his mission for the ambassador before the Americans once again kicked him out of the Highlands.

At the end of his visit, he gave his report to the ambassador with a warning that if the Rhade were starving in the camps they would be more volatile and could rise up again and turn on the Vietnamese.

'They have the means and strength to do this using the ex-FULRO forces which now exist as regional type forces in Darlac Province,' he wrote. After he handed in his report to the embassy, Petersen returned to Australia, his second, and last, tour of duty at an end. His war was over, but his fight with the CIA, battles with bureaucrats in the Australian Army, his involvement with shadowy characters in the spy world and his support for the Montagnards continued.

Petersen did not mention this in his report to the ambassador, but he had also learned that as soon as he left the Highlands in 1965, the CIA had gone ahead and introduced assassination squads to the province, as they had done across the country. Petersen's refusal to be part of what would become known by

1967 as the Phoenix Program, one of the most notorious aspects of American conduct during the Vietnam War, had no hope of stopping the Americans from embracing this tactic – they were out to win the war any way they could, regardless of the cost.

14

PHOENIX RISING

It started off with a certain military logic. It was impossible to tell who was the enemy in Vietnam – the VC dressed just like local villagers in black pyjama-like smocks. They lived among the villagers. They could be innocent farmers and local officials by day, communist Viet Cong by night. VC tactics were often horrific, using torture and terrorism to force reluctant villagers to supply them with food and shelter and they were quick to assassinate village chiefs and their families to terrorise them into providing support.

The CIA decided the only way they could win was to beat the VC at their own game – match terror with terror. They would have to get dirty and go undercover to hunt down and break the Viet Cong 'infrastructure' – Viet Cong political officers, tax collectors, intelligence gatherers, provincial chiefs and enforcers.

The tactic was not new. It had its origins with American secret service operatives fighting communists in Laos in 1960. One operative was the colourful Ralph Johnson, a veteran of the Flying Tigers, the ragtag outfit that flew in support of the nationalist Chinese against the Japanese after the attack on Pearl Harbor. Johnson was a smooth-talking wheeler-dealer and notorious ladies' man who was later reputed to have had an affair with the wife of Air Marshal Ky's glamorous wife.[1] After World War Two Johnson was involved in spying activities in the Philippines and Indonesia before being sent to Laos. In the rugged, jungle-covered Laotian mountains he organised Montagnard tribesmen into commando units to take on communists coming over the mountain borders from China and North Vietnam, copying tactics of infiltration and assassination from the communists.

In 1960 he was transferred to South Vietnam and started setting up similar commando units, called Mountain Scouts. They were a ruthless bunch of handpicked ex-soldiers and police officers. A year later he was joined by Stu Methven, who had also been involved in setting up indigenous commando units in Laos.

The terror tactics of the VC sickened even the toughest CIA operatives. Senior officer Peer de Silva was shocked at what he saw when he arrived in Vietnam in 1964. Out on patrol with a CIA-funded unit he discovered a village chief, his pregnant wife and a young boy impaled on sharp poles. 'To make sure this horrible sight would remain with the villagers one of the terror squads used his machete to disembowel the woman, spilling the foetus onto the ground,' de Silva wrote in his 1978 autobiography, *Sub Rosa – The CIA and the Uses of Intelligence*.

But de Silva also recognised terror had its uses. 'This implacable use of terror in its own way served an intelligence purpose. A bloody act of terror in a populated area would immobilize the population nearby, make the local inhabitants responsive to the Viet Cong and, in return, unresponsive to the government element requests for cooperation,' he wrote.

It was Stuart Methven who took the US response a big step further, towards adopting similar terror tactics. Methven told American author Douglas Valentine that, after seeing the terrorist actions of the Viet Cong, he decided to take the most aggressive and cutthroat of the Scouts and hired mercenaries and fierce warrior Nung tribesmen to form a unit within the Scouts called Counter Terror (CT) teams. Shrouded in secrecy and with an aura of fear and terror, these were small tight units of five to 20 hard men whose mission was to go into communist-controlled areas to capture Viet Cong leaders. In 1962 Methven was told by CIA station chief Cliff Strathern to install the Mountain Scout and CT programs in the northern provinces of South Vietnam.

Methven told Valentine it was easy to persuade Vietnamese province chiefs to pick up the program as the units were paid for with CIA money and supplies. It also gave the provincial chiefs a force that was nominally under their personal control rather than that of the government in Saigon or the army. The US military became more involved in the CT units, beefing them up in size and expanding their operations into hunter–killer missions. They began what became known as 'snatch and snuff' operations – go in and identify VC, then kidnap or kill them. The CT men frequently dressed in black pyjamas and committed acts of terror on villagers to make them think they were Viet Cong. US military advisers or CIA operatives were nearby directing the operation.

It was at this stage that Australian Army Captain Ian Teague was assigned to give formal military training to the Vietnamese and Montagnard units the CIA were running. These became the successful People's Action Teams (PATs).

When CIA officer de Silva visited the Quang Ngai training centre for the PATs, he was impressed. He got the CIA station chief, William Colby, to approve it and soon it was up and running with CIA money pouring in. Assassination squads got the green light. They were to be a radically new approach of small, specially trained teams dedicated to counter-terror activities. They would be dressed like the Viet Cong in black pyjamas armed with folding stock carbines which could be hidden in their clothing and grenades in their pockets.

The program changed its name several times over the next few years and involved many different strands and types of units. It was all later to come under the umbrella of the Phoenix Program.

Although it may have made military sense, and certainly made sense to the CIA, the program started to go wrong almost immediately. It was just as Barry Petersen predicted. The problem lay in the sort of people who were to do this cutthroat work: Poor intelligence gatherers; the worst murderers and killers from criminal gangs; crazed mercenaries and drugged up, psychologically damaged ex-soldiers; Viet Cong turncoats; prison inmates allowed out so long as they killed; greedy, envious and scheming Vietnamese officials; incompetent and inexperienced US advisers – all came to play a major role in this secret dirty war.

A CIA operative running paramilitary raids in Laos called Anthony Poshepny, also known as Tony Poe, told his militia to cut off the ears of men as proof of their victories in battle. Poe collected them in a green cellophane bag and on one of his infrequent visits to CIA headquarters in Vientiane dumped them on the desk of his stuffed-shirt deputy chief.[2]

American author Douglas Valentine spoke to Elton Manzione, whom he described as a highly trained US Special Forces soldier who often carried out secret missions for the CIA. Much of this was with CT groups along the border with Laos and the Demilitarised Zone. Manzione said many were criminals the Vietnamese could not handle in their jails. 'So they gave them to us. Some actually had an incentive plan – if they killed X number of Commies they got X number of years off their prison terms.'[3]

Manzione said the CT teams dreamed up dirty tricks to strike terror into the hearts of villagers that not even his tough breed of men in Special Forces had come up with. They preyed on superstitious fears: Buddhists believed they could not enter heaven unless their liver was intact, so Manzione would sneak into a VC camp, garrot his victim and then use his dagger to cut out the man's liver. He said some of the CT would even devour their enemies' vital organs.

He makes the incredible admission that they were not always sure who they were killing or which side their victims were really on. But Manzione insisted counter-terror was one way of winning over uncommitted civilians.

'We left our calling card nailed to the forehead of the corpses we left behind. They were playing-card-sized, with a light-green skull with red eyes and red teeth dripping blood set against a black background. We hammered them into the third eye, the pituitary gland, with our pistol butts. The third eye is the seat of consciousness for Buddhists, and this was a form of mutilation that had a powerful psychological effect.'

This bizarre practice appears to have had the approval, or at least the knowledge, of senior officials in Washington. CIA officer Pat McGarvey told US journalist Seymour Hersh that some psychological warfare guy in Washington thought of a way to scare the local villagers. 'When we killed a VC they wanted us to spread eagle the guy, put out his eye, cut a hole in the back of his head, and put his eye in there. The idea was that fear was a good weapon.' Ears were also cut off and hammered to houses to let villagers know that Big Brother was listening. McGarvey said the Phoenix system was wide open to corruption and false accusation. 'One guy who was a source of information about the VC relieved his family of three generations of debt. He turned in phony reports fingering as Viet Cong people his family owed money to.'[4]

It sounds like a nightmare, but the program had approval from the very top. CIA and military psychological warfare experts believed the terror tactics would drive people into a state of infantile dependence. Manzione said US Special Forces working with CT teams were told to ignore the normal military rules of engagement and to keep the CT teams separate from other forces and US advisers. Senior military officers turned a blind eye.

One of the tried and tested interrogation methods, according to Manzione, was to take three prisoners up in a helicopter, say to one 'Talk!' then throw him out before he even had a chance to answer. Do it to the second one, and the third could not stop talking.

The CT teams came up with one better. 'We wrapped det [detonator] cord around their necks and wired them to a detonator box. Basically what it did was blow their head off. The interrogator would tell the translator, usually a South Vietnamese intelligence officer, "Ask him this." He'd ask him, "Who gave you the gun?" And the guy would start to answer, or maybe he wouldn't – maybe he'd resist – but the general idea was to waste the first two. They planned the snatches that way. Pick up this guy because we're pretty sure he's VC cadre – these other two guys just run errands for him. Or maybe they're nobody; Tran the farmer, and his brother Nguyen. But bring in two. Put them in a row. By the time you get to your man, he's talking so fast you got to pop the weasel just to shut him up . . . I guess you could say that we wrote the book on terror.'[5]

Manzione said he quit the counter-terror squads after he found out he'd killed two young women by mistake on a raid into North Vietnam. In darkness he'd gone to the right hut to kill the target, he silently knifed one in her sleep and shot the other in the head. Then he found out the target wasn't there. He sat on an ammunition dump with a grenade in his hand, the pin pulled, until his controllers agreed to send him home. He'd had enough. 'We were no longer the good guys in the white hats defending freedom – we were assassins pure and simple.'[6]

Some historians dispute Manzione's story. Mark Moyar, associate professor at the US Marine Corps University in Quantico, Virginia, said military records showed Manzione was never in Special Forces, and had left Vietnam in 1964, two years before Phoenix began. To this Manzione states that the military falsified his records after he spoke out against the war. Moyar does not just debunk Manzione, he also defends Phoenix, arguing it was never an assassination program, but an intelligence gathering effort.[7] In his book *Phoenix and the Birds of Prey*, Moyar argues Phoenix was inaccurately derided by the anti-war movement and was actually an effective weapon against the Viet Cong.

There are many claims and counter claims about whether Phoenix was a terror and assassination operation, and the debate still rages today as the program has been resurrected to some degree for operations in Iraq and Afghanistan. However, there is enough evidence to establish Phoenix was out of control in Vietnam and atrocities were committed there on a large scale.

It didn't start that way. Given the job of spreading versions of his PAT and CT teams to every province in Vietnam, Stu Methven's first step was to build a permanent training base for the teams in 1963. Methven knew of an old Catholic seminary on the Vung Tao peninsula, on the coast west of Saigon and not far from the Australian base at Phuoc Tuy. By January 1965 it had grown into a base capable of training 5000 people at a time.

Australians were involved in the Phoenix program from the beginning. Some, like Captain Ian Teague, were integral to its early days, helping set up the model for militia teams, that later became the model for the assassination squads under the Phoenix umbrella. Between 1963 and 1972 several members of the Australian Army Training Team served as trainers at the CIA-run Vung Tao base, and also as advisers to units under the Phoenix program across the country.

Captain Peter Jarratt was the first to run the Vung Tao base in April 1964. Even though he was an Australian Army officer, for several months he was the CIA case officer at Vung Tao. One of the first contacts Jarratt had with the US army on arriving in Vietnam caused him alarm. 'I was taken aback at my first briefing from the Americans. There were 50 to 60 people there and General Charles Timmes took over the briefing, telling us: "God is on our side and we will defeat the Godless communists. God is looking over our shoulder and protecting and guiding us. We will prevail." Well, I'm an atheist, and I was worried the Yanks were relying on God to get them through this war. I later found out Timmes had parachuted into France on D-Day and fought his way across France and Germany, so he was probably right to think God was looking after him.'

When Jarratt visited Petersen in Ban Me Thuot he was impressed by his Montagnard operation. But he was told by his CIA handler, Tom Powers, that the Vung Tao operation would be very different from that run by Petersen. Within a short time at the base called Cat Lo, 15 kilometres from the military airstrip at Vung Tao, Jarratt was training 200 people for the PAT units devised by Ian Teague. A showpiece for the CIA, Jarratt had a constant stream of dignitaries visiting Cat Lo from Saigon. On the Australian side there was the then defence minister, Paul Hasluck, and ASIS chief Sir Walter Cawthorn. Senior CIA officers including Stu Methven, Lou Conein and John Negroponte made frequent visits. Like Petersen, Jarratt resisted pressure to set up assassination squads.

According to Jarratt, the Vietnamese officer Captain So, who was answerable to the province chief, urged him to set up a dirty tricks unit. 'He pushed me to set up black propaganda teams which would pretend to be Viet Cong and go into a village and shoot it up to turn the village against the VC. Captain So also talked about forming assassination squads. I refused, saying we were not ready for it at that stage.'

Jarratt was immediately cut out of several CIA operations and when they started training the men in secret on the base, he was not allowed near them. He believes they were assassination squads. 'I would have had nothing against assassination squads providing they were run properly and actually went after the people they were supposed to. The problem was keeping control and making sure the provincial chief did not use them to bump off rivals. We were there to fight the Viet Cong, not to target civilians. Assassination teams targeted civilians who had a certain political thinking.'

Rather than assassins, Jarratt could have done a lot with a team of spooks, literally. One side of his camp was permanently safe from attack because it was protected by a ghost. 'I noticed our guards never went through a cemetery which lined one side of the camp. They walked around it every time. I asked the Vietnamese commander why they did that, and he said they would never go there because a ghost of a woman dressed in white haunted the cemetery. I figured the Viet Cong wouldn't go into the haunted cemetery either, and we never had trouble from that side of the camp. With a division of ghosts we would have had peace across the entire country!'

The Vung Tao training bases expanded rapidly after Jarratt left in November 1964. CSD chief Tom Donahue leased another former Catholic seminary as headquarters and by January 1965 built a new training camp for 5000 called Ridge Camp. It was essentially Teague's program on steroids, but Australians were not invited to train troops there. The CIA recruited tens of thousands of villagers from across the country, sent them to Vung Tao, trained them, paid them, and sent them back to the provinces to combat the Viet Cong from the villages. The big problem was the operation expanded so fast the CIA sent the units to villages that were completely foreign to them. Teague's central tenet had been that PATs had to be based in their home villages so they knew who was who. Donahue's expanded operation sent them everywhere, losing that vital village link.

Captain Don McDowell, who succeeded Jarratt at Cat Lo, said the men he saw being trained at Ridge Camp were 'a bunch of thugs'. 'I always thought if we wanted to win the hearts and minds of the Vietnamese we needed the softly-softly group I was training at Cat Lo. They went to villages and administered medical aid, spread propaganda and civic action such as building and repairing homes. Their only military training was for self-defence.'

McDowell was not impressed with the CIA operatives he came across in Vietnam. 'Many were failures from the Bay of Pigs fiasco in Cuba and the failed operation in Laos. They were not the type we would have hired for our intelligence operations.'

A year later Australian Army Captain Jack Leggett came close to being murdered by a CIA operative after the Australian refused an order to assassinate four unarmed Vietnamese women. Leggett was a CIA-appointed case officer for Phuoc Tuy province, running Phoenix-style operations, including Provincial Reconnaissance Units (PRU), a Vietnamese militia conducting more aggressive operations than the PATs; they did carry out assassinations. But Leggett insisted the PRU operate as an Australian-controlled unit. When the CIA sent him two American sergeants to act as advisers Leggett infuriated his CIA bosses by sending them packing.

'They were killers,' Leggett recounted over coffee in a Canberra cafe in 2009. 'The American sergeants had already been kicked out of other units for their attitude. They kept on saying they just wanted to "kill gooks", and they treated the Vietnamese terribly. The CIA did not like it when I told them I wanted them out, but I would not have them in my units.'

A short time later a CIA adviser to the local Vietnamese Police Special Branch, a former US Navy petty officer called BJ Johnson, told Leggett they had intelligence a group of Viet Cong couriers were coming through a valley carrying important documents. Johnson was a tough guy aged in his 50s, extremely gung ho and eager to make a name for himself in the CIA as he was at the end of military age. Special Branch was run by the CIA as a separate, secretive unit inside the Vietnamese Police. They did the dirty work inside the interrogation centres, torturing prisoners and carrying out executions.

'Johnson wanted me to take my PRU and ambush these couriers,' Leggett said. 'It sounded like a legitimate operation so I cleared it with the province chief, and we got ready. We had about a week's notice, so I did a reconnaissance of the area and found the closest we could get to a feasible ambush site was about 300 metres. That meant it became more of an assassination with a sniper rifle than an ambush.'

Leggett quickly discovered none of his unit could shoot accurately at 300 metres; he would have to do it himself. He practised until he was confident he could quickly take out five targets with five shots. 'Then some further intelligence came through that these five Vietnamese we were to hit were all women. They had been taking food in, and coming out with documents. They were very low echelon, and for me that information changed the entire nature of the operation.

'I told Johnson I wouldn't do it. I was not going to kill a group of unarmed women. I told him I had not trained for years as an army officer to assassinate unarmed women. He hit the roof. He was furious. He said he'd take it to the senior adviser, an American lieutenant colonel, and have me disciplined for refusing a mission. I told him he could go to the Pope himself, I was still not going do it.'

Like Petersen, Leggett was in an unusual position. Johnson was of equal rank in the CIA, and did not have the authority to order him to carry out the operation. Even the American CIA senior adviser in the province did not have the power to order it, as Leggett was an Australian Army officer. If the matter went to the Australian commander in Vietnam, Leggett maintains he had the right to refuse the operation as it went against the Australian military rules of engagement.

'Things got rather heated. I told Johnson that even if I could live with myself for killing five unarmed women, it would not make one iota of a difference to the outcome of the war. I told him the PRU would not be used for the operation. There were dozens of ways this could be done instead of killing them.

They could have been followed to their village and arrested. For some reason Johnson insisted on them being assassinated. He went off in a fury.'

At 11pm that same night the alarm bell rang on the front door of Leggett's house. The two Vietnamese guards stationed at the front gate rang the bell twice to signify an American was coming up the driveway. Leggett went outside and was stunned to see Johnson holding a pistol pointing straight at him. Johnson was just 2 metres away at the bottom of the steps. He was very drunk, and for some reason was dressed in the Vietnamese black pyjama-style clothes.

'I am going to get you, you bastard. I am going to blow your fucking head off,' Johnson yelled. He levelled the pistol at Leggett. It waved a bit in his drunken state, but at that range he couldn't miss, Leggett recounted.

'You are a lousy, coward foreigner,' Johnson shouted at Leggett. 'How dare you refuse the operation. You ruined the careers of two fine American soldiers when you kicked them out. Who the bloody hell do you think you are? You have no fucking right to tell me what you will or won't do. Now you are going to fucking die.'

Leggett knew this drunken CIA agent was quite prepared to kill him. Life was cheap in Vietnam, and men like Johnson found it easy to kill. Leggett was in a bad position. He was standing on the porch with the light silhouetting him against the front door, whereas Johnson stood in almost complete darkness. Leggett's mind raced. Should he dodge to one side and run before Johnson gets a shot away, or should he charge the gunman? He tried to talk his way out of it.

'Look, BJ, let's talk about this tomorrow. I am sorry you feel like this, but why don't you go home and we'll talk in the morning.'

Johnson took a step closer and pointed his pistol directly at Leggett's head. His finger tightened on the trigger. 'You fucking bastard,' Johnson screamed.

Leggett thought he was about to die.

'BJ, before you pull that trigger think very carefully, because two of my soldiers are right behind you with guns pointed at you.'

Johnson gave a drunken snort. 'I'm not falling for that old trick.'

Just then the two soldiers from the gate who had followed Johnson up the drive cocked their guns, giving the unmistakable double-click sound. Johnson froze. He could kill the Australian, but even in his drunken rage he realised he would also be shot dead.

Leggett said in the calmest voice he could muster: 'Now BJ, put the pistol in your pocket and go home. We'll talk in the morning.'

With the guns aimed at his back, Johnson backed down and was escorted to the front gate by the two soldiers. Not a word was ever said about the incident. Johnson did not mention it when he saw Leggett a few days later, carrying on as though nothing had happened, and Leggett never raised it with him. BJ Johnson was killed during the Tet Offensive in 1968.

By 1967 all the various counter-terror operations were gathered under the CIA code name 'The Phoenix Program'. Vast amounts of CIA money were thrown at the program and it expanded rapidly. Australians continued to be heavily involved.

From 1968 to 1970, Australian Army Warrant Officer Ernest 'Ossie' Ostara was an adviser to a Provincial Reconnaissance Unit in Binh Dinh province, about 150 kilometres northeast of Ban Me Thuot. Using intelligence gleaned from the Phoenix Program, Ostara mapped every village with a red dot over houses in which suspected VC lived, and blue dots for those loyal to the South Vietnamese government. Ostara reported his PRUs killed around half a dozen VC officials per month and captured another 30 or so.[8]

In 1970 the CIA handed over control of the Phoenix Program to the US military. Captain Bill Deane was one of the last Australians training Montagnard in PRU teams across four Highland provinces, including Petersen's earlier stomping ground of Darlac Province. Deane found Vietnamese provincial chiefs were more concerned about provoking the Viet Cong if they used the Montagnard units, so they were effectively grounded. The units had also become too big and bogged down with heavy equipment. Four years after Petersen was forced out of the Highlands, Deane came to the conclusion that Petersen's original tactic of keeping the Montagnard force to small teams of eight had been correct.[9]

Petersen's instincts about the dangers of forming special assassination squads were proved well founded. A few years after he was pulled out of the Central Highlands, Phoenix operatives were being derided in the US as the CIA's mercenary killers. In a 1970 report in the American mass circulation *True* magazine titled 'The CIA's Hired Killers', gutsy female war correspondent Georgie Anne Geyer wrote: 'The US has trained an elite corps of assassins to eliminate the Viet Cong's "shadow government".' She gave a graphic description of a raid which killed eight VC and captured another 26.

With the US desperate to placate an increasingly disillusioned public at home, worn out with this neverending war, a Congressional inquiry was held into the Phoenix Program. CIA station chief William Colby provided the Senate Foreign Relations Committee with figures claiming 21 000 VC officials had been eliminated by Phoenix in its first year of operations. But the figures were dodgy. Even Colby admitted many of the kills credited to Phoenix were actually battlefield casualties, and there was no way of knowing how many were genuine Viet Cong and how many were innocent civilians. However, he rejected a suggestion by Democrat Senator J William Fulbright that it was a 'program for the assassination of civilian leaders'.

Public revulsion at the Phoenix Program grew as it was revealed CIA-supported forces under Phoenix were dressing up as Viet Cong and committing terror acts on villagers to put the blame on the communists.

US Lieutenant Colonel Anthony Herbert in his 1973 book *Soldier* tells how he reported for duty in November 1965 with the Special Operations Group (SOG). 'They wanted me to take charge of an execution team that wiped out entire families and make it look as though the VC themselves had done the killing.'[10]

After the 1968 Tet Offensive, pressure grew from Washington to achieve results in Vietnam. President Lyndon B Johnson demanded some sign that America was winning. So when the

American put in charge of Phoenix, Robert Komer, introduced quotas, all of a sudden units started bringing in bodies and saying they were VC just to meet the quota.[11]

Phoenix was said to be directly linked to one of the worst atrocities of the Vietnam War – the March 1968 massacre in the village of My Lai of up to 504 unarmed civilians, including many women, babies, children and old men. Led by Lieutenant William Calley, the US army platoon that murdered the entire village was acting on information provided by Phoenix intelligence that there were Viet Cong in the village. The officers had been briefed on maps that showed the village coloured red – meaning it was under the control of the Viet Cong. On the basis of that intelligence, My Lai was to be treated as a Viet Cong stronghold, and therefore as a 'free-fire zone'. The aim was to wipe it off the face of the Earth.

This is not to say the CIA directly ordered the My Lai massacre, but in the atmosphere generated by a CIA-sanctioned assassination program and the declaration of 'free-fire zones', where everyone was an enemy, it became easy for soldiers – American, Australian or Vietnamese – to regard every villager, even children, as objects to be annihilated. Instructors at US army training centres routinely dehumanised the Vietnamese, describing them as gooks, slants or dinks as trainees shot, bayonetted and otherwise practised killing.[12]

My Lai was not an aberration. From late 1968 to mid-1969 the US Army's 9th Infantry Division, under the command of Major General Julian Ewell, conducted a brutal campaign in the densely populated Mekong Delta aimed at eliminating the Viet Cong that amounted to a My Lai massacre every month. In the first stage leaflets were dropped across the area saying all the people who lived there had to leave and go to special camps set up by the Saigon government. In the second stage, US patrols would go in and anyone found in the areas would be regarded as a potential enemy. With military headquarters demanding ever larger body counts, the areas became 'free-fire zones'. Peasant farmers who had simply refused to leave their land were killed in their thousands.

Forty years after the war, American journalist Nick Turse uncovered evidence in the US National Archives that up to 5000 Vietnamese civilians were killed in this campaign, which was called Operation Speedy Express. In an article he wrote in December 2008 for *The Nation*, Turse said the army not only covered up the atrocities, but promoted those in charge. One of the company commanders was David Hackworth. 'A lot of innocent civilians got slaughtered because of Ewell's drive to have the highest count in the land,' Hackworth wrote in a 2002 memoir, *Steel My Soldiers' Hearts*. Hackworth arrived in Vietnam in 1965 at about the time Petersen was forced out of the Highlands. He became one of America's most decorated soldiers but, like Petersen, was deeply disillusioned with the way the US was running the war, particularly the inadequate training of troops. In 1971 Hackworth caused a furore when he said in a TV interview that US casualties were 30 per cent higher because of poor training and that up to 20 per cent of US casualties were due to friendly fire. He blasted US headquarters for demanding enemy body counts that led to officers falsifying combat reports. Hackworth stated the US army had 'lost the war'.

The US command was furious and set out to destroy Hackworth's reputation. A few weeks later he was flying in a brand-new helicopter with an experienced pilot he knew well when suddenly the chopper lost all hydraulic power and crashed into enemy territory. Hackworth survived and was rescued, but he suspected it was no accident. He knew what the darker shadowy elements in US military and intelligence were capable of. He told reporters he feared an assassin's bullet or a knife in the back. Then, when Hackworth was leaving the country, he discovered a car bomb in the jeep he was about to use to drive to the airport. In the US he was followed, his phone was tapped and his home frequently searched. He eventually migrated to Australia and settled in Queensland, where he wrote up his accounts in his 1989 book, *About Face*.

The chopper crash and attempted bombing may have been coincidence, but Hackworth's experience adds further credence to warnings that elements in the CIA were ready to kill Petersen if he did not leave the Highlands.

A prominent American military man to die in an accident after publicly criticising the US army was John Paul Vann. In 1969 he was a former lieutenant colonel in charge of pacification efforts in the Mekong Delta. He complained to General Westmoreland of massacres by troops in Speedy Express who were using night-vision goggles to shoot from helicopters at anyone they saw, making no attempt to tell friend from foe. The US military hierarchy found Vann a thorn in their side, and must have breathed a sigh of relief when he was later killed in a helicopter crash.

One American adviser, Jeffrey Record, wrote in a 1971 *Washington Monthly* article that he saw helicopter gunships strafe a herd of water buffalo being tended by six or seven children. Within seconds the tranquil paddy was 'transformed into a bloody ooze littered with bits of mangled flesh. The dead boys and the buffalo were added to the official body count of the Viet Cong'.[13]

In 1970 General Ewell served as the top US military adviser at the Paris peace talks. After the war he retired and worked with the Pentagon devising 'future operational concepts'. No one was ever charged over the atrocities in Operation Speedy Express.[14]

A similar horror story of indiscriminate killing in areas deemed 'free-fire zones' is contained in *Tiger Force*, a book by journalists Michael Sallah and Mitch Weiss examining the operations of a Special Forces unit in the northern region of Vietnam around Quang Ngai. Many of the men in Tiger Force went battle-mad, one of them cutting off a baby's head. One of the worst offenders, Sergeant William Doyle, later joined the Phoenix Program. When Tiger Force was investigated for war crimes after the war Doyle screamed in rage that the unit did nothing more than they had done under the Phoenix Program, and the people at the top such as CIA director Richard Helms had known exactly what Phoenix operatives were doing out in the field.[15]

Word first leaked to the public about the Phoenix program in 1968. The American press began calling Phoenix a CIA assassination program, and the PRU as its 'hired killers'.[16]

Several soldiers started speaking out publicly against the Phoenix Program. One recruit, Francis Reitemeyer, refused to depart for Vietnam after he was told he was to be part of Phoenix, knowing that it targeted civilians for assassination. Reitemeyer told civil rights lawyers that during training he was told he would have a 'kill quota' of 50 bodies a month, and it was acceptable to 'resort to the most extreme forms of torture'.[17]

The Phoenix Program gave the CIA the chance to practise interrogation and torture techniques. Interrogations were carried out at the National Interrogation Centre in Saigon or at provincial interrogation centres where CIA interrogators worked alongside CIA-trained and funded South Vietnamese Special Branch police. One of those CIA interrogators, John Patrick Muldoon, said the Special Branch were already experienced in torture methods they knew from Asia and the former French colonialists, namely water torture and the use of electricity. A popular saying of the CIA-trained interrogators was *khong danh cho co* – 'If they are innocent, beat them until they become guilty.'[18]

The most violent Phoenix interrogations were carried out at the provincial interrogation centres, away from the eyes of senior CIA officials in Saigon. The cells were mass-produced concrete bunkers under the direction of John Patrick Muldoon and Tucker Gouglemann, CIA chief of Special Branch field operations. Former US Special Forces ran many of the provincial interrogation centres for the CIA, but few of them were trained interrogators.

British author Gordon Thomas uncovered evidence that in the summer of 1966 the CIA conducted bizarre experiments on VC prisoners that sounded more like the nightmare experiments of Nazi scientist Joseph Mengele. Two CIA doctors and a private physician went to Vietnam to see if a person's ideological views could be transformed via repeated doses of electric shocks. For several weeks they experimented on prisoners in a heavily guarded section of the Bien Hoa Hospital in Saigon. One prisoner was strapped to a table and shocked six times every twelve hours. After seven days of this treatment the man died. Dr Lloyd Cutter told Thomas he conducted several thousand electro-shock treatments at the hospital. After three weeks the prisoners were all dead and the CIA doctors flew home. Thomas documented that there were more CIA medical experiments on prisoners a year later, inserting tiny electrodes into various parts of the prisoners' brains. They used different frequencies to try and trigger different responses. One frequency caused the victim to vomit, another to defecate uncontrollably. One experiment tried to trigger a violent response and get prisoners to attack each other. That experiment failed and after a few weeks the team flew back to Washington. The subjects were executed and their bodies burned to ashes.[19]

CIA agent Barton Osborne told a US Senate committee that by late 1968 Phoenix had become 'a bad genocide program'. He told how he watched as a prisoner was killed by hammering a six-inch dowel into his ear. 'It was tapped through the brain until he died,' he told the congressmen. He saw a woman prisoner who was kept in a cage until she starved to death. He testified that at his provincial interrogation centre not one prisoner survived interrogation during his 18 months in the Phoenix Program.

The 1972 US Congressional inquiry concluded: 'The people of these United States have deliberately imposed upon the Vietnamese people a system of justice which admittedly denies due process of law . . . we appear to have violated the 1949 Geneva Convention for the protection of civilian people.' The inquiry found 'torture is a regularly accepted part of the interrogation . . . US civilian and military personnel have participated for over three years in the deliberate denial of due process of law to thousands of people held in secret centers built with US dollars'.[20]

It was a cry that was to be heard again 34 years later as the horrors of the US run prison at Abu Ghraib in Baghdad were revealed.

Public opinion was turning so strongly against Phoenix and the assassination squads that pressure was on congressmen to demand answers in their 1970 hearings. Colby denied Phoenix was an assassination program, claiming it was a program devised to find and eliminate an enemy hiding among innocent civilians. However the CIA preferred living in the shadows, not in the glare of Senate hearings and on the front pages of newspapers. By the end of 1970 Phoenix was transferred to the Vietnamese. Once in their hands it became an instrument of political repression: the government used it to eliminate political opposition and local officials used it to get rid of rivals – political, family and business.

The fact remains that the CIA's adoption of the Phoenix Program did help the Americans' war effort. The sheer number of enemy and civilians killed thwarted the Viet Cong and the North Vietnamese. After the war several North Vietnamese military leaders conceded Phoenix had severely damaged them and resulted in thousands of Viet Cong deaths. General Tran Do told historian Stanley Karnow that Phoenix had been 'extremely destructive'. Nguyen Co Thach, united Vietnam's first foreign minister, said Phoenix 'wiped out many of our bases'. One veteran Viet Cong leader, Madame Nguyen Thi Dinh, said they never feared a division of troops, but the infiltration of spies into their ranks 'created tremendous difficulties for us'.[21]

Ted Serong, who had quit the Australian Army to work with the CIA and the Phoenix Program, was unapologetic. 'Yes, we did kill teachers and postmen. But it was the way to conduct the war. They were part of the Viet Cong infrastructure. I wanted to make sure we won the battle.' Serong likened the atrocities to traffic laws, declaring 'everyone goes over the speed limit from time to time.'[22]

When Petersen had his run-in with Methven, refusing to set up assassination squads, Serong had already left the Australian Army. Had he still been in charge of the Australian Army Training Team he would undoubtedly have put pressure on Petersen to agree to the assassination squads.

'The only counter to terror is counter-terror,' Serong later said in an interview with *Time* magazine. 'Our job then was to organise special groups who would behave towards the opposition as the opposition were behaving towards our people. It was not a very salubrious operation. As I said to my own people at the time, this is a gutter fight and the only way to fight is to get down in the gutter. We had started a counter-terror program in another area run by an Australian. It worked very well. So, in effect, what Methven was saying to Petersen was, "Look, your Australian buddy over there is doing this. Get off your backside and get things running in parallel."'[23]

Phoenix was an ugly mess that Barry Petersen was wise to stay out of. It might have cost him his post at Ban Me Thuot, but history was to prove him right. For an army man like him, duty and honour were equally important. Barry Petersen can look back on his army life and know there are some lines he never crossed.

15
STIRRED, NOT SHAKEN

At the end of his second tour of Vietnam in June 1971, Barry Petersen returned to Australia. Once home, he suffered from what nearly all soldiers, sailors and airmen returning from war go through when they get back to normality – not necessarily post traumatic stress, but trouble adapting to the workaday world of civvie street.

To go from the high tension, pressure and excitement of dodging bullets in the jungle to living in a small cabin-sized room in the suburbs of Canberra was particularly difficult. No more the camaraderie of war and living in constant danger of being killed. Petersen was a single man and his military-issue home was a tiny, one-room apartment in a military hostel. The bland drab uniformity of the Australian capital and the bureaucrats who largely inhabited them were a far cry from the longhouses and rice wine ceremonies of Vietnam's Central Highlands.

By mid-1972 President Nixon was desperately trying to extricate himself from the disaster of the Vietnam War. Henry Kissinger had started secret peace talks in Paris with the North Vietnamese even though American B-52s were still bombing North Vietnam. Five men linked to Nixon's White House had just been arrested for breaking into the Democratic Party's national headquarters in the Watergate building in Washington. Protest marches against the war were growing bigger and bigger.

After his last combat stint, Petersen was assigned to doing the paperwork equipping the Australian forces in Vietnam. It was an important job, and it was good to have an experienced hand decide what the troops on the ground really needed. Some officers itched to get to Canberra, where promotion often came faster while rubbing shoulders with the right people. Petersen found it so boring he thought he was going out of his mind.

Part of his military duties included making up the numbers in the Canberra diplomatic cocktail party circuit. One evening he took a friend, Dr Julia Potter, to a reception at the Swedish Embassy. As he sipped his drink the Swedish first secretary brought over a solidly built block of a man.

'Barry, I would like you to meet the Soviet Union charge d'affaires, Mr Smirnov,' the Swedish diplomat said.

'Mr Smirnov I would like to introduce Major Barry Petersen and Dr Potter.'

The Soviet diplomat beamed and shook Petersen's hand saying: 'Ah, Major Petersen, you had a very interesting tour of duty in South Vietnam.'

Petersen was taken aback. 'To which tour do you refer, Mr Smirnov?'

'To your first tour, when you were with the Montagnard tribes. That must have been fascinating.'

Petersen was shocked. How could the second most senior Soviet diplomat in Australia know about his time in the Central Highlands?

Perhaps the Soviet Embassy had clipped Gerald Stone's story seven years earlier, but Petersen was staggered the Soviets would still remember it. Did they have a file on him? Did they know he was working for the CIA at the time?

Petersen changed the subject, but the conversation made him realise he was not just another major in the Australian army but a person of interest to the Soviet Union. After reporting the exchange with Mr Smirnov to his superiors, he was stuck in the shadowy world of spy agencies and spooks. Barry Petersen was to discover it was a murky world, and that once you are caught up in it, you never really escape.

A short time later an opportunity came for him to return to Malaysia as an instructor to their army. He seized the chance; he couldn't stand life in the dreary corridors of Defence Headquarters and he had loved his time in Malaya in the late 1950s. He spoke the language, relished the climate and loved the people. His job was at the Malaysian School of Training on the west coast and he moved into an old rambling two-storey colonial house on an isolated beach near the defence training school. For him, this was more like the life he wanted to live.

A few months after Petersen moved in he was working upstairs when he heard people moving around on the ground floor. He went down just in time to see two hefty-looking men leaving through the open front door. He called out but they kept going. He shouted out he was calling the police, and one of the men turned and said in a thick Russian accent that he apologised, and that he was looking for someone else.

Something about their manner, not just the fact that they had entered his home unannounced, bothered him. Petersen had heard Soviet spies were active in the area, and he decided to find out about the men. He traced them to a hotel in the nearby town of Port Dickson, but they had just checked out. However they had given their address as care of the Soviet Embassy in Singapore. These were obviously not the smartest spooks but Petersen took no chances. He had his house searched for electronic bugs but nothing was found. But this was not the last time his senses were on alert. His next brush with Soviet spies was even more strange.

In 1975, when Petersen was almost at the end of his Malaysian posting, communist terrorists fired rockets into five military camps, two of which were close to Petersen's house. It was a step up in aggression – two weeks earlier, 12 Malaysian soldiers had been killed by communist-laid mines and booby traps. Investigators found the mines had been smuggled from Vietnam into Malaysia through Thailand.

Late on the night of the second attack Petersen's phone rang. A man who had no distinguishable accent, said: 'Major Petersen, I'm calling because you can help us . . . we are prepared to pay for your help . . . $20 000 for the information you can provide.'

Petersen couldn't believe his ears. He asked the caller to repeat what he had just said.

'Never mind that. We want you to help us and we will pay you handsomely.'

Petersen thought it must be the bluntest offer a spy had ever made. He played along to find out more.

'What sort of information do you want?' he asked.

'Military information.'

He burst out laughing at the ineptitude of the bribery attempt.

'I am an army officer. Surely you don't seriously expect me to give you any military information?'

The caller's voice hardened. 'If you provide the information we want, you will receive $20 000 cash. If you don't, then you will die.'

A chill ran up Petersen's spine. It sounded like a corny line from a B-grade film. But he was all on his own in an isolated house. The neighbouring homes were weekenders used by wealthy Chinese so there was no one nearby to help him.

'Who are you?' Petersen said down the phone, guessing the answer.

'Our people were responsible for the rocket attacks on the Malaysian army bases and the recent success against the security forces near the Thai border. Major Petersen we have been watching you for some time. We have photographs of you and we know your car. We know all about you and your movements. We know that you are alone in your house this weekend. Even now we are watching your house.'

Petersen was answering the phone in the open doorway leading onto the upstairs veranda. He slid to the floor and lay down . . . just in case. To keep the man talking, he asked what sort of military information he wanted.

'We want details of the security patrols and ambushes around the Port Dickson garrison, the locations of all the ammunition bunkers, and the number of troops in the garrison.'

Petersen saw a way out. 'But I'm a foreign officer, I don't have access to that kind of information.'

The voice on the other end was very hard. 'You can get it for us,' it said simply. 'By tomorrow afternoon.'

The caller told Petersen to drive into town the next day and pick up a person waiting at a particular bus stop in Port Dickson at 2pm precisely. That person would guide Petersen to a meeting place, where he would hand over the information and get the cash in return.

'Do it, or you will die. Don't try to call the police or the army. We will know if you do,' the man said, and hung up.

Petersen was worried. If he tried to drive out of his house, the only way to town was a deserted jungle road along the coast. He had to assume the communists would be waiting for him. He had to risk calling for help even if they had somehow tapped his phone.

He tried calling the Australian Embassy but could not reach anybody. He called a local Chinese friend and in veiled language asked him to contact the Malaysian base commander and the senior Australian military officer, Colonel Victor Stevenson. But no one called him or came to the rescue that long and sleepless night. In the morning Petersen decided to risk driving to town where he met Colonel Stevenson. Together they went to see the Malaysian base commander, Colonel Mohammed Ariff. Colonel Ariff asked Petersen to keep the rendezvous so they could arrest the terrorists.

'Would you like a pistol for your protection?'

Petersen declined the offer, thinking it would only invite trouble. Police briefed him on what to do. The plan was to have 60 undercover cops stationed around the bus stop. One would be in a battered taxi facing the bus stop arguing with the driver over the fare. 'If shooting starts get out of your car and roll underneath it,' Petersen was told.

Petersen nervously drove to the rendezvous point and at precisely 2pm pulled up near the bus stop. He waited and waited, but no one came up asking for a lift. After a while police let him know they were calling off the surveillance. Who knows what had happened. They thought it might have been a test, to see if he could be trusted. Perhaps the undercover cops had been spotted. Maybe it was a hoax after all. Or maybe whoever had called Petersen got their information from someone else.

Because no one knew what could happen next, Petersen was provided with guards until he ended his tour of duty in Malaysia a few weeks later. His phones were monitored, but the mysterious, unsubtle spy was never heard from again.

Shortly before he left Malaysia, on 12 March 1975, Petersen heard the news on the radio that Ban Me Thuot had fallen to the advancing North Vietnamese. It hit him like a bomb. He was in his house alone, and burst into tears. 'I wept and wept. I had never done that before. It really hit me. All those people I had worked with, people who had trusted me with their lives. Many of them had saved my life several times over. They had put their lives on the line to defend the South; they did not want to live under communism and fought to stop them taking over their country. They were betrayed by the Americans who had promised to protect them.'

Petersen monitored the events in Vietnam closely and worried about his friends.

Ban Me Thuot was the first target of the invading North Vietnamese army. Petersen had been right, the Highlands and Ban Me Thuot were absolutely vital to the survival of Saigon. The North Vietnamese generals picked it as it was not as well defended as other Highland towns, but managed to trick Saigon into thinking its main thrust would come in the Hue/Da Nang region of central Vietnam. The North Vietnamese quietly amassed three divisions in the Highlands west of Ban Me Thuot, far outnumbering the single ARVN regiment in the town. The rural intelligence network run by Petersen that would have picked up such a large movement of men and equipment had broken down long before and the North Vietnamese attack caught the ARVN by surprise. Any soldiers in the area fled. The road to Saigon was wide open. Word of the defeat in the Highlands spread quickly and ARVN troops simply ran away from key defensive positions in central Vietnam.

After the Australian forces pulled out of the country in 1972 and the last American combat troops left in 1973, it was only a matter of time before the government fell. The US called it Vietnamization, handing over the defence of the country to the South Vietnamese. It was window dressing. Without the power of the United States, the collapse of South Vietnam, with a government corrupt to the core, was inevitable.

Petersen listened, devastated, as the news came in of the slaughter of the people of Ban Me Thuot as they fled towards Saigon. Of the 250 000 people fleeing the Central Highlands, only about one-third made it to the coast. Petersen later learned that many of the Montagnard troops turned on the fleeing South Vietnamese, using military techniques he had taught them to ambush retreating troops. Many of his Tiger Men joined the FULRO independence fighters, hoping they would win some concessions from the North Vietnamese conquerors. Once again they were to be betrayed. Many of those Petersen had worked with were executed by the Viet Cong; others spent years in 'reeducation camps'. Many of those who had escaped over the border were killed when Vietnam invaded Cambodia in 1978 in retaliation for raids on Vietnam by Cambodian Khmer Rouge fighters.

A few weeks after Saigon fell, Petersen received a letter from the Philippines. 'It had been sent on to me by the defence attaché at the Australian Embassy in Kuala Lumpur. It was my former translator Y-Jut saying he had approached the defence attaché in Manila asking to contact me. The war correspondent Denis Warner wrote in his book *Not With Guns Alone* that Australian Embassy people in Saigon simply abandoned their staff. When I was trying to get Y-Jut into Australia, officers who were senior to me said: "Why are you worried about this Montagnard and his family? What are they to you?"

'I thought it was a terrible attitude. I couldn't understand how they could just wipe their hands of people who had been loyal to them.

'Y-Jut told me he had managed to flee overland with his family to Nha Trang on the coast then the CIA flew him and his family from the beach by helicopter to a US Navy vessel. He had continued working for the CIA after I left, and they did get a lot of their people out. Like most refugees Y-Jut and his family were taken to the nearest land. He was in a camp in the Philippines waiting to find out what would happen to him. He confirmed that he got no help from the Australian Embassy and was asking me to help get him to Australia.'

As soon as Petersen returned home he went to the Immigration Department. 'I told them Y-Jut had been a valuable employee in Vietnam who had risked his life for Australian troops and that I wanted to get him to Australia. But they just laughed at me. They said I had no hope.

'I replied that if I didn't get any positive results within six weeks I would go to the press. When nothing happened I wrote to Denis Warner who had been writing stories about the plight of the Vietnamese refugees.'

Petersen reminded Warner they had met in Vietnam and told him of Y-Jut's position. He had since been taken to the United States with his family, but he was destitute and unemployed. Petersen wrote to Warner: 'The message I wish to get home to the public is that here is one of the Vietnamese who personally risked his life for Australians for quite a lengthy period. Surely we Australians owe something to him. He personally saved my life on more than one occasion and more than proved his devotion and loyalty to me over a dangerous two-year period. He is, because of his loyal service to us, perhaps more entitled than most to the right to permanent residence here in Australia.'

Petersen fought for some time to get the Labor government of Gough Whitlam to listen. He built an extension onto his Queensland home to provide Y-Jut and his family with a place to stay and lined up a job for him so he could sponsor him and his family to Australia. But the government would not move.

Australian TV journalist Ray Martin was based in the US at the time and went to Seattle to interview Y-Jut and his family. A tug of war began as the Americans were not prepared to let Y-Jut go to Australia. It would have been a blow to their pride. Y-Jut had worked with US Special Forces as a translator after Petersen left and they regarded it as their duty to look after him. After stories of his shoddy living quarters and unemployment appeared in the media in Australia, American Vietnam veterans were stirred into action and found him a job and a house to live in. Y-Jut told Petersen the Americans were telling him Australians were all racist. He then said his wife had fallen ill and was receiving treatment in Seattle, so he had decided to stay there. Petersen felt he had done all he could but was disillusioned by the lack of support from the Australian government to his pleas. After so many years of service to his country it must have been a bitter pill to swallow.

Petersen's time in the army was coming to an end. When he returned to Australia from Malaysia he informed his superiors he had developed osteoarthritis and so needed to stay in a hot climate to keep healthy. Perhaps it was his body finding an excuse never to go near Canberra again. He was promoted to Lieutenant Colonel and posted to the 1st Military District Headquarters in balmy Queensland.

Petersen also became head of the Queensland division of the Australian Army Training Team Vietnam Veterans' Association. He felt strongly that the South Vietnamese allies had been betrayed and abandoned after the war. In 1976 he proposed to his association members that they invite South Vietnamese veterans to march with them on Anzac Day. This was unheard of at the time. The team members agreed, but the RSL in Brisbane refused to allow South Vietnamese ex-soldiers to join the traditional Anzac Day march. They may have thought that was the end of the matter, but Petersen was stubborn and knew how to use the media. The story was leaked, creating the necessary outrage. The RSL backed down and in 1976 former South Vietnamese soldiers who had escaped to Australia proudly joined the members of the AATTV in the Anzac Day march in Brisbane. It is now commonplace for South Vietnamese ex-servicemen to march in Anzac Day parades across Australia, along with allied veterans of other wars.

Petersen finally retired from the army in 1979. He left with the rank of Lieutenant Colonel after 26 years of service. Many of his colleagues believe he should have reached a higher rank in the military hierarchy. It was true, he had had a remarkable career, carrying out unique roles as a captain that required superior skills of diplomacy as well as battle command experience as a major. He was an acknowledged leader of men in extraordinary, difficult situations. His hands-on knowledge of military intelligence and accurate predictions of the way the Vietnam War would develop should have had him marked to go right to the top.

But the military machine does not work on logic and Lieutenant Colonel Petersen had a black mark against him. Somewhere in the bowels of the military system, suspicion still hung over Petersen's role with the Montagnard and his relations with the CIA. On top of that, Petersen refused to play the necessary military snakes and ladders game to gain a promotion. He never did ingratiating well. Nor was he a cunning practitioner of office politics, having severely bitten the hand of his boss and paymaster in Vietnam, the CIA. Even today he doesn't suffer fools gladly, and he found plenty of those in the ranks of the military.

His dislike of Canberra and his refusal to return there also limited his advance. Just prior to his retirement he was asked about a post that would have given him a promotion to full colonel, but got the word that this post only went to married officers. Petersen said he would not get married just for the sake of convenience, and it was then he decided it was time to strike out on a new career path and bow out of the military. With his service retirement pay he set up a farm and landscape gardening business near Cairns, then a fast-growing town.

However, even after he left the army and embarked on a peaceful career among trees and pot plants, Petersen was to be frequently dragged back into the murky world of spooks. He was living in Cairns in 1984 when he got a phone call out of the blue from a former army captain called Gary Roy Scott. Scott had a bizarre offer for Petersen to earn big money by training the indigenous tribesmen of Irian Jaya (the Indonesian province on the western half of the island it shares with Papua New Guinea) to fight for independence.

'I asked Scott if it was authorised by ASIS and he replied, "Yes. It's worth $5000 a month and there's $150 000 insurance if you get killed".

'I thought this was bloody stupid. What use would that be to me if I was dead?

'I rang my contact in ASIS and he said it certainly was not sanctioned by ASIS and if it did have any backing it must be from some renegade group. He suggested I take it to the Australian Federal Police.' Petersen did just that.

The AFP asked Petersen to play along with Scott while they monitored the situation and eventually arrested Scott, charging him under the *Crimes (Foreign Incursions and Recruitment) Act* with trying to recruit mercenaries to overthrow the government of Indonesia. It was a sensational case and Petersen found himself dragged into the news as he gave evidence against Scott in court. In 1987 Scott was convicted of trying to recruit the former army officer and sentenced to 12 months' jail.

After that, one would think those in the shadowy world of mercenaries would know to steer clear of Barry Petersen. But it wasn't the case. A couple of years later he received another mysterious phone call, this time from a man living in Cairns who originally came from the Seychelles, a poverty-stricken island group east of Africa. The man said he had read about Petersen in a 1987 *Time* magazine article about his experience with the Montagnard. Petersen will not reveal the man's name.

'He wanted me to help him recover the Seychelles from their Marxist government. I thought, oh no, not again!

'I told him I was too old for this sort of thing. But he wanted to meet me anyway. I checked with my contact at ASIS and they hadn't heard anything about this bloke. When I rang the Federal Police officer I had dealt with earlier on the Gary Roy Scott case he said they had heard these Seychelles guys were sniffing around ex-military people and were keen to check them out.

'I arranged to meet this man at the Pier, a shopping and restaurant complex in Cairns. I would sit facing outward to the mountains and the police would dress up as tourists with cameras pretending to take pictures of the view. The guy would have no option but to sit opposite me facing inward so they could get a good photograph of him.

'Well, we did meet. This guy told me I would be right for life after this operation as I would have so much money. I said that may be true until the next coup and then he and I would be up against a wall being shot. I didn't see the police but they later told me they got the pictures they needed. Eventually the whole scheme fell through.'

The saga didn't end there. In 1992 an AFP officer threatened to subpoena Petersen to force him to cooperate in an arrest he planned on the Seychellean man. 'I wasn't keen as I had become rather friendly with him and his wife over the years. I thought he was harmless and a bit of a dreamer. Besides I disliked doing what I was doing, as I had been reporting what I learned to the AFP. The Seychellean bragged to me he had an informant inside the AFP, a woman. I was worried because she might learn I was informing on him to the AFP, and I could be in danger if she told him.'

It was all very dirty and murky, and Petersen was getting fed up with it. The final straw was when the AFP officer tried to threaten him into testifying against the Seychellean. Petersen got stuck into the officer, saying he was already working undercover for another AFP officer and would cease to cooperate any further.

'That was it. I pulled out and walked away. I didn't need this kind of cloak-and-dagger hassle anymore. As far as I know the Seychellean was never arrested.'

For Barry Petersen a quieter life beckoned.

16

BETRAYAL

Almost ten years after he left the army, Barry Petersen published his memoirs. Titled *Tiger Men*, it recounted his time with the Montagnard and how he was sacked by the CIA. Petersen may have thought he was telling the whole story, but it was after his book's publication that Peter Young told him the CIA had been prepared to kill him if he did not leave the Central Highlands quietly and quickly.

Petersen was outraged. In 1979, when he saw the film *Apocalypse Now* he had seen some amazing similarities to his own life. The controversial blockbuster directed by Francis Ford Coppola could easily have been based on much of his own tour of duty in Vietnam: the parallels between himself and the Colonel Kurtz character played by Marlon Brando were striking.

Like Kurtz, Petersen was sent into the mountain jungles of Vietnam by the CIA to build a guerilla force of fierce Montagnard tribesmen to fight the communists.

Like Kurtz, Petersen's mission was top secret. Two years before the Australian government told the public it was going to send combat troops to fight in Vietnam, this young officer was already leading a force of more than a thousand tribesmen guerillas against the Viet Cong, copying the communist hit-and-run tactics to great effect. Petersen's mission for the CIA was so secret that only a few in the Australian government knew of it. Just a handful of Australian military knew this Australian Army officer was operating under orders from the CIA rather than Australian military command.

Like Kurtz, the Highland guerilla force of Montagnard tribesmen became more loyal to Petersen than the CIA masters pulling strings behind the scenes and the largely corrupt South Vietnamese military government.

Like Kurtz, the tribesmen came to regard Petersen as a demi-god. In a traditional ceremony they made Petersen a paramount tribal chief and bestowed on him the name of Dam San, a legendary warrior who became so powerful he tried to fight the power of the sun.

But Barry Petersen had no idea that, like Kurtz, the CIA were wary of his growing influence in the Highlands and feared Petersen was getting out of control. He knew he had ruffled feathers when he refused a CIA order to set up assassination squads, and sent back a CIA agent in disgrace after he'd tried to set up assassination squads behind his back. But Petersen never imagined that, like Kurtz, the CIA were prepared to kill him because he would not fight the war their way.

For Petersen this was an extreme act of betrayal. He had risked his life for the CIA fighting communists in the remote Highlands. He had done his best and succeeded in holding back Viet Cong from a strategically important region. He had helped thwart a Montagnard rebellion against the South Vietnamese. He had been recognised for his bravery and accomplishments with medals from both the Australian and South Vietnamese governments.

But now he learned the CIA had been ready to kill him. He was furious, and mystified. Was it because he had refused to play their dirty games with the assassination squads? Was it because he blocked CIA plans to put in people who were incompetent or whose personality and approach did not fit the unique requirements of the mission? Was it because he had grown too close to the Montagnard and sympathised with their cause? Was it because he had embarrassed the CIA when the US ambassador asked why an American could not do what he had done in the Highlands? Was it because he had gone too far with the Montagnard, that he was regarded as being out of control by the CIA? Was he seen as a loose cannon who knew too much about CIA operations?

Petersen would never really know but the answer is most probably all of the above. Peter Young believes the CIA was furious with Petersen as he bucked their control and was seen as 'going native', being more loyal to his Montagnard troops than to his CIA masters. It was common knowledge that he had infuriated some very senior Vietnamese with his popularity among the Montagnard forces. He was pursuing political agendas that were not in line with those of the CIA. In CIA eyes Petersen had become a renegade, and renegades were not tolerated, especially if they knew a lot of secrets.

Stu Methven published a book in 2008, *Laughter in the Shadows – A CIA Memoir*, in which he revealed what was really going on behind the scenes when Petersen was sacked.

Methven describes how he got into 'serious trouble' with General Vinh Loc, who blasted him after the Montagnard rebellion and blamed CIA support for training Montagnard militia troops for fomenting the uprising. General Loc demanded to see Methven after the rebellion and slammed down a set of photographs on the table. They were gruesome pictures of mutilated and decapitated bodies of the massacred Vietnamese soldiers. Vinh Loc pointed to the photographs and told Methven furiously: 'This is what comes of your meddling with the Montagnards and stirring them up against the Vietnamese!'

General Loc told Methven he was going to report him to US ambassador General Maxwell Taylor – the same ambassador who had praised Petersen for his Montagnard program and wanted to know why an American could not do it. Methven does not mention Petersen in his book, even though the Australian was at the same meeting.

Ambassador Taylor immediately summoned Methven. Also present was the American military commander General William Westmoreland. Methven was facing the two most senior Americans in Vietnam. It was not going to be pleasant. Methven began by rebutting General Loc's accusations, pointing out that the Montagnard troops he had been involved with had not joined the rebellion. In fact, it was Petersen's troops who stayed out of the rebellion, but Methven ignored this fact.

Methven said the rebellion was a sign of the growing hostility between the Montagnard and the Vietnamese, and that FULRO was encouraging the rebels. He warned FULRO was still active and might spark another rebellion by declaring independence for the Montagnard in the Highlands.

Ambassador Taylor, who had been Westmoreland's commander in World War Two, was furious. He was angry at Westmoreland because the army's Special Forces had not prevented their Montagnard militia from killing the Vietnamese soldiers. One Special Forces unit had slept through a massacre in their own camp.

Ambassador Taylor then turned his fury on Methven. 'He… said the last thing he needed in the middle of a war that was already hard enough to justify and explain was a "tribal rebellion", a war within a war. He then gave us our marching orders which were to rein in FULRO and ask them to tamp down, at least for the time being, this call for independence, and to make sure there would be no more massacres in our Special Forces camps!'[1]

From this account by Methven, it is clear that after the rebellion and the resulting anger from senior Vietnamese like General Loc, the US simply wanted to wash its hands of the whole Montagnard mess. Methven must have come out of that meeting with his ears still ringing. The CIA operation financing outfits such as Petersen's Truong Son Force came to an end. The training and control of Montagnard militia forces were eventually taken from the CIA and handed to the US military. Petersen was seen as far too sympathetic to the Montagnard as well as tied up with FULRO. He had to go, and he had to go quietly without stirring up the Montagnard once again.

Petersen was steeped in army discipline and although he had already rejected CIA pressure to set up assassination squads, he was in no position to kick up a fuss when the CIA ordered him out of the Highlands. They were the ones supplying the money for the operation. If the money and supplies stopped there simply was no way the Tiger Men could continue even if they did have enormous respect for Petersen. He had tried to appeal against the CIA decision, arguing his mission was a success and he was the best person for the job. But once his own Australian commander told him it was all over, that he had to leave the country quickly, Petersen was disciplined enough to realise his time was up. Had he kicked up a fuss, spoken to journalists in Saigon or tried to use his contacts with the South Vietnamese to fight to stay on, then Petersen may very well have met with the 'accident' that Peter Young discovered was waiting in the wings. It was that military discipline which may have just saved his life.

17
BACK TO ASIA

Petersen had never married and with few real ties in Australia he found himself drawn back to South East Asia. He felt more comfortable with the people there. In 1990 he started to look for a place in Asia where he could live and work.

In 1987 he had been invited by a documentary filmmaker, Evan Ham, to return to Vietnam for the first time since the war. Ham wanted to record Petersen's reaction as a Vietnam veteran to what he saw in the country in which he had fought 16 years earlier. The few foreigners allowed into Vietnam at that time were restricted to the Hanoi area. The Vietnamese authorities knew what Petersen had done during the war. He heard that the Vietnamese Foreign Minister, Nguyen Co Thach, made the decision to allow him into Vietnam but Petersen was warned there were to be 'no Rambo actions'.

Petersen found that Hanoi was still suffering badly 12 years after the war ended. The pits dug alongside the roads that people used during air raids had not been filled in. Buildings were still badly damaged because no one could afford to repair them. The communist government had not yet allowed free enterprise, which meant there were no street stalls.

'The North Vietnamese seemed to know all about me and my time in Ban Me Thuot. I must admit I was apprehensive about how they would react to me, but they treated me politely and with respect,' Petersen said. Their visit coincided with a group of American ex-servicemen led by a former colonel who wanted to offer medical assistance to their former foe. They had artificial limbs which they wanted to donate. Petersen said he watched with frustration as once again the Americans bungled the goodwill gesture. 'They seemed to be going well and the Vietnamese were interested, but then the Americans dropped in the big word "however", and said they would like to resolve the question of American soldiers missing in action from the war. Typical bloody Americans. They couldn't just come and offer medical help, they had to have strings attached. Afterwards one of the Vietnamese came up to me and said, "Vietnam lost hundreds of thousands of people who will never be traced, gone up in smoke in napalm bombs and blasted to bits by B-52 bombs – and they are worried about 1800 of their troops missing. Why can't they just get on with life?"'

That year Petersen decided to set up a small business in Cairns importing Vietnamese ceramics and made several subsequent trips there. The business was not a great success, and lasted only a couple of years.

Copies of his memoirs had made their way over to Vietnam and during one visit for ceramics he met a Vietnamese general called Hoang Phuong, who told him he had been in charge of the North Vietnamese army infiltrating the Darlac Province where Petersen's Tiger Men operated.

'General Phuong revealed to me he had fought against me. This brought me up with a start as I was a bit anxious how he would react to me as a former enemy. But there were no hard feelings. He said that mistakes were made by both sides, and that he hoped we would learn from those mistakes and never have another war like that.

'I found the former enemy, particularly combat soldiers, do not bear a grudge against other combat soldiers. That is true with everyone. The ones who fought generally say let bygones be bygones. If you were a front line soldier you very much understand what the front line soldier on the other side went through.'

In the same year he started his new business Petersen made a trip to Vietnam with scriptwriter Ro Hume, who was researching a possible movie on Petersen. The actor Mel Gibson had read his memoirs and was interested in turning Petersen's wartime story into a movie or TV mini series. Petersen and Hume travelled to Ban Me Thuot planning to seek out some of his old friends among the Vietnamese and Montagnard.

Vietnamese officials kept an eye on Westerners, particularly former enemy combatants, so Petersen and Hume adopted the cover of being journalists doing research for a documentary on the amount of foreign aid Vietnam needed to recover from the war.

Petersen's first CIA handler, Bryan Mills (LEFT), catching up on some sleep during an Air America flight between Saigon and Ban Me Thuot.

Montagnard independence leader Y-Bham Enuol (RIGHT) became a friend of Petersen's. His letter appealing to South Vietnam's president to keep Petersen in the Central Highlands was the final straw for CIA and Vietnamese leaders, who thought Petersen was far too close to the Montagnard.

From left, the legendary US intelligence operator Lieutenant Colonel Lou Conein, who gave the green light for the coup against President Diem; CIA handler Stuart Methven, who asked Petersen to turn his troops into assassins; US Special Forces Captain Vernon Gillespie; and Petersen's translator and fixer Y-Jut Buon To. They are standing in front of an Air America plane after the Montagnard rebellion.

If not for the constant threat of war, the Montagnard people would have gone about their lives in their traditional way using elephants as work animals (ABOVE) and farming the lands they lived on. Many of the young men of the Highlands villages became part of Barry Petersen's Tiger Men and trained at the Buon Enao base (BELOW).

Tiger Men (ABOVE) proudly show off the tiger badge on their berets Petersen gave them to make them feel their unit was special. The name came from the Viet Cong who offered rewards for killing them.

Senior Tiger Man fighter Y-Kren Nie with the tiger badge.

Barry Petersen on operations with the Tiger Men

Captain Barry Petersen in the bush near Buon Enao in his tiger beret, with Warrant Officer Bevan Stokes behind him. On the right is translator Y-To.

Bevan Stokes (FAR RIGHT) at the American base at A Shau with the Nung bodyguard who saved his life.

Y-Liu Buon Ya (CENTRE), who was being groomed to lead the Tiger Men, with Montagnard troops preparing for an operation.

Petersen's driver Vuong in the tiger-striped camouflage uniform which caused the Viet Cong to dub Petersen's Montagnard unit the Tiger Men. Vuong is holding Petersen's pet sun bear at his house in Ban Me Thuot.

Petersen stands inside a tiger skin he was given as a gift by the Rhade tribe.

Captain Ian Teague sleeps with Petersen's leopard cub Fatima during a visit. Fatima was later killed by poisoned chicken Petersen believed was meant for him.

Barry Petersen in traditional Montagnard dress at his official farewell from the Central Highlands in 1965, drinking the ceremonial rice wine.

Petersen at his farewell. He had to have two tribal costumes stitched together to fit him.

Barry Petersen at the 2008 Remembrance Day ceremony in Bangkok.
The Military Cross is the first medal of 13 on his chest.

In Ban Me Thuot Petersen was delighted to meet people who had been on his personal staff 25 years earlier. They met secretly and had a wonderful reunion. But they were being watched by the local secret police who became suspicious. For a while the travelling pair were placed under house arrest.

Petersen managed to slip away and went to his old Tiger Men training camp at Buon Enao, which after the war had been turned into a communist reeducation centre. By the time he saw the old camp it was empty and abandoned. Bevan Stokes' base at Lac Thien was also deserted and dilapidated. Every sign it had once been a thriving Montagnard camp was gone. The old airstrip had almost completely been reclaimed by the jungle.

Petersen and Hume were invited to stop at a Montagnard village where they were offered the fermented rice wine in a formal ceremony. Petersen didn't recognise any of the tribespeople in the village, but apparently the village chief recognised him. As they were leaving the old man held his hand and bent over it in the traditional manner of honouring a paramount chief.

Petersen was deeply moved that his ties from all those years ago still meant something.

The secret police who were keeping watch on them had been suspicious about who this visiting Australian really was and must have been extremely puzzled when the village chief paid him homage.

Petersen had never really felt comfortable in Australia since the Vietnam War. His soul seemed at home in Asia, and in 1995 he moved to Bangkok where he started up a business advising Western companies how to negotiate Asian bureaucracy and taxes and establish themselves in South East Asia. He's retired from that now, but he continues to live in Bangkok and his former Thai employees have become his extended family.

He hasn't forgotten his past and is still active in helping the Montagnard when he can. He's urged the United Nations High Commissioner for Refugees (UNHCR) to stop using Vietnamese to interview Montagnard refugees as they felt it was intimidating. Petersen said one Montagnard he helped was interrogated by a Vietnamese working for UNHCR and demanded to know the names and addresses of all his relatives in Vietnam, his address in Bangkok and to name those who were helping him in Bangkok.

Petersen admits he helped a few Montagnard get over borders quietly and without notice. He's been asked to publicly advocate for Montagnard independence, but he's reluctant to do so as he feels it only brings retribution on the Montagnard still in Vietnam. Many of the Montagnard who escaped Vietnam settled in North Carolina near the Special Forces base at Fort Bragg. He is pleased the Special Forces soldiers felt a duty to look after their Montagnard allies.

However, Petersen is sceptical about what advocates for the Montagnard really achieve for them. 'There are a lot of Americans who associate themselves with the Montagnard and promise they can do this or that. Some claim to be ex-Special Forces or former CIA, but aren't. The Montagnard support movement attracts some people who like to think they are playing cloak and dagger and are still fighting the Vietnam War.

'I feel obliged to do what I can for the Montagnard. There is not much I can do from here now, though. If I do have contact with my old friends in Vietnam it can endanger them.

But I will do what I can to help anyone who manages to get out of Vietnam. These people helped me a lot during the war and were very loyal to me. I feel I should do my best for any of their people who might manage to get out. Maybe I am subconsciously paying them back for helping me during the war. I don't see it that way, nor as if I am clearing my conscience. I know what they went through, and what they are still going through.' For Petersen, the loyalty he was shown deserves his continued respect – and he will always be there to help the Montagnard if he can.

18
OLD SOLDIERS NEVER DIE

Barry Petersen stoically insists he does not suffer nightmares from his experiences in Vietnam. He knows he is one of the few. Other veterans' lives fell apart after the war. But Barry insists that the only times he relived memories of blood and death was in the quiet of the night immediately after the action. Back then, it was not the fighting, but what happened after, that affected him.

'You'd search the bodies after a killing, looking for letters, maps, anything that could provide valuable intelligence. But you'd also find photos of family, wives, girlfriends. You'd know them as real people with family and lovers back home who would miss them. You'd realise they were no different to you, just soldiers doing what they are told.'

Not everyone can separate themselves so well. One of those still suffering nightmares is Petersen's one-time offsider, Warrant

Officer Bevan Stokes. In 2008 when he talked for the first time about the war he fought in the Central Highlands under Barry Petersen's command, Stokes broke down, staring silently at the floor as the memories came flooding back. 'I've never spoken about this before. I've never told my wife . . . I have nightmares sometimes,' he said in a quiet voice. His eyes screwed up and slowly he broke into deep, racking sobs. 'You shouldn't talk about it . . . It's best not said, but this is the truth of what happened. I remember shooting a young bloke. There was blood everywhere, but none on his face. He looked so young. His eyes opened up and he looked at me . . . he looked straight into me. He didn't have anger or hate in his expression. He just stared into my eyes as he bled to death. It's like he was asking me over and over . . . "Why?"'

Stokes paused for a long time, then sighed. 'I often wonder what sort of man that young Vietnamese kid would have become. War is a bastard of a thing. That kid had a gun and he would have killed me. But I can't get his eyes looking at me out of my head.'

Petersen believes this intimate experience with killing is the reason those who have been in combat are more readily prepared to accept their former enemy as equals in times of peace. He feels veterans who display a hatred of the enemy never really saw them in combat. 'Those who know the horror of battle are far more ready to forgive their former enemy.'

An old song from World War One says, 'Old soldiers never die, they simply fade away.' It's certainly true of men like Bevan Stokes and Barry Petersen. While Stokes continues to be haunted by his wartime experiences, Petersen keeps the ghosts at bay. He is now in his mid-70s, living by himself in a small fourth-floor apartment in Bangkok. He is battling cancer he believes was caused by his exposure to Agent Orange during the war. He has close friendships with the staff of the small accounting firm he set up when he moved to Bangkok, and they have become his extended family, helping him with everyday chores. He may not see ghosts but he is surrounded by memories. His living room is decorated with Montagnard pipes and cloths, even a bow and arrow. He gave the best of his Montagnard collection to the Australian War Memorial, including the traditional handwoven chieftain's garb he wore for his farewell ceremony. It was on display in Canberra for many years, but is now tucked away in a warehouse. Files, maps, old reports and newspaper clippings concerning the ongoing persecution of the Montagnard fill his bookshelves and cover his writing desk. Petersen may not have nightmares, but he has not forgotten what happened in the Highlands and the loyalty and friendship he was shown fires him up as he watches history repeating itself.

It angers him when he sees the same mistakes made in the Vietnam War being repeated four decades later. He was frustrated and furious when he saw Australian politicians blindly following the Americans into war in Iraq and Afghanistan without thinking how it would end, and how the soldiers would get out of it. 'Was Iraq worth the life of one young Australian or American soldier?' he asks.

Petersen is right. History does keep repeating itself and leaders keep repeating the mistakes. Losing the war in Vietnam deeply scarred the United States psyche and presidents ever since have been anxious to stress they would never take America into another Vietnam. In 1991, after President George HW Bush forced Iraq out of Kuwait in the first Gulf War, he declared America had finally buried Vietnam in the desert sands of Arabia and, 'By God, we've kicked the Vietnam syndrome once and for all.' How wrong he was.

In Gulf War 2 Vietnam's Phoenix Program was resurrected from the ashes. US military officers started writing academic papers with titles like 'Phoenix Rises Again', arguing that Phoenix wasn't all bad and should be dusted off for use in Iraq. One American adviser in Baghdad told journalist Seymour Hersh, who did much to expose the atrocities committed in Vietnam under Phoenix, that America would have to fight terrorism with terrorism and 'scare the Iraqis into submission'.[1]

One of the key men bringing Phoenix back to life was the then Secretary of Defense, Donald Rumsfeld. Under his watch, US Special Forces and CIA operatives would go in and kill insurgents identified by Iraqi intelligence. *Newsweek* reporter Michael Isikoff said a CIA-supported squad of Kurdish paramilitary fighters conducted a deadly series of drive-by shootings and ambushes of Iraqi military and Baath Party officials. 'These were in effect targeted assassinations against identified regime figures,' Isikoff wrote.[2]

While Petersen may have faced assassination for refusing to be part of the Phoenix Program, many of those who were involved in it went on to bigger and better things. Even after the atrocities were exposed and the program discredited, many of its toughest operatives became big players in CIA and military covert operations. Some emerged from the shadows to become key figures in power politics in Washington and other capitals.

Petersen's contemporaries were not as keen to step away from the action as he had been.

Rumsfeld had been a key adviser in President Richard Nixon's White House, arguing Phoenix was the best way to fight the war. He went on to be President Ford's Secretary of Defense and was brought back by President George W Bush as Defense Secretary for Gulf War 2, where once again he pushed Phoenix-style operations and assassination squads.

Another man who was in the thick of the political games in Vietnam also went on to work for President Richard Nixon's White House. Lucien Conein ran Nixon's war against the international drug trade. He was reportedly involved in setting up secret 'Action Teams' – assassination squads – who would kill the drug lords of South America and Asia.

The ties back to Vietnam are easy to follow and the ruthless nature of US policy did not change. Rumsfeld promoted Phoenix veteran Thomas O'Connell to assistant secretary for Special Operations, putting him in charge of the highly trained shadowy Special Forces squads engaged in Phoenix-style hunter–killer operations such as Delta Force, Seal Team 6 and Grey Fox.

Phoenix Program chief William Colby was promoted in 1973 to director of the CIA and was later a lawyer for the shadowy Nugan Hand Bank in Australia – a clearing house for the drug trade and CIA money laundering. It was run by Phoenix veterans including former US Special Forces soldier John Hand, who co-founded the mysterious bank in 1973. The bank collapsed in 1980 when its Australian co-founder, lawyer Frank Nugan, was shot to death.

Another associate of the bank, Theodore 'Ted' Shackley, had been one of Phoenix's chief operators as CIA station chief in Saigon. He was later heavily involved in the overthrow of Chilean President Salvador Allende and the Iran-Contra scandal, illegally selling arms to Iran to fund anti-communist rebels in Nicaragua.

A political officer in the Saigon embassy closely involved in Phoenix, John Negroponte, later became the first US ambassador to Iraq after the invasion and in 2007 Assistant Secretary of State.

Stu Methven was posted to Indonesia and later became CIA station chief in the Congo where he organised CIA support for a war against Marxists in Angola. After the September 11 terrorist attacks in 2001 on New York and Washington old Phoenix operators found their skills were in high demand. Many experienced covert operators jumped ship to make big money in booming private security firms such as Blackwater (effectively a private mercenary army). The controversial private security operation's vice chairman is Cofer Black, a former CIA agent sent to the Congo to follow Stu Methven in arming rebels in Angola. The span of Phoenix is far and wide.

Australian troops in Afghanistan adapted a technique from the Phoenix Program, identifying and categorising every adult male in the town and villages around the base, each labelled according to their loyalty. Every shopkeeper was photographed and his political views placed in a category, even those who refused to be questioned. Every house is marked on a map as being friendly or not friendly.[3]

And just like they did with the Montagnard, the US is funding armed local militias in remote areas of Afghanistan, and they tried the same in Iraq by recruiting thousands of Sunni fighters. But there are some new initiatives in their approach now. To win over local chieftains the CIA is passing out Viagra. The old chiefs come back with a smile on their face and in return for more of the little blue pills they have to supply information about the Taliban or agree to set up a CIA-backed militia force in their area.[4]

A key advocate of bringing back Phoenix has been David Kilcullen, a former lieutenant colonel in the Australian Army, and a key defence analyst called upon to advise on counterterrorism around the world. In 2007 he was the senior counterinsurgency adviser to General David Petraeus in Iraq during planning for the so-called surge of 2008. He argues for a 'global Phoenix program' to dismantle the worldwide terrorist jihadist structure in the same way Phoenix was designed to dismantle the Viet Cong hierarchy. He argues Phoenix has been much maligned and had been highly effective in Vietnam.[5]

In 2009 Barry Petersen listens and watches as the key US and Australian playmakers demonstrate their continued mis-steps and the CIA constantly repeats its mistakes. In his mind the CIA have failed too many times to control the resurgence of Phoenix: they did not predict major developments such as the Soviet invasion of Afghanistan, the opening of the Berlin Wall, the economic collapse of the Soviet Union or the September 11 terrorist attacks.

Barry Petersen has earned the right to his opinions. Despite his misgivings on the way the war was fought, he does not think the US and Australia were wrong to go in to Vietnam when they did. He still believes in the Domino Theory and the idea that if the Western military had not been in Vietnam in those crucial years Thailand and Malaysia could have fallen to the communists. But he feels the big mistake was turning the

Vietnam War into an American war. They should have stood back and supported the Vietnamese in fighting their own war. 'The Vietnamese knew all along how to fight that war better than the Americans,' Petersen says. 'It has been the same in Iraq and Afghanistan. We have learned nothing from history. I was so angry when I saw then Prime Minister John Howard go to war on the shirt-tails of George Bush. We never learn.

'In retrospect I wish I had told the army chiefs and authorities in 1963 that it would be better to send more skilled advisers to train up the Vietnamese rather than send combat troops. A war of that nature is best fought by the people themselves, not by foreigners. They might be welcomed at first but after a short time will be seen as occupiers. It happens time and again.'

History shows Petersen made the right decision to stay well out of what would become the CIA's Phoenix Program. He did not make this decision to avoid fighting the enemy or getting his hands dirty. He demonstrated time and again he was prepared to do that, and he has the medals to prove his bravery. Petersen displayed this courage in standing up to the CIA when he felt it was against his moral code of conduct and his country's rules of engagement with the enemy.

Petersen is certainly guilty of being stubborn. He may have cared too much about what happened to the Montagnard tribesmen he was sent to train for war. He may even have fallen victim to flattery by the high esteem in which he was held by the Montagnard. But had the Australian and American military hierarchy taken more notice of his tactics on the way to fight a guerilla war in Vietnam the conflict may have taken a very different turn.

Just as the tiger escaped Barry Petersen's gun during the hunt in the jungle in 1963, so Barry Petersen probably escaped a CIA bullet in 1965 when he left the Highlands quickly and quietly. He survived a remarkable life and carved a legend, the legend of the Tiger Man of Vietnam.

ENDNOTES

CHAPTER 2   TORTURE TRAINING

1. Michael Sexton, *War For the Asking – How Australia Invited Itself to Vietnam*, Penguin, Sydney, 1981, page 53.

CHAPTER 3   VIETNAM AND THE CIA

1. David Halberstam, *The Best and the Brightest*, Ballantine Books, New York, 1969, page 198.
2. Stanley Karnow, *Vietnam – A History*, Penguin Books, New York, 1997, page 246
3. Alfred McCoy, *The Politics of Heroin – CIA Complicity in the Global Drug Trade*, Lawrence Hill Books, New York, 1991, page 197.
4. Ian McNeill, *The Team – Australian Army Advisers in Vietnam 1962–1972*, University of Queensland Press, Brisbane, 1984, page 32.
5. Paul Ham, *Vietnam – The Australian War*, HarperCollins, Sydney, 2007, page 93.

6 Anne Blair *There to the Bitter End – Ted Serong in Vietnam*, Allen & Unwin, Sydney, 2001, page 38.
7 AJ Langguth *Our Vietnam – The War 1954–1975*, Simon & Schuster, New York, 2000, page 184.
8 Lieutenant Colonel Barry Petersen, 'Report on Attachment to US Agency, August 1963 – October 1965, Republic of Vietnam', Australian War Memorial, AWM PR89/097.

CHAPTER 4   THE CIA COUP

1 Anne Blair, op cit, page 46.
2 Stanley Karnow, op cit, page 311.
3 ibid, page 308.
4 Seymour Hersh, *The Dark Side of Camelot*, Little, Brown, Boston, 1997, page 418.
5 Stanley Karnow, op cit, page 326.

CHAPTER 5   TIGER HUNT

1 Peter Smark, 'Australians Fight Their Way Out of a Comic Opera', *The Australian* 17 August 1964.
2 Bruce Davies and Gary McKay, *The Men Who Persevered*, Allen & Unwin, 2005, page 39.
3 Paul Ham, op cit, page 100.

CHAPTER 6   MONTAGNARD REBELLION

1 Stanley Karnow, op cit, page 351.
2 ibid, page 353.
3 ibid, page 354.
4 Papers of Barry Petersen dated 30 July, 1964, Australian War Memorial, AWM PR89/097.
5 Anne Blair, op cit, page 97.
6 Howard Sochurek, 'American Special Forces in Action in Viet Nam', *National Geographic*, January 1965.

CHAPTER 7 THE JOHNNIE WALKER MIRACLE

1 Christopher Robbins, *Air America*, Corgi Books, London, 1979, page 162.

CHAPTER 9 FIRED

1 Author interview with Ian Teague, 2008.
2 Ian McNeill, op cit, page 382.
3 Barry Petersen *Tiger Men – An Australian Soldier's Secret War in Vietnam*, Macmillan, Melbourne, 1988, page 121.
4 Stanley Karnow, op cit, page 361.
5 Alfred McCoy, op cit, page 212.

CHAPTER 10 FAREWELL

1 Lieutenant Colonel Barry Petersen, op cit.
2 Papers of Barry Petersen, Australian War Memorial, AWM PR89/097.
3 Barry Petersen *Tiger Men – An Australian Soldier's Secret War in Vietnam*, op cit, page 157.
4 Alfred McCoy, op cit, page 215.

CHAPTER 11 A PAIN IN THE ASS

1 Tim Weiner, *Legacy of Ashes – The History of the CIA*, Anchor Books, New York, 2008, page 189.
2 Interview with Brigadier OD Jackson, Army Historical Program, Australian War Memorial, AWM 107.

CHAPTER 12 ACTION IN EXILE

1 Lieutenant Colonel Barry Petersen, op cit.
2 Stanley Karnow, op cit, page 163.

CHAPTER 13 RETURN TO VIETNAM

1 Gregg Zoroya and Alan Gomez, 'War Zone Massacre an Uncommon Event', *USA Today*, 12 May, 2009.
2 *New York Times*, 16 May, 1971.
3 US National Archives, statistical information about casualties in the Vietnam War: http://www.archives.gov/research/vietnam-war/casualty-statistics.html
4 Paul Ham, op cit, page 531.
5 David Hackworth, *About Face*, Touchstone, New York, 1989, page 775.

CHAPTER 14 PHOENIX RISING

1 Douglas Valentine, *The Phoenix Program*, William Morrow and Co, New York, 1990, page 44.
2 Tim Weiner, op cit, page 292.
3 Douglas Valentine, op cit, page 61.
4 Zalin Grant, *Facing the Phoenix*, Norton & Co, New York, 1991, page 297.
5 Douglas Valentine, op cit, page 63.
6 ibid, page 12
7 Mark Moyar, *Phoenix and the Birds of Prey*, Bison Books, Nebraska, 2007, page 225.
8 McNeill, op cit, page 405
9 ibid, page 401.
10 Anthony Herbert, *Soldier*, Holt Rhinehart & Winston, New York, 1973, page 105.
11 Douglas Valentine, op cit, page 191.
12 AJ Langguth, op cit, page 497.
13 Nick Turse, 'A My Lai a Month', *The Nation*, 1 December, 2008.
14 ibid.
15 Michael Sallah and Mitch Weiss, *Tiger Force*, Hodder, London, 2006, page 295.
16 Douglas Valentine, op cit, page 264.
17 ibid, page 311.
18 Michael Otterman, *American Torture*, Melbourne University Press, Melbourne, 2007, page 67.

19 Gordon Thomas, *Journey Into Madness: The True Story of Secret CIA Mind Control and Medical Abuse*, Bantam, New York, 1989, page 400.
20 Douglas Valentine, op cit, page 382.
21 Stanley Karnow, op cit, page 617.
22 Ken Edwards, 'Vietnam Revisited', *Time Magazine*, 10 August, 1987.
23 ibid.

CHAPTER 16   BETRAYAL

1 Stuart Methven *Laughter in the Shadows – A CIA Memoir*, Naval Institute Press, Annapolis, 2008, page 101.

CHAPTER 18   OLD SOLDIERS NEVER DIE

1 Seymour Hersh 'Moving Targets', *The New Yorker*, 15 December, 2003.
2 Michael Isikoff and David Corn, *Hubris: The Inside Story of Spin, Scandal, and the Selling of the Iraq War*, Crown Publishing, New York, 2006, page 211.
3 Cameron Stewart, 'Aussies Keep Spy Files on Afghans', *The Australian*, 1 December, 2008.
4 Joby Warrick, 'Little Blue Pills Among the Ways CIA Wins Friends in Afghanistan', *Washington Post*, 26 December, 2008.
5 David Kilcullen, 'Countering Global Insurgency', *Small Wars Journal*, September–November 2004.

A TIMELINE OF CONFLICT

At the end of the Vietnam War, the Vietnamese people had effectively been part of various conflicts for more than 100 years. Barry Petersen and his involvement with the Montagnard was only a brief interlude in a violent history.

1627	French Jesuit missionaries spread influence in Vietnam.
1847	French forces clash with Vietnamese mandarins as they try to push out the missionaries.
1852	Napoleon III sends military force to Vietnam to protect missionaries and gain trade concessions.
1861	French forces capture Saigon and gain religious, trade and political concessions.

A TIMELINE OF CONFLICT

1863	The French extend control over Cambodia.
1883	France takes control over much of Vietnam.
1890	Ho Chi Minh born in central Vietnam.
1914	World War One breaks out and several hundred thousand Vietnamese go to France in labour battalions.
1919	Ho Chi Minh unsuccessfully tries to petition US President Woodrow Wilson at the Versailles Peace Talks for self-determination for Vietnam.
1920	Ho Chi Minh joins Communist Party and goes to Moscow.
1932	The French puppet emperor Bao Dai ascends throne.
1934	Barry Petersen born in Queensland.
1940	Japan invades Vietnam but leaves French administration in charge.
1941	Ho Chi Minh secretly returns to Vietnam and forms Viet Minh to fight both Japan and France.
1945	*15 August* Japanese surrender and transfer of power to Viet Minh. *2 September* Ho Chi Minh declares the independence of Vietnam. *13 September* British forces under General Douglas Gracey land in Saigon and use rearmed Japanese troops to help return authority to the French.
1946	France renegs on peace deal with Ho and Viet Minh forces attack French troops in the north.
1949	The French appoint puppet Bao Dai as nominal leader of Vietnam as war continues.

1950	14 *January* Ho declares Democratic Republic of Vietnam is the only legitimate government. China and Soviet Union recognise Ho's government. 26 *June* The Korean War starts. 26 *July* US President Harry Truman grants US$15 million in military aid to France for use in Indochina.
1954	13 *March* Battle at Dien Bien Phu begins as Viet Minh mount largest attack on French forces. 7 *May* French defeated at Dienbienphu. *July* Geneva Peace Accord divides Vietnam at 17th Parallel pending nationwide elections. 8 *September* South East Asia Treaty Organization (SEATO) formed, including US, UK, France, Australia, New Zealand, Pakistan, Thailand and Philippines. 9 *October* French forces leave Hanoi. US gives South Vietnam US$100 million in aid. US Navy helps hundreds of thousands flee from North to South.
1955	The US begins training South Vietnamese army. Australia sends an infantry battalion and artillery units to Malaya to join British units. 20 *July* The South Vietnamese government under Ngo Dinh Diem rejects Geneva Accords and refuses to participate in nationwide elections. US backs his decision. 23 *October* Diem deposes Bao Dai in referendum to become prime minister. Diem proclaims Republic of Vietnam with himself as president.
1956	Diem cracks down on Viet Minh and other dissidents.
1957	Viet Cong start war on Diem regime, killing 400 officials.
1958	North Vietnam starts using the Ho Chi Minh Trail to deliver arms, men and supplies to the Viet Cong.

A TIMELINE OF CONFLICT

1959	*31 August* Lieutenant Barry Petersen posted to Malaya for Malaya Emergency.
1960	Resistance in Vietnam to Diem's repressive regime grows beyond communists. *11 May* Attempted coup against Diem fails.
1961	*17 April* With approval from President John F Kennedy, the CIA launches disastrous invasion of Cuba with anti-Castro expats. US expands military aid to Diem regime including around 500 military advisers. *12 November* Lieutenant Petersen completes posting to Malaya.
1962	*8 February* US military advisers reach 2394. US Military Assistance Command set up in Saigon. *27 February* Two South Vietnamese pilots bomb Diem's palace. Diem survives. *March* Captain Barry Petersen approached by Colonel Ted Serong to ask if he would be interested in going to Vietnam to train native tribesmen in military tactics. *May* US Admiral Harry Felt, visiting Australia, requests nominal commitment of Australian military advisers. *24 May* Australia's Menzies government announces deployment of Australian Army Training Team Vietnam (AATTV), a group of 30 experienced jungle fighters, officers and senior NCOs, to go as instructors. *30 July* Colonel Ted Serong, commander of AATTV, tours Vietnam and sets up arrangements with US military and CIA for deployment of the team. *3 August* Thirty AATTV members arrive in Vietnam. *October* President Kennedy forces Soviet Union to withdraw missiles from Cuba. *31 December* US military strength in Vietnam reaches 11 000.

1963

2 January Viet Cong units defeat South Vietnamese forces at Ap Bac on the Mekong Delta.
January Captain Barry Petersen undergoes torture survival training in Sydney.
8 May Buddhist riots in the central Vietnamese city of Hue.
11 June Venerated monk Thich Quang Duc immolates himself in Saigon in protest at Diem persecution of Buddhists, sending shockwaves around the world.
27 August Petersen arrives in Saigon and told by Serong he will be seconded to CIA to train Montagnard.
September Petersen taken by CIA contact to Ban Me Thuot.
1 November Diem overthrown in US-approved coup and murdered along with his brother.
6 November General Duong Van Minh takes over as president.
22 November President Kennedy assassinated.
December 15 000 US military advisers in Vietnam along with few dozen Australians.

1964

30 January President Minh ousted in coup by General Nguyen Khanh.
8 June Australia increases AATTV to 80.
20 June General William C Westmoreland takes over as commander of US forces in Vietnam.
2 August North Vietnamese patrol boats attack US destroyer *Maddox* in Gulf of Tonkin. US warplanes bomb North Vietnam.
Viet Cong increase attacks on US bases.
14 August Australia sends six Caribou transport aircraft to Vietnam.
19 September Montagnard rebellion in Petersen's Darlac Province.
November Riots break out in Saigon protesting against the Khanh regime.
24 November The Australian Liberal government brings in conscription.

January AATTV is increased to 100.

5 February Colonel David Jackson takes over command of AATTV from Serong, who leaves the Australian Army to work for the CIA.

7 February The Viet Cong make a daring attack on US base at Pleiku. The US bombs North Vietnam.

18 February With US approval Khanh is forced to leave the country as Dr Phan Huy Quat forms new government.

2 March Operation Rolling Thunder, the intense bombing of North Vietnam, begins.

8 March First US combat troops arrive in Vietnam.

March Petersen sent to Australia for short visit to brief chiefs of ASIS, Army and Foreign Affairs Department. Menzies congratulates him during a brief meeting. He is repeatedly asked how combat troops would fare in Vietnam.

29 April The Australian Prime Minister, Sir Robert Menzies, announces sending combat troops to Vietnam.

11 June Air Vice Marshal Nguyen Cao Ky takes over as prime minister and General Nguyen Van Thieu as president.

July President Lyndon B Johnson increases US combat forces to 200 000.

August Petersen forced out of Highlands by CIA. Spends two months in Saigon.

14 October Petersen leaves Vietnam.

13 November Warrant Officer Kevin Wheatley of the AATTV is posthumously awarded the Victoria Cross.

20 November to 20 December Petersen posted to Borneo.

1965

1966

January Harold Holt becomes Prime Minister of Australia.

8 March Australia boosts the size of its combat forces, settling in Phuoc Tuy province.

10 March Anti-government and anti-American riots break out in northern Vietnamese provinces.

December US troops strength reaches 400 000.

1967

7 April Major Peter Badcoe of the AATTV is killed in action and awarded the Victoria Cross.

October Massive anti-war rallies in the US and Australia.

December US troops reach 500 000.

Australian Prime Minister Harold Holt drowns.

1968

January John Gorton appointed Prime Minister of Australia.

30 January North Vietnam and Viet Cong launch the Tet Offensive.

16 March A US platoon massacre 504 unarmed civilians including women and babies at the village of My Lai.

4 April Martin Luther King is assassinated in Memphis.

5 June Robert Kennedy is assassinated in Los Angeles.

2 July General Creighton Abrams is appointed US commander.

November Richard Nixon is elected US president with a promise to withdraw forces from Vietnam.

December US troop strength reaches 540 000. The US annual death toll in Vietnam is the highest yet at 16 869. The Australian death toll is 98.

1969

31 January US forces reach a peak of 542 400.
18 March Nixon begins secret bombing of Cambodia. The US invents the term 'Vietnamization' to describe troop withdrawals.
8 May Massive anti-war demonstrations in Australia.
11 May Warrant Officer Ray Simpson of AATTV awarded Victoria Cross.
24 May Warrant Officer Keith Payne of AATTV awarded Victoria Cross.
8 June Nixon announces the withdrawal of 25 000 US troops.
3 September Ho Chi Minh dies aged 79.
18 September Anti-war marches in Australia.
15 November Huge anti-war demonstrations in the US.
16 November Revelation of 1968's My Lai massacre.

1970

20 February Secret peace talks begin in Paris.
22 April Australia announces one of its three battalions in Vietnam will not be replaced when its deployment ends in November.
29 April Petersen returns to Vietnam as a regular combat officer, a major in charge of a company.
30 April Nixon says South Vietnamese and US forces have attacked communist sanctuaries in Cambodia.
4 May National guardsmen kill four students during an anti-war protest at Kent State University in Ohio.
12 November The US army's Lieutenant William L Calley goes on trial for his part in the My Lai massacre.
December US force down to 280 000 as withdrawals continue.

1971

February South Vietnamese forces backed by US Air Force attack communist strongholds in Laos.

10 March William McMahon becomes Prime Minister of Australia.

29 March Lieutenant Calley convicted of premeditated murder of civilians at My Lai.

30 March McMahon announces gradual reduction of Australian forces in Vietnam.

24 April 500 000 anti-war protesters fill Washington.

1 June Petersen completes second tour of Vietnam.

18 August McMahon announces all Australian combat troops will be out of Vietnam by Christmas.

December US troop strength down to 140 000.

1972

25 January Nixon reveals that Henry Kissinger has been secretly negotiating with North Vietnam for a peace deal.

30 March North Vietnam launches offensive across the demilitarised zone.

15 April Nixon orders the bombing of Hanoi and Haiphong.

April Viet Cong launch an offensive in Phuoc Tuy province, once protected by Australian troops.

17 June Nixon's Watergate burglars are arrested.

August Thieu rejects Kissinger's ceasefire agreement.

12 August The last US combat troops leave Vietnam leaving 43 500 US air force personnel.

7 November Nixon is reelected.

2 December Labor wins Australian election and Gough Whitlam becomes prime minister. His first action is to free conscientious objectors from jail. Whitlam orders Australian troops out of Vietnam.

18 December The AATTV are the last to leave Vietnam.

18 December Nixon orders further bombing of North Vietnam.

A TIMELINE OF CONFLICT

1973
27 January US and North Vietnam sign a ceasefire agreement in Paris.
26 February The Whitlam government becomes the first Western nation to formally recognise the socialist government of the united Vietnam.
29 March The last US troops leave Vietnam.
1 April The last US prisoners of war released.
14 August The US Congress forces Nixon to stop bombing Cambodia.

1974
January Thieu says war against North Vietnam has started up again.
9 May Impeachment process begins against Nixon over Watergate.
9 August Nixon resigns, replaced by Gerald Ford.

1975
11 March The North Vietnamese capture Ban Me Thuot.
15 March Thieu orders his troops to abandon northern provinces to defend Saigon.
23 April Ford declares the war 'finished'.
25 April Thieu flees to Taiwan.
29 April Evacuation of last Americans begins.
30 April The North Vietnamese capture Saigon; the South Vietnamese government surrenders.

1976
Jimmy Carter wins US election.

1977
The day after his inauguration, President Carter pardons most of 10 000 draft dodgers.
25 December Vietnam invades Cambodia.
Thousands of 'boat people' flee Vietnam.
SEATO is dissolved.

1979
February China invades Vietnam.

1989
September Vietnam withdraws last troops from Cambodia.

1991	The Soviet Union ends aid to Vietnam.
1994	President Clinton removes US trade embargo on Vietnam.
1995	The US opens diplomatic relations with Vietnam.
2008	The US opens talks to sell arms to Vietnam, mostly spare parts for vehicles, planes and helicopters abandoned after the war.

BIBLIOGRAPHY

Blair, Anne *There to the Bitter End – Ted Serong in Vietnam*, Allen & Unwin, Sydney, 2001.
Belfield, Richard *Terminate With Extreme Prejudice*, Macmillan, Sydney, 2005.
Burchett, Wilfred *Vietnam Will Win!* Guardian Books, New York, 1968.
Cowie, Peter *The Apocalypse Now Book*, Da Capo Press, New York, 2001.
Davies, Bruce and McKay, Gary *The Men Who Persevered*, Allen & Unwin, Sydney, 2005.
De Silva, Peer *Sub Rosa – The CIA and the Uses of Intelligence*, Times Books, New York, 1978.
Gardner, Lloyd C and Young Marilyn B (editors) *Iraq and the Lessons of Vietnam*, The New Press, New York, 2007.
Grant, Zalin *Facing the Phoenix*, Norton & Co, New York, 1991.
Hackworth, Colonel David *About Face*, Touchstone, New York, 1989.
——*Steel My Soldiers' Hearts*, Rugged Land, New York, 2002.
Halberstam, David *The Best and the Brightest*, Ballantine Books, New York, 1969.
——*The Making of a Quagmire*, Ballantine Books, New York, 1988.
Ham, Paul *Vietnam – The Australian War*, HarperCollins, Sydney, 2007.

Herbert, Anthony *Soldier*, Holt Rhinehart & Winston, New York, 1973.

Hersh, Seymour *The Dark Side of Camelot*, Little, Brown, Boston, 1997.

Hickey, Gerald Cannon *Shattered World – Adaptation and Survival among Vietnam's Highland Peoples During the Vietnam War*, University of Pennsylvania Press, Philadelphia, 1993.

——*Village in Vietnam*, Yale University Press, New York, 1964.

Isikoff, Michael and Corn, David *Hubris: The Inside Story of Spin, Scandal, and the Selling of the Iraq War*, Crown Publishing, New York, 2006.

Karnow, Stanley *Vietnam – A History*, Penguin Books, New York, 1997.

Kwitny, Jonathan *The Crimes of Patriots – A True Tale of Dirty Money and the CIA*, Norton & Co, New York, 1987.

King, Peter (ed) *Australia's Vietnam – Australia in the Second Indo-China War*, Allen & Unwin, Sydney, 1983.

Langguth, AJ *Our Vietnam – The War 1954–1975*, Simon & Schuster, New York, 2000.

——*Hidden Terrors*, Pantheon Books, New York, 1978.

McCoy, Alfred *The Politics of Heroin – CIA Complicity in the Global Drug Trade*, Lawrence Hill Books, New York, 1991.

McGehee, Ralph *Deadly Deceits – My 25 Years in the CIA*, Sheridan Square Publications, New York, 1983.

McNeill, Ian *The Team – Australian Army Advisers in Vietnam 1962–1972* University of Queensland Press, Brisbane, 1984.

Maddock, Kenneth (ed) *Memories of Vietnam*, Random House, Sydney, 1991.

Methven, Stuart *Laughter in the Shadows – A CIA Memoir*, Naval Institute Press, Annapolis, 2008.

Moyar, Mark *Phoenix and the Birds of Prey*, Bison Books, Nebraska, 2007.

Otterman, Michael *American Torture*, Melbourne University Press, Melbourne, 2007.

Petersen, Barry *Tiger Men – An Australian Soldier's Secret War in Vietnam*, Macmillan, Melbourne, 1988.

Robbins, Christopher *Air America*, Corgi Books, London, 1979.

Sallah, Michael and Weiss, Mitch *Tiger Force*, Hodder, London, 2006.

Sexton, Michael *War For the Asking – How Australia Invited Itself to Vietnam*, Penguin, Sydney, 1981.

Sklar, Holly *Washington's War on Nicaragua*, South End Press, Boston, 1988.

Snepp, Frank *Decent Interval*, Random House, New York, 1977.

Stockwell, John *In Search of Enemies – A CIA Story*, Andre Deutsch, London, 1978.

Sullivan, John F *Of Spies and Lies – A CIA Lie Detector Remembers Vietnam*, University Press of Kansas, Lawrence, 2002.
Thomas, Gordon *Journey Into Madness: The True Story of Secret CIA Mind Control and Medical Abuse*, Bantam, New York, 1989.
Toohey, Brian and Pinwill, William *Oyster – The story of the Australian Secret Intelligence Service*, Mandarin Australia, Melbourne, 1989.
Valentine, Douglas *The Phoenix Program*, William Morrow and Co, New York, 1990.
Warner, Denis *Not With Guns Alone*, Hutchinson, Melbourne, 1977.
——*Wake Me If There's Trouble – An Australian Correspondent at the Front Line*, Penguin, Melbourne, 1995.
Weiner, Tim *Legacy of Ashes – The History of the CIA*, Anchor Books, New York, 2008.
——*Blank Check – The Pentagon's Black Budget*, Warner Books, New York, 1990.
Willey, Keith *Tales of the Big Country*, Rigby, Sydney, 1972.

MOVIE

Apocalypse Now, 1979. Directed by Francis Ford Coppola, starring Marlon Brando, Robert Duvall and Martin Sheen. Released by United Artists.
Apocalypse Now Redux 2001, released by Miramax Films.

JOURNAL ARTICLES

'American Special Forces in Action in Viet Nam', Howard Sochurek, *National Geographic*, January 1965.
'A My Lai a Month', Nick Turse, *The Nation*, 1 December, 2008.
'Australians Fight their Way Out of a Comic Opera', Peter Smark, *The Australian*, 17 August, 1964.
'Aussies Keep Spy Files on Afghans', Cameron Stewart, *The Australian*, 1 December, 2008.
'Blackwater's Private CIA', Jeremy Scahill, *The Nation*, 9 June, 2008.
'Countering Global Insurgency', David Kilcullen, *Small Wars Journal*, September–November 2004.

'The Dark Art of Interrogation', Mark Bowden, *The Atlantic Monthly*, October 2003.
Joby Warrick, 'Little Blue Pills Among the Ways CIA Wins Friends in Afghanistan', *Washington Post*, 26 December, 2008.
'Moving Targets', Seymour Hersh, *New Yorker*, 15 December, 2003.
'The Spook Who Would be a Congressman', by Douglas Valentine, *Counterpunch* online newsletter, 4 November, 2000.
'The Tiger Man of Banmethuot', Gerald Stone, *Daily Mirror*, 7 September, 1965.
'Vietnam Revisited' Ken Edwards, *Time Magazine*, 10 August, 1987.
'What a Lovely War', Stein, Jeff, *Vietnam Generation Journal*, Volume 4, number 3–4, 1992.
Gregg Zoroya and Alan Gomez, 'War Zone Massacre an Uncommon Event', *USA Today*, 12 May, 2009.

PAPERS

Colonel Christopher Costa, US Naval War College, May 2006.
Lieutenant Colonel Barry Petersen, 'Report on Attachment to US Agency, August 1963 – October 1965, Republic of Vietnam', Australian War Memorial, AWM PR89/097.
Papers of Barry Petersen dated July 30, 1964, Australian War Memorial, AWM PR89/097.

ACKNOWLEDGEMENTS

This book could not have been written without the generous cooperation of Barry Petersen. Not only did he give weeks of his time answering endless questions, but he also allowed me to use his private collection of papers and photographs. I spent more than a week in Bangkok interviewing Barry, including being taken to a notorious seedy bar in Patpong Road where fading spooks and shady mercenaries of all types hang out to swap war stories.

I thank Barry for his patience in explaining a war to a bloke who was not there, and for diligently answering hundreds of follow-up questions via email and phone even as he battled a cancer he believed was caused by Agent Orange. The good news as this book goes to press is that he is winning the fight.

I would also like to thank the many former soldiers of the Australian Army Training Team Vietnam (AATTV) who agreed to be interviewed for this book, including Peter Young, Ian Teague, Bevan Stokes, Jack Leggett, Peter Jarratt and Don McDowell. I thank Rick Ryan and his colleagues at the AATTV Association for their help in putting me in touch with several of the veterans. They are one of our most highly decorated units and an incredible bunch of men.

I am indebted to Vietnam war correspondents Gerald Stone and Denis Gibbons, who recounted their dramatic exploits with Captain Petersen during the war. Former South Vietnamese army colonel, Le Van 'Peter' Thanh, now living in Canberra, gave a valuable Vietnamese perspective. Former Australian diplomat Roy Fernandez explained what went on behind the scenes in Saigon. And, of course, thank you to retired CIA agent Stu Methven who, like most Americans, believes in the right to free speech and answered my questions.

I would like to thank Douglas Valentine for giving permission to quote from his book, *The Phoenix Program*, arguably the most thorough research on the subject, and also Michael Sexton, for allowing me to use the documentation he dug up for his book *War for the Asking*, proving Australia was taken into the Vietnam War on a lie. It wasn't the last time.

All the unsourced quoted statements in this book come from interviews I did with people in 2008–2009. Sources of other quotes are notated.

I would also like to thank several people who helped this book become a reality: Sandra Harrison for her eagle eye; sub-editors at the *Sun-Herald* for beating into shape my original newspaper feature on Barry; Paul Ham; Matthew Benns, Terry Smyth and my brother Peter for their much-valued advice; my daughter Hannah for endless cups of tea and my wife Esther for her unflagging support.

Finally, thanks to my publisher, Vanessa Radnidge, for trusting a newspaper reporter to write a story longer than 2000 words, and my editor Jacquie Brown for helping to beat this book into shape.

INDEX

A Shau base, 91–92, 94–95, 98, 100
AATTV. *see* Australian Army Training Team Vietnam
Afghanistan, 257, 267, 314, 317
Africa, 15, 83, 220–221, 317
Air America, 50, 62, 119, 121, 123, 141, 144–146, 176, 191
Allende, Salvador, 317
Anderson, Dorsey, 189–190
Anderson, Professor Terry, 97
Angola, 220, 317
Apocalypse Now (film), 300–301
Ariff, Colonel Mohammed, 290
ARVN (Army of the Republic of Vietnam)
  in Ban Me Thuot, 292
  conditions in, 11, 108
  drug rackets in, 228
  FULRO and, 190–192
  mentioned, 2, 46
  Montagnard militia, 93
  Montagnard rebellion, 122–123, 127
  US military advisers to, 39–40, 45, 55, 97
  veterans in Australia, 296
  Viet Cong infiltration of, 97
  Vietnamese militia, 91–92, 271
ASIS (Australian Secret Intelligence Service)
  CIA, 41, 159, 188
  formation of, 21–22, 237
  Petersen debriefing, 155–161
  Scott, 297–298
assassination squads. *see* Counter Terror (CT) units
Australia. *see also* Australia in Vietnam
  in Afghanistan, 314, 317
  in Iraq, 314
  in Malaya, 17–18

National Service, 16
press, 168
Republic of Vietnam, 161–162, 167–168
Australia in Vietnam. *see also* Australian Army Training Team Vietnam
anti-war demonstrations, 244–245
Battle of Long Tan, 251
casualties, 96–99
CIA command, 3, 5, 23–24, 41, 48, 94
conscription, 165, 168
decision to send combat troops, 160–161, 164–168, 292, 319
deployment of combat troops, 211, 240–241, 247–254
fragging, 238–239
as military advisers, 18
reasons for involvement, 19–20, 155, 166
The Australian, 91, 168
Australian Army Training Team Vietnam (AATTV). *see also* Australia in Vietnam; People's Action Teams
ASIS, 156–157
Australian Army attitude to, 223
CIA, 183–184, 224
deployment, 91, 95, 196, 211
Diem and, 65–66
formation of, 18, 40–41, 45
role, 92
Veterans' Association, 295–296
Australian Defence Force, 3, 24–36, 33, 35, 106, 223
Special Operations, 18, 20–21
Australian Federal Police, 298–299
Australian Labor Party, 168
Australian War Memorial, 230, 314

B

Ban Don, 123
Ban Me Thuot
after Diem, 71–73
Americans in, 54–57
bombing of bar, 150–151
description of, 47, 50–53, 255
falls to North Vietnamese, 198, 291–293
Montagnard rebellion, 118, 122, 123, 126–127
morgue, 142, 143–144
Vietnamese in, 63, 69, 104–105, 136, 179
Bao Dai, Emperor, 54
Barry, Glen, 239
Bartlett, Charles, 67–68
Bay of Pigs, 270
Benefield, Jack, 194, 199, 201–202
Bianchetti, Father, 115
Binh Dinh province, 275
Black, Cofer, 317
Blackwater, 317
Blair, Anne, 130–131
Boer War, 17
Boileau, Captain Guy, 171–172
Borneo, 231, 234
Bouchart, Bill, 112–114
British in Malaya, 17–18
British in Vietnam, 234–238
Brockett, Lieutenant David, 174
Brooks, Major Edwin, 133
Browne, Colonel Laurence E, 188, 191, 213
Browne, Malcolm, 38
Buddhists in Vietnam, 37–38, 40, 43–44, 63, 66, 264–265
Bui Huy Gia, Major, 116, 120
Bui Thi Vu, 59
Buon Brieng, 123–125
Buon Enao, 72–74, 89, 309

menagerie of animals, 75–76
Montagnard rebellion, 119, 120, 126, 127–132, 137–138
Buon Mbre, 121
Buon Mi Ga, 123
Buon Sarpa, 118, 123, 126, 127, 129, 132–135
Burgess, Pat, 203–204, 228
Burma, 78, 90, 181
Bush, George HW, 315
Bush, George W, 316, 319

C

Calley, Lieutenant William, 277
Cambodia, 79, 114, 135, 136, 188, 242, 257, 293
Canaday, Captain Donald, 212
Cat Lo base, 268–269, 270
Catholics in Vietnam, 37, 43, 63
Cawthorn, Major-General Sir Walter, 22, 157–161, 164, 268
Cham, 135–136
Charles, Prince, 221
Chiang Kai-shek, 235
Chile, 317
China, People's Republic of, 114, 166, 168, 235
Chinese crime syndicates, 216
Chinese in Malaya, 17–18
Church, Lieutenant Colonel, 247
CIA (Central Intelligence Agency)
AATTV, 183–184, 224
airline. *see* Air America
ARVN, drug rackets with, 228
ASIS, 41, 159, 188
Australians, command, 3, 5, 23–24, 41, 48, 94
Counter Terror (CT) units. *see* Counter Terror (CT) units
Covert Action Branch, 177, 193
CSD (Combined Studies Division), 23–24, 45, 48–49, 170–174, 202
Diem, overthrow of, 64–65, 68–70
expansion of, 199
failures, 318
funds for paramilitary operations, 52–53, 58, 93, 102, 146–147, 149–150, 178–179, 200
journalists, 147–148
in Laos. *see* Laos
Montagnard militia, set up, 79, 163
opium trade, 44, 216
Petersen as conduit to, 116–117
Petersen as threat to, 214–217, 220, 224, 228, 300, 302–304, 305
Petersen, relations with, 140–141, 146–149, 187–188
propaganda material, 77
psychological operations, 63
Serong, 46, 48, 154, 184
supplies, 146–147, 148
turf wars, 187, 195
US Operations Mission, 155
Vietnamese Police Special Branch, 271–274, 281
Co Than, 151
Colby, William, 46, 263, 276, 316
Colombo Plan, 15
Conein, Lucien, 68–70, 110, 148, 149, 268, 316
Congo, 220–221, 317
Conway, Warrant Officer Kevin, 98–99
Coronel, Marcel, 114
Counter Terror (CT) units. *see also* Phoenix Program
as assassination squads, 222, 269

Australians at training bases, 267–269
CIA funding, 172–174, 222, 258–259
CIA introduce, 258–259
CIA operatives, 263–264, 270–274
establishment of, 262–267
interrogation and torture methods, 266, 281–282
Methven's role in, 174–176, 262, 267, 268
US military involvement, 262–263
US Special Forces working with, 265
Crimean War, 22, 24
Cutler, Sir Roden, 239
Cutter, Dr Lloyd, 281–282

D

Da Nang, 49–50, 98–99, 214
Dam San base, 179–180, 204
Darlac Province, 79. *see also* Ban Me Thuot
Davies, Bruce, 96
de Gaulle, Charles, 114
de Silva, Peer, 187, 261–262, 263
Deane, Captain Bill, 275
Defense Intelligence Agency, 113
Department of External Affairs, 161–165
Devitt, Captain Jim, 174
Diem. *see* Ngo Dinh Diem
Domino Theory, 39, 41
Donahue, Tom, 178, 186, 189, 193–195, 199–200, 270
Dottle, Captain James, 212–213
Doyle, Sergeant William, 280
Duong Van Minh, 65, 70, 110

E

Evans, Bill, 193–194
Evans, Brigadier FR, 232
Ewell, Major General Julian, 277–278, 280

F

Fernandez, Roy, 209, 226–227
Fitzgerald, Major Jack, 215, 227–228
Flying Tigers, 261
Force Populaire, 52
Ford, Gerald, 316
Fort Bragg (US), 240, 310
Fraser, Major General Colin, 243
French Foreign Legion, 7
French in Vietnam
    Dien Bien Phu, 99, 245
    interests, 51
    Japanese, 68, 234
    Montagnard rebellion, 136
    US and Britain, support by, 235–236
    Viet Cong, support for, 112–116, 149, 150
    Viet Minh, 6–7, 44
French missionaries, 77
Freund, Colonel John, 127, 132–135
Fulbright, Senator J William, 276
FULRO, 135, 138, 188–192, 201, 202, 256, 258, 293, 304

G

Geelong Grammar School, 221
Geneva Convention, 282
Gerardie, Pierre and Madame, 115–116
Germans, 118
Geyer, Georgie Anne, 276
Gibbons, Denis, 205, 207–208

Gibson, Mel, 308
Gillespie, Captain Vernon, 123–125, 133–135
Gougleman, Tucker, 281
Gracey, General Douglas, 235–236
Green Berets, 54, 55

H

Hacking, Sergeant Bill, 96–97, 108
Hackworth, Colonel David, 254, 278–279
Hagerty, Captain Bob, 96
Halberstam, David, 38
Ham, Evan, 306
Ham, Paul, 97
Hand, John, 316
Hasluck, Sir Paul, 167, 268
H'Chioh Nie, 74
Healy, Captain John, 23–24, 41, 42, 45, 159
Helms, Richard, 280
Herbert, Lieutenant Colonel Anthony, 276
Hersh, Seymour, 265, 315
HMAS *Sydney*, 208
Hmong, 176
Ho Chi Minh, 68, 234–235, 236–237, 244
Ho Chi Minh Trail, 4, 46, 52, 78, 88, 105, 150, 168, 176, 189
Hoang Phuong, 308
Hoang Thong, 52
Howard, John, 319
Hue, 96–97
Hume, Ro, 308–309

I

Indian Army Corps, 235–236
Indonesia, 220, 231, 234, 261, 317
Iran-Contra scandal, 317
Iraq, 257, 267, 283, 314–316, 317
Irian Jaya, 297–298
Isikoff, Michael, 315

J

Jackson, Brigadier David, 164, 188, 194–195, 204, 208–209, 230–231
Japanese
 attack on Pearl Harbour, 261
 in Burma, 90, 181
 French and, 68, 234
 in Vietnam, 68, 149, 234–236
Jarratt, Captain Peter, 268–269
Jesuits, 115
Jockel, Gordon, 19
Johnson, BJ, 271–274
Johnson, Lyndon B, 185, 276
Johnson, Ralph, 261

K

Karnow, Stanley, 110, 235, 283
Kelly, Bob, 172
Kennedy, John F, 38–39, 44, 67–68, 70, 184
Kennedy, Robert, 67, 154
Kersting, Colonel Donald, 127–129
Khmer Rouge, 293
Kilcullen, David, 318
Kissinger, Henry, 286
Komer, Robert, 277
Korean War, 16, 24
Kurds in Iraq, 315
Kuwait, 315
Ky. *see* Nguyen Cao Ky, Air Marshall

L

Lac Thien, 103, 105–108, 174, 309
Lan, General, 194, 200–201
Laos
 Air America, 191

CIA-funded Montagnard militia, 79, 93, 175–176, 261, 270
French interests, 114
Montagnard population, 78
opium trade, 44, 145–146, 191, 216
US and civilian casualties, 257
Lawrence of Arabia, 181
Le Van Thanh, Colonel, 71, 111, 224–225
Leggett, Captain Jack, 270–274
Loan, General, 216
Lodge, Henry Cabot, 68, 70, 110–111, 184
Long Thanh, 141
Lu Lan, General, 190
Ly Tran Ly, Madame, 51

M

McCone, John, 154
McCoy, Alfred, 44
McDowell, Captain Don, 222–224, 270
McGarvey, Pat, 265
McKay, Gary, 96
McPherson, Lieutenant David, 250
Mai Huu Xian, General, 69–70
Malaya, 17–18, 58, 90, 98, 237
Malaysia, 287–291
Mannix, Archbishop Daniel, 65
Mansfield, Senator Mike, 44
Manzione, Elton, 264–267
Martin, Ray, 295
Mekong Delta, 277–278, 279
Melbourne Club, 158
Menzies, Sir Robert, 3, 18–20, 158–159, 166–168, 211
Mercurio, Noel, 114
Methven, Stuart
  CIA, Covert Action Branch, 122, 163, 168–170, 178

CIA, Petersen as threat to, 218
Co mission to Montagnard, 126–127, 132, 137
in Congo, 220–221, 317
Counter Terror (CT) units, 174–176, 262, 267, 268
in Indonesia, 220, 317
in Laos, 261
Laughter in the Shadows – A CIA Memoir, 303
Petersen, relations with, 147–148, 180–181, 240
Petersen, removes from Highlands, 193–194, 195
Smith, 178
Taylor, 183, 185–186
Vietnam, role in, 218–221
Vinh Loc, 191–192, 304–305
MI6, 234, 237–238
Mills, Bryan, 48–50, 52–53, 57, 59, 62–64, 73, 102, 109, 122, 163
Milner, Colonel John, 18
M'Nong, 103–104, 105, 107, 121, 126
Mobutu, Joseph, 220–221
Montagnard hill tribes. *see also* Cham; Hmong; M'Nong; Muong; Nung; Rhade
  autonomy, desire for, 105–106, 111–112, 131–132, 162–163. *see also* FULRO
  characteristics of, 77–78, 105
  customs, 79, 80–83, 103–104, 181–182, 205–207, 309
  forced to resettle in camps, 4, 51, 54, 78, 256–257
  hatred of Vietnamese, 122, 169–170, 303–304
  refugees, 310–311
  Vietnamese, hatred of, 87–88

Montagnard militia. *see also*
Truong Son Force
  Americans, attitude to, 97
  ARVN, 93
  CIA set up, 79, 163
  Diem's attitude to, 47–48
  FULRO and, 189–192, 256, 258, 293, 304
  in Laos, 79, 93, 175–176, 261, 270
  Malays work with, 238
  Montagnard rebellion, 118–132, 161–162, 303–304
  snap-shooting course, 95
  Thang Thanh, attack on, 2–5
  US advisers train, 39, 55
  US military take over, 304
  US Special Forces run, 90, 109
  weapons, 89, 107
Morris, Arthur Malcolm, 161–163, 247, 255
Mountain Scouts, 261–262
Moyar, Mark, 267
Muldoon, John Patrick, 281
Muong, 177
Murdoch, Rupert, 168
My Lai massacre, 242, 277

N
Nam Dong Special Forces Camp, 98–99
Negroponte, John, 268, 317
Nelson, Private Graham, 255
Nesbitt, Warrant Officer Adrian, 184
Neville, Danny, 89
Ngo Dinh Can, 43
Ngo Dinh Diem
  Montagnard forced into resettlements, 4, 51, 54
  overthrow of, 64–65, 68–70, 110–111
  political prisoners, 111
  regime, 37–40, 43–45
  Serong, 64–66, 155
  Special Forces bodyguard, 63
Ngo Dinh Nhu, 43–44, 66–67, 68–70
Ngo Dinh Thuc, 43
Ngo Dzu, General, 256
Ngoc (bomber), 151
Nguyen Cao Ky, Air Marshall, 44, 191, 209, 261
Nguyen Co Thach, 283, 306
Nguyen Dinh Thuan, 47
Nguyen Huu Co, General, 126–132, 135
Nguyen Khanh, General, 109–111, 132, 135, 149
Nguyen Thi Dinh, Madame, 283
Nguyen Van Nhung, Major, 110–111
Nguyen Van Thieu, General, 202–203
Nhu. *see* Ngo Dinh Nhu
Nhu, Madame, 43, 67
Nicaragua, 317
Nie Tren, 179
Nixon, Richard, 242, 286, 316
Noone, Dick, 237–238
North Vietnam, 44–45. *see also* Viet Cong/North Vietnamese army
  aerial bombing of, 185, 187, 211, 286
  attitude to Montagnard, 78–79, 188
  Hanoi, 306–307
  negotiations with Nhu, 66–67
  Vietnamese Special Forces, 141–142, 145

Nugan, Frank, 316
Nugan Hand Bank, 316
Nui Dat, 211, 241, 243, 247
Nung, 55, 91–92, 100, 262

O
O'Connell, Thomas, 316
Oliver, Wynn, 177, 194, 203
Ong Bui Diem, 209–210
Ong Nguyen Binh, 71–73, 119–120
Operation Speedy Express, 278–280
opium trade, 44, 145–146, 191, 216
Osborne, Barton, 282
Ostara, Warrant Officer Ernest, 275

P
Paltridge, Shane, 167
People's Action Teams (PATs), 172–174, 263, 267–268, 270. see also Counter Terror (CT) units
Petersen, Arthur ('Fred'), 14
Petersen, Barry
  2RAR command, 240–241, 247–254
  Agent Orange, exposure to, 314
  ASIS, 155–157, 160
  awards, 139, 153, 200–201, 251, 254–255
  Ban Me Thuot, returns to, 255, 308–309
  in Bangkok, 309–310
  in Canberra, 285–287
  CIA, as conduit to, 116–117
  CIA, as threat to, 214–217, 220, 224, 228, 300, 302–304, 305
  CIA, relations with, 140–141, 146–149, 187–188
  CIA remove from Highlands, 193–198
  counter-terror teams, refuses, 169, 174, 284
  Cutler, aide-de-camp to, 239
  early life, 14–16
  Fort Bragg, 240
  guerilla warfare, 89–90
  in Hanoi, 306–307
  Ingleburn, 238–239
  Jarratt, 268
  joins army, 16–17
  in Malaysia, 287–291
  memoirs Tiger Men (1988), 220, 300, 308
  Methven, 147–148, 180–181, 240
  Montagnard, attitude to, 79–80, 183, 194–195
  Montagnard, farewells, 204–207
  Montagnard militia, 4–5, 90. see also Truong Son Force
  Montagnard rebellion, 127–132
  Montagnard rice wine ceremony, 80–83
  operational fund, 52–53, 62
  in Queensland, 295–296
  rank, 295, 296–297
  report, 232–234
  retires, 296–297
  Serong, 45–48, 88, 119, 138–139
  in Singapore, 232
  Special Operations, joins, 20–21, 94
  Stokes, 99–100
  Teague, 174
  Thang Thanh, commands attack on, 1–3, 5–13
  tiger hunting, 83–86
  'Tiger Man of Vietnam', 13
  underground resistance plan, 198–199

VC, 85–86, 108, 213
Vietnam, arrives in, 40–42
Vietnam, leaves, 231
Vietnamese Armed Forces Command, 254
Y-Bham Enuol, 111–112
Petersen, Hans Christian, 15–16
Petraeus, General David, 318
Pham Tuong, Captain, 52, 61, 64
Phan Huy Quat, 168
Phan Tan Truoc, 71–73, 77, 102
the Philippines, 261, 293
Phoenix Program. *see also* Counter Terror (CT) units
  in Afghanistan, 257, 267, 317
  Australians in, 267–269
  call for global program, 318
  CIA funding, 274–275
  CIA operatives, 315–317
  CIA secrecy over, 222
  Congressional inquiry into, 276, 282
  interrogation and torture methods, 266, 281–282
  in Iraq, 257, 267, 283, 315–316, 317
  My Lai massacre, 242, 277
  quotas introduced, 277, 280
  Special Operations Group, 276
  transferred to Vietnamese, 283
  US military take over, 275
  Viagra initiative, 318
  in Vietnam, 263, 283–284
Phuoc Tuy, 211, 241, 243, 247, 271
Pleiku, 150, 257
Plimsoll, Sir James, 164
Poe, Tony, 264
Poland, 118
Poshepny, Anthony, 264
Potter, Dr Julia, 286
Powers, Tom, 268

Provincial Reconnaissance Units (PRU), 271–272, 275, 280

Q

Quang Ngai, 65–66, 171, 174, 263, 280

R

Record, Jeffrey, 279–280
Reed, Warren, 224
Reitemeyer, Francis, 280
Republic of Vietnam. *see also* Vietnam/Vietnamese
  Australia, 161–162, 167–168
  Montagnard population, 78. *see also* Montagnard hill tribes
  province chiefs, 262
  United States and, 93, 187
Rhade, 5–13, 54, 58, 64, 77–78, 79. *see also* Montagnard hill tribes
  in Buon Brieng, 125
  at Buon Sarpa, 135
  in Dam San, 179–180
  in Truong Son Force, 102–103
Ridge Camp, 270
Roy, Warrant Officer John, 202
Royal Australian Air Force, 211
RSL, 296
Rumsfeld, Donald, 315–316

S

Sallah, Michael, 280
Santamaria, BA ('Bob'), 65
School of Military Intelligence (Middle Head), 24–36
Scott, Gary Roy, 297–298
Scotton, Frank, 172
SDECE (*Service de Documentation Extérieure et de Contre-Espionnage*), 115–116
September 11, 317

Serong, Colonel Ted, 4–5
 Australian Army, relations with, 223
 CIA, 46, 48, 154, 184
 Diem, 64–66, 69, 155
 Montagnard rebellion, 122, 127–132, 137
 Petersen, 45–48, 88, 119, 138–139
 Phoenix Program, 283–284
 Stokes, 99
 Stone, briefing to, 213, 228–229
 Teague, 170–171, 173–174
 use of media, 91, 92–94
Sexton, Michael, 19–20, 167
Seychelles, 298–299
Shackley, Theodore, 316–317
Sihanouk, Prince Norodom, 114, 136
Singapore, 232
Smark, Peter, 91, 92–94
Smith, Bill, 175–178, 194
Smith, Lieutenant Colonel Wayne, 257–258
So, Captain, 269
Sochurek, Howard, 124–125, 133, 135, 139
South Vietnam. *see* Republic of Vietnam
South Vietnamese army. *see* ARVN
Soviet Union, 22, 24, 114, 118, 220, 235, 286–288
Spellman, Cardinal Francis, 44
spycraft, 23, 42, 59, 117, 156
Stevenson, Colonel Victor, 290
Stokes, Bevan, 91–92, 94–100, 102–109, 119, 137, 147, 174, 313
Stone, Gerald, 204, 211–213, 228–229
Strathern, Cliff, 48–49, 262
Swan Island (Vic), 22

T

Taylor, General Maxwell, 183, 184–187, 197, 303
Teague, Captain Ian, 170–174, 222, 227, 263, 270
Terry, Captain, 123
Thailand, 237
Thang Thanh, 1–3, 4, 5–13
Thayer (in American military intelligence), 215
Thich Quang Duc, 37–38, 40, 43
Thieu. *see* Nguyen Van Thieu, General
Thomas, Gordon, 281
Thompson, Captain Allan, 174
Tiger Force, 280
'Tiger Men'. *see* Truong Son Force
tigers, 83–86, 208
Times of Vietnam, 66
Timmes, General Charles, 268
Tran Do, General, 283
Tran Kim Tuyen, Dr, 44
Truman, Harry, 236–237
Truong, Captain, 124–125
Truong Son Force
 in Buon Enao, 72–73
 expansion of, 102–103, 140, 168, 178–179
 formation of, 73–74, 77, 89–90
 missions, 101, 174–178
 Montagnard rebellion, 127–128
 officers in, 101–102
 tactics, 151–153
 Taylor visits, 185–187
 as 'Tiger Men', 5, 108–109
Turse, Nick, 278

U

United Nations High Commissioner for Refugees (UNHCR), 310

United States in Vietnam, 19. *see also* CIA; Phoenix Program
  1964 elections, 67–68
  aid, 40, 63, 131, 134
  American deaths, 187, 242, 278
  American drug use, 242–243
  American war, 245–246, 319
  anti-war demonstrations, 242
  Bouchart, 114
  civilian casualties, 256–257
  Claymore mines, 248–249
  combat troops leave (1973), 292
  deployment of combat troops, 211, 242
  fear of peace, 110–111
  fragging, 97, 242
  'free-fire zones', 277–278, 280
  MACV, 230
  military advisers, 39–40, 44–45, 55
  military intelligence units, 227
  Montagnard rebellion, 123–125
  Operation Delta, 141–142, 145, 188
  Potsdam Conference, 235
  Republic of Vietnam and, 93, 187
  Saigon embassy, bombing of, 150
  soldiers missing in action, 307
  strategic hamlets strategy, 157
  tactics, 90, 98–99
  treatment of local populations, 106, 180
  US Special Forces, 90, 93, 94–95, 97, 109, 265
  use of napalm, 180
  'Vietnamization' policy, 242, 243, 292

V
Valentine, Douglas, 262, 264
Vann, John Paul, 279

Viet Cong/North Vietnamese army. *see also* Ho Chi Minh Trail
  agents, 138
  Americans, attitude to, 86–88
  Australians, post rewards for, 108, 213
  Battle of Long Tan, 251
  captured, 11
  Counter Terror (CT) units, 172–174
  FULRO, 189
  interrogation of, 74
  killed, 197, 243
  in Long Khanh, 243
  Montagnard autonomy and, 105–106
  Montagnard defections to, 135
  Montagnard in, 87–88, 117–118
  Nam Dong, attack on, 98–99
  Petersen, 85–86, 108, 213
  Phoenix Program, 283–284
  propaganda, 10
  A Shau base, overrun, 95
  supremacy, 210–211
  tactics, 5, 89–90, 151–153, 248–254
  terror tactics, 260, 261–262
  Tet Offensive, 227, 243, 245
  Thang Thanh, 2
  villagers and, 4, 8–9, 39, 46–47, 105, 170, 171
  weapons, 6, 89
Viet Minh, 68, 149, 234, 235–237
Vietnam/Vietnamese. *see also* North Vietnam; Republic of Vietnam
  Americans, attitude to, 201, 210, 307
  aristocracy, 51
  attitude to war, 243–244

Buddhists, 37–38, 40, 43–44, 63, 66, 264–265
Cambodia, invades, 293
Catholics, 37, 43, 63
civilian casualties, 278–279
fall of Saigon, 293
Montagnard, 5, 78, 101–102, 118
Montagnard attitude to, 87–88, 122, 169–170
North and South, division into, 44–45, 235
Saigon, 42–43, 246–247
spies in, 109
Vietnamese Police Special Branch, 271, 281
Vietnamese Special Forces, 141–142, 145, 237–238
Vinh, Colonel, 177, 178
Vinh Loc, General, 191–192, 201, 220, 303
Vu, Bui Thi, 62
Vung Tao base, 267–268, 270
Vung Tao Province, 222–224

W

Warner, Denis, 203, 221–222, 293, 294
Watergate, 286
Weiss, Mitch, 280
West Papua, 297–298
Westmoreland, General William, 99, 187, 227, 279, 303–304
Whitlam, Gough, 294
Willey, Keith, 248–249
Wilton, Lieutenant General Sir John, 161, 164
Wingate, Orde, 181
Wood, USAF Sergeant Jim, 146–147

Y

Y-Bham Enuol, 111–112, 117, 120–121, 126, 135, 188–189, 202
Y-Bu, 9
Y-Jhon Nie, 123–125, 134
Y-Jut Buon To, 10, 73, 82, 111, 120, 121, 127–130, 132, 293–295
Y-Liu, 6–7
Y-Tin Hwing, 64, 65, 84, 85, 119, 137, 143
Y-To Nie, 137–138
Y-We Eban, 188–189
Young, Captain Peter, 45, 50, 159, 214–216, 220, 221, 226–228, 240, 300, 305

Z

Ziemer, Reverend Rob, 58